Recovery of Interest
Practice and Precedents

Recovery of Interest
Practice and Precedents

Peter K. J. Thompson, MA, LLB
of Lincoln's Inn, Barrister

London
Butterworths
1985

United Kingdom	Butterworth & Co (Publishers) Ltd, 88 Kingsway, LONDON WC2B 6AB and 61A North Castle Street, EDINBURGH EH2 3LJ
Australia	Butterworths Pty Ltd, SYDNEY, MELBOURNE, BRISBANE, ADELAIDE, PERTH, CANBERRA and HOBART
Canada	Butterworth & Co (Canada) Ltd, TORONTO and VANCOUVER
New Zealand	Butterworths of New Zealand Ltd, WELLINGTON and AUCKLAND
Singapore	Butterworth & Co (Asia) Pte Ltd, SINGAPORE
South Africa	Butterworth Publishers (Pty) Ltd, DURBAN and PRETORIA
USA	Butterworth Legal Publishers, ST PAUL, Minnesota, SEATTLE, Washington, BOSTON, Massachusetts, AUSTIN, Texas and D & S Publishers, CLEARWATER, Florida

© Butterworth & Co (Publishers) Ltd 1985

British Library Cataloguing in Publication Data

Thompson, Peter K. J.
    Recovery of interest: practice and precedents.
    1. Debtor and creditor—Great Britain
    2. Interest—Law and legislation—Great Britain
    I. Title
    344.106'77   KD1740

ISBN 0-406-26140-7

Typeset by Latimer Trend Ltd, Crescent Avenue, Plymouth
Printed and bound in Great Britain by Billing & Sons Ltd, Worcester

Preface

The law relating to the recovery of interest first engaged my attention twenty years ago when, as a practising barrister, I was instructed to seek awards of interest under s 3(1) of the Law Reform (Miscellaneous Provisions) Act 1934, for various creditors who had been kept out of their money. I discovered that this provision was less than satisfactory for the purpose. In cases where there had been a bona fide dispute about the principal debt, an order for the honest, but unsuccessful, defendant to pay interest on top could be obtained without difficulty. But where the defendant had no kind of a defence and had obtained a lengthy period of credit by lies, evasion and prevarication he could forestall any application for interest under the Act by paying up the principal debt within 14 days of receiving the writ, and that was that. There was the further oddity that no procedure existed in the county court for obtaining an award of interest under the Act once judgment had been obtained in default or on an admission; and although such a procedure was devised for the High Court the extra time and costs involved weighed heavily against its being used except when very large sums were at stake. For all these reasons s 3(1) of the 1934 Act was of little practical value in the process of debt-collecting and the number of applications made under it in 1965 must have been very small indeed.

Since then there have been many changes. The most important and influential changes have been in the economic scene: an unprecedented rate of inflation, on the one hand, and a steep rise in the cost of borrowing money, on the other. Businessmen have reacted by resorting, increasingly, to contractual provisions whereby either interest is payable on default, or the monetary obligation itself is linked to a foreign currency or a domestic index. These changes have, in turn, served also to highlight the anomalies and deficiencies in the law regarding the recovery of non-contractual interest, as it was in 1965. It has had to be reformed; and a number of important steps have been taken by Acts of Parliament, by rules of court, by practice directions and by decisions of the courts. These provide the subject-matter of this book.

The main areas in which the law relating to interest has been changed in the past twenty years are as follows:

(1) *Moneylending and consumer credit*

The Consumer Credit Act 1974 has repealed the Moneylenders Acts and the Hire-purchase Act 1965 and introduced a much broader scheme for consumer credit which is now fully in force, the last remaining provisions coming into operation on 19 May 1985.

(2) *Debt-collecting actions and arbitrations*

Non-contractual interest is now much more readily available in proceedings for debt-recovery than it was under the 1934 Act.

(3) *Interest on damages*

Awards of interest on damages have become the norm and there is a fast-growing body of case law on the situations in which interest should, or should not, be awarded, and on the period and the rate, with particular reference to personal injury litigation and commercial cases.

(4) *Interest on judgments and awards*

Rates of interest on High Court judgments and arbitration awards are no longer tied to 4% (set by s 17 of the Judgments Act 1838) and have been increased to reflect rises in the cost of borrowing. This has important implications for the law of enforcement. Other significant developments are that the way has been prepared, by primary legislation, for county court judgments to carry interest, as a matter of course, and for the 'portability' throughout the Common Market of judgments of our High Court and county courts with interest thereon at our rates, not at the rates applicable in the State where they are to be enforced.

(5) *Money in court*

As for money in court, a major recent change is that the accrual of interest has, since 1983, been automatic; and certainly interest at the automatic rate (deposit rate) is better than no interest at all. But it is not necessarily the best that can be obtained within the courts' ever-growing investment powers, which it is often advantageous to invoke.

(6) *Debts proved in insolvency*

The provisions of the Bankruptcy Act 1914 regarding the recovery of interest in an insolvency have been criticised severely and will eventually be replaced by the simpler provisions of the new Insolvency leglislation. For the present, however, the old provisions still apply and it is a matter of making the best of them.

(7) *Tax*

The basic proposition that interest is taxable income still obtains but some interest has been made exempt (in the context of personal injury litigation) and the questions when, and by whom, tax must be deducted out of payments of interest continue to present difficulites.

The broad aim of this book is to bring the practitioner up to date with recent developments, as above, and to suggest solutions to the new problems which are presented. Its scheme follows more or less the same sequence as this Preface; and the Appendices at the end bring together all the Acts, rules and directions which are most closely connected with the recovery of interest, together with a few precedents for use in the High Court and county court.

I did not realise, when I started to write this book, how complicated this branch of the law has become. But I have had more than a little help from my friends and am particularly grateful to Sir Jack Jacob QC, Roy Gregory QC, Mr Registrar Lowis and Dr A. N. Brice; I sought their views on an earlier draft and they gave me excellent advice, by which the final product has been much improved.

1985   Peter K. J. Thompson

Contents

Table of statutes

References in the right-hand column are to paragraph and page numbers. Numbers printed in italic type refer to pages of the Appendices. Set out Acts are printed in bold italic type.

Table of statutes

Compulsory Purchase Act 1965 . . . . 10.09

Consumer Credit Act 1974 . . 1.09, 2.09, 2.12, 2.13, 2.34, 9.15

s 1 . . . . *144*

8 . . . . 2.09, *145*

(2) 2.09, 2.12, 2.14, 2.15, 2.17

9 . . . . 2.13, *145*

10 . . . . *145*

(1)(a), (b) 2.16

11, 12 . . . . *146*

13, 14 . . . . *147*

15 . . . . *148*

(1) 2.16

16 . . . . . . 2.13, 2.14, 2.15, 2.16, *148*

17, 18 . . . . *149*

20 . . . . *151*

(2) 2.14

19 . . . . . . 2.15, *150*

21 . . . . . . 1.10, *151*

40 . . . . *151*

55 . . . . . . 2.12, *152*

56 . . . . *152*

57, 58 . . . . *153*

59 . . . . *154*

60, 61 . . . . . 2.12, *154*

62, 63 . . . . 2.12

64 . . . . . . 2.12, *156*

65 . . . . . . 2.12, *157*

66 . . . . *157*

67 . . . . . . 2.13, *157*

68 . . . . . . 2.13, *157*

69 . . . . *158*

70 . . . . *159*

71 . . . . . . 2.13, *159*

(2), (3) 2.13

72 . . . . *160*

73 . . . . *161*

74 . . . . . . 2.13, *162*

75 . . . . *163*

76 . . . . . . 2.12, *163*

(1) 229

77 . . . . . . 2.12, *164*

78 . . . . . . 2.12, *165*

79, 80 . . . . . 2.12, *166*

81 . . . . . . 2.06, *166*

Consumer Credit Act 1974— *contd*

s 82 . . . . *167*

83–85 . . . . *168*

86 . . . . *169*

(2) 237

87 . . . . . . 2.12, *169*

88 . . . . . . 2.12, *170*

89 . . . . *170*

90 . . . . . . 2.12, *171*, 237

91 . . . . . . 2.12, *171*

92 . . . . *172*

(1), (2) 237

93 . . . . . . 2.14, 2.35, *172*

94 . . . . . . 2.15, *172*

95 . . . . . . 2.15, *173*

96 . . . . . . 2.15, *173*

(3) 2.15

97 . . . . . . 2.12, *173*

98 . . . . . . 2.12, *174*

(1) 229

99 . . . . *174*

100 . . . . . . 2.12, *174*

101 . . . . *175*

102 . . . . *176*

103 . . . . . . 2.12, *176*

105 . . . . . . 2.12, *177*

(7) 2.12

106 . . . . *178*

107 . . . . . . 2.12, *178*

108 . . . . . . 2.12, *179*

109, 110 . . . . . 2.12, *180*

111 . . . . . . 2.12, *180*

(2) 2.12

112, 113 . . . . *181*

123 . . . . . . 2.12, *182*

124 . . . . . . 2.12, *182*

(1), (2) 2.12

125 . . . . . . 2.12, *183*

126 . . . . . . *183*, 237

127 . . . . . . 2.12, *183*

128 . . . . *184*

129 . . . . *184*

(1)(b) 237

(2)(a) 237

130 . . . . *185*

(6) 237

131 . . . . . . *185*, 237

132 . . . . *186*

133 . . . . *186*

(b) 237

xv

Table of statutes

Table of statutory instruments

References in right-hand column are to paragraph and page numbers. Numbers printed in italic type refer to pages of the Appendices. Page references to set out Instruments are printed in bold italic type.

Table of cases

PARA

S

T

W

Chapter 1

Historical introduction

Early history

1.01   The recovery of interest has always been controversial. Aristotle reached the conclusion that the recovery of interest was unnatural and should not be allowed, for the slightly curious reason that coins cannot grow or beget other coins.[1] The Early Church in England reached the same conclusion but by a different route based on the Scriptures. According to Glanvil usury was punishable by the Ecclesiastical Courts both as a sin and as a crime.

1 Aristotle's *Politics* (c 330 BC), 1.10.

CHANGING ATTITUDES TO USURY

1.02   But theological opinions softened a little. St Thomas Aquinas recognised as valid the payment by the borrower of compensation for the loss (or, later, risk of loss) borne by the moneylender (*damnum emergens*) in addition to repaying the loan; and in the fifteenth century the payment, on top of that, of compensation to the moneylender for being deprived of the use of his money (*lucrum cessans*) was 'accepted by the best theologians'.[1] Despite this subtle shift in opinions a statute of 1487 nevertheless declared that 'bargains grandyt in usurye' were void. But with the rise of Protestantism, supported chiefly by the rich middle class, and the dawn of capitalism, came a major change in attitude to money and investment. It came to be accepted that commerce could not be sustained without risk capital and that such capital would not be laid out except for some kind of return, whether in the form of interest or a share in the profits or something else.[2] The setting up of business partnerships and the mercantile practices which developed abroad in relation to bottomry bonds, insurance, bills of exchange, bills of

1

lading and banking itself, could not be ignored. And even while commercial moneylending was formally condemned, respectable means were devised of achieving the same ends. For example, the redeemable rentcharge was freely used as a means by which a land-owner could repay a loan with interest. The legal conclusion, under the Tudors, was that moneylending should be permitted, so long as the terms were not exorbitant. As Francis Bacon wrote in 1597, 'Since there must be borrowing and lending, and men are so hard of heart that they will not lend freely, usury must be prescribed'.[3] Various rates of interest were prescribed by statute from time to time,[4] the highest being 10% per annum.

1 Ashley *Economic History*, vol i, Pt II, 401.
2 W. S. Holdsworth *History of English Law*, vol VIII, Chapter 4.
3 Essay on Usury.
4 1545 37H8 c9; 1571, 13 Eliz 1, c8; 1623, 21 Jac I c17; 1660, 12 Charles II, c13; 1713, 12 Ann, c16.

1.03   The fixing of a legal rate for borrowing allowed Church and State to maintain its disapproval of usury and, at the same time, to allow the financing of mercantile ventures by which the national economy was sustained. But the simple expedient of drawing a line above which moneylending ceased to be lawful and became usury vexed academic lawyers. Francis Bacon acknowledged the need to strike a fair balance between grinding the tooth of usury 'that it bite not too much' while, at the same time leaving a way open for monied men to lend to the merchants 'for the continuing and quickening of trade'. But he favoured a two-tier system, the one applying as a general rule and fixing the rate of interest on loans at something reasonably low for ordinary people and the other being a special regime of licensed moneylending for certain people at certain places but without restriction on the rate of interest. The suggestion was never adopted in his lifetime, although now, four centuries later, we have something rather like it. But between his time and ours the country had first to experience unlicensed moneylending with no legal limits at all. This came about with laissez-faire and the acceptance of the arguments of, amongst others, Jeremy Bentham, whose published letters[1] on behalf of 'The liberty of making one's own terms in money bargains' put the case for the right to borrow money at high rates as a fundamental civil right with which the State should not interfere. He was particularly scornful of Dr Adam Smith's contention that a legal rate of interest prevented money being squandered by profligates and by projectors. In more moder-ate vein William Blackstone, writing a little earlier[2] pointed to the inconsistency in the law in trying to curb charges for the loan of money, but not for the loan of a horse. Opinion settled in favour of removing all restraints on moneylending and this came about in 1854 with the Usury Laws Repeal Act, which provided many good plots for the Victorian novelists, until the passing of the Money-lenders Act 1900.

1 Published in 1787, some being addressed to Dr Adam Smith and criticising his work *The Wealth of Nations*, published in 1784.
2 *Commentaries*, first published between 1765 and 1769; 4th edn (1876) vol 2, p 408.

INTEREST AS DAMAGES

1.04   The recovery of interest came before the courts in another form as well, as a side-effect of the growth of commerce. So long as the creditor used the old form of action, Debt, as a means of recovering what he was owed, he was limited to recovering the contractual debt itself: no questions could be raised as to ancillary loss or out of pocket expenses. But the emergence of assumpsit[1] opened up fresh possibilities. This was a new kind of action on the case, based on the debtor's breach of his promise to pay that which he owed; thus interest could be claimed as a head of loss flowing from the debtor's wrongful withholding. This bold innovation was pressed to the full in the eighteenth century. In 1780 Lord Mansfield CJ summarised the position as follows:[2]

> Though by the common law, book-debts do not of course carry interest, it may be payable in consequence of the usage of particular branches of trade; or of a special agreement, or, in cases of long delay under vexatious and oppressive circumstances, if a jury in their discretion shall think fit to allow it.

1 *Slade's Case* (1602) 4 Co Rep 91a.
2 *Eddowes v Hopkins* (1780) 1 Doug KB 376.

1.05   Lord Mansfield's observations prompt two comments. First there is the reference to a 'special agreement', which was not necessarily a moneylending agreement. Since interest might in some circumstances be awarded as a head of damages there could be no objection to the parties making a pre-estimate of the damage which might flow from delayed receipt of the money due and providing in the agreement for interest to accrue at a specified rate on a default. Second, in the residuary category of 'long delay under vexatious and oppressive circumstances' the award of interest could not be regarded as matter of absolute entitlement: the jury had a *discretion* whether to award it or not.

1.06 By 1789 interest in the form of damages was being awarded as a matter of course, at least in the City. In *Craven v Tickell*,[1] the Lord Chancellor, Lord Thurlow, commented that 'It is the constant practice at Guildhall (I do not speak from my own experience, but from conversations I have had with the Judges on the subject) either by the contract, or in damages, to give interest upon every debt detained'. But in 1807, in *De Havilland v Bowerbank*[2] Lord Ellenborough CJ decided that the time had come to rein in the discretion to award interest, in the light of 'some extremely capricious determinations'. He said that 'My great object is to have a fixed rule and to exclude discretion' and his fixed rule was to confine awards of interest to cases where there had been an express promise to pay interest or at least a contract for the payment of money on a certain day as on bills of exchange or promissory notes. Best CJ strove to keep the discretion alive in *Arnott v Redfern* in 1826[3] but the 'fixed rule' was reinstated in *Page v Newman* three years later.[4] No wonder that in 1833 the law reporter who wrote up *De Havilland v Bowerbank* was moved to add, as a footnote, that 'It would fortunately be a very difficult matter to fix upon another point of English law on which the authorities are so little in harmony with each other'. In that same year Lord Tenterden's Act[5] was passed, which empowered juries to award interest as a matter of statutory discretion wherever the debt was payable on a certain day under a written instrument or there had been a written demand for payment which informed the debtor that interest would be claimed. The common law *discretion* to award interest on debts never recovered from this intervention and was eventually pronounced dead in 1893 in *London, Chatham and Dover Rly Co v South Eastern Rly Co*.[6] But the common law *entitlement* to interest, eg by contractual provision, is central to the current law on the recovery of interest. It is considered in some detail in Chapter 2.

1 (1789) 1 Ves 60.
2 (1807) 1 Camp 50.
3 (1826) 3 Bing 353.
4 (1829) 9 B & C 378.
5 Civil Procedure Act 1833, s 28. See too s 29 which allowed interest to be awarded on damages for trespass to goods or conversion. Lord Tenterden CJ was the author of the Act and, incidentally, the presiding judge in *Page v Newman*, above.
6 [1893] AC 429. See para 3.02, below.

1.07 Moreover, awards of interest were not confined to the common law. The Court of Admiralty recognised from the start that the loss sustained through tortious damage to a ship necessarily involved the loss of the use of the capital which was tied up in it;

4

accordingly interest calculated on the value of the ship, if sunk, or on the cost of repairs, was treated as part of the damages recoverable in tort. Likewise the courts with equitable jurisdiction saw no difficulty in ordering the fraudulent trustee to make restitution not only of the fund that had been misappropriated but the interest made thereby, of which the fund had been deprived; anything less would have allowed the defendant to keep the profits made from his breach of trust. So in one way or another the recovery of interest was established as a feature of civil litigation in all the various courts. The recovery of interest in Admiralty and in Equity has survived to the present without major changes: the position is considered further in Chapter 3.

STATUTORY INTEREST

1.08   There were three significant statutes on the recovery of interest in the nineteenth century. Two have been mentioned already, namely the introduction, by the Civil Procedure Act 1833, of the statutory discretion to award interest on unpaid debts in certain circumstances and the Repeal of Usury Laws Act 1854. Between these two came the Judgments Act 1838, section 17 of which is still in force today. By this Act it was provided that judgments and orders of the High Court should carry interest at 4% per annum. This was to be the first of many statutes which created an *entitlement* to interest. Subsequent developments in the right to interest on judgments are considered in Chapter 5. Mention should also be made of the Bankruptcy Acts of 1883 and 1890 which provided, amongst other things, for statutory interest on debts proved in a bankruptcy: these provisions were carried over into the existing law which is considered in Chapter 9.

Twentieth-century developments

USURY AND THE CONSUMER CREDIT ACT 1974

1.09   The Moneylenders Acts of 1900 and 1927 endeavoured to bring usury under legal control once more, this time by subjecting the business of moneylending to certain restrictions and by giving the lender the power to seek relief in the courts from extortionate bargains. These Acts have now been superseded by the Consumer Credit Act 1974 which establishes a two-tier system, although not quite as Francis Bacon had envisaged: consumer credit business now requires a licence[1] and individuals are given protection against being exploited in the matter of interest charges. But the protection does not apply to corporate customers nor to transactions in excess of

£15,000: here the customer has won back the liberty of making his own terms in money-bargains. This and other aspects of the modern law on the recovery of contractual interest are discussed in the next Chapter.

1 So does consumer hire business: both are covered by Consumer Credit Act 1974, s 21. Section 147 provides in the same way for the licensing of credit brokerage, debt-adjusting, debt-counselling, debt-collecting, and the operation of a credit reference agency. See Appendix A for the text.

DISCRETIONARY INTEREST BY STATUTE

(a) Debt-collecting

1.10   The statutory discretion to award interest in certain situations under sections 28 and 29 of the Civil Procedure Act 1833 was widened by section 3(1) of the Law Reform (Miscellaneous Provisions) Act 1934 to enable awards to be made in respect of almost any debt or damages that did not carry interest anyway; and the changes made by the Administration of Justice Act 1982, which are examined in Chapter 4, have widened the discretion yet further. But at bottom the nature of the remedy has remained the same; it was and still is a discretion in the court to make an award, not an entitlement of the creditor. He has a cause of action in respect of the debt or damages but not for an award of statutory interest, which is more like an award of costs than anything else.[1] But the procedural and other changes made since the publication of the Law Commission's Report on Interest in 1978[2] have now put the creditor in almost the same position as if he had a cause of action for interest as well. He cannot now obtain an award of statutory interest unless he includes a claim for it in his pleadings, just as if it were contractual interest;[3] and the defendant who wishes to pay money into court to satisfy the claim for debt or damages must pay money in to satisfy any pleaded claim for interest under the statute as well, just as if the plaintiff had a cause of action for that too.[4] And even if the defendant pays off the debt or damages before the case comes to trial or judgment the unsatisfied claim for interest under the statute remains, like the smile of the Cheshire cat, and the creditor may proceed to judgment for that alone although the substantive cause of action has already been satisfied.[5] If Lord Thurlow were to return and to have conversations with the Judges or, better still, with the officials in the Central Office he would probably be told that it is now the constant practice, as it was in his time, to give interest upon every debt detained. There is, however, one respect in which the claim for a discretionary award for interest differs from the claim to interest for which a cause of action exists. The difference is that a creditor may start proceedings for contractual interest alone where everything else has already been paid before proceedings are started[6] but an application for a statutory award may not be made in such a case. The situation, which is discussed further in Chapter 4, has been criticised as unsatisfactory.[7] But, for good or ill, the statutory discretion seems now to have brought the recovery of interest to almost exactly the same point as the judicial discretion in its heyday, so that an award of interest is to be had for the asking by any litigant with a good cause of action in debt or damages, but not otherwise.

1 The *Harbutt's 'Plasticine'* case [1970] 1QB 450, at 452, per John Stephenson J. *Jefford v Gee* [1970] 2 QB 130, [1970] 1 All E R 1202, CA.
2 Cmnd 7229
3 RSC Ord 18, r 8(4); CCR Ord 6, r 1A. See Appendix B.
4 RSC Ord 22, r 1(8); CCR Ord 11, r 1(8). See Appendix B.
5 Supreme Court Act 1981, s 35A; County Courts Act 1984, s 69. See Appendix A.
6 *Florence v Jenings* (1857) 2 CBNS 454.
7 *President of India v La Pintada Cia Navegacion SA* [1984] 2All ER 773, [1984] 3 WLR 10, HL.

(b) Personal injury litigation

1.11 The statutory discretion to award interest in respect of damages for personal injuries has existed since 1934, but remarkably, seems to have been exercised on no more than a few isolated occasions before 1970, when the Court of Appeal laid down guidelines, in *Jefford v Gee*[1] on the approach which the courts should take to such matters in the future. The extent of the change may be measured by comparing the outcome in1970 of *S v Distillers Co (Biochemicals) Ltd*[2] with that of *Croke v Wiseman*[3] in 1982. In the former the court approved settlements of proceedings brought on behalf of certain children whose mothers had taken the drug thalidomide. General damages were approved at various five figure amounts, but the question of interest to compensate for the four year waiting period since the issue of the writ was left entirely out of account. In *Croke v Wiseman* on the other hand a child, tragically injured by medical negligence, was awarded compensation broadly in line with that approved in the thalidomide cases but with a further five figure sum on top by way of agreed interest for the three year waiting period between issue of the writ and judgment. It is debatable whether the interest factor has done anything to speed up the settlement of civil claims,[4] but on any view a plaintiff's claim for personal injuries is now worth significantly more, by reason of the addition of interest, tax-free,[5] than it would have been if the courts had continued to leave it out of account as they did down to 1970. The present position is examined in detail in Chapter 5.

7

1 [1970] 2 QB 130, [1970] 1 All ER 1202, CA.
2 [1969] 3 All ER 1412, [1970] 1 WLR 114.
3 [1981] 3 All ER 852, [1982] 1 WLR 71.
4 The Winn Committee's Report on Personal Injuries Litigation (1968, Cmnd 3691),
suggested that the addition of interest would stimulate early settlements: the Law
Commission, in paras 271–272 of their Report No 56 on Personal Injury Litigation—Assessment of Damages (1973 HC 133) expressed doubts as to whether it
had had this effect.
5 See paras 11.03–11.04, below.

INTEREST ON JUDGMENTS
1.12   There have been two important legislative changes in
relation to interest on judgments, both of them comparatively
recent. By the first, in 1970,[1] the rate payable on High Court
judgments may now be fixed and refixed by the Lord Chancellor at
different rates from that of 4% provided by section 17 of the
Judgments Act 1838. Rates have varied since then, as set out in
Appendix E. By the second, in 1981,[2] the Lord Chancellor has been
enabled to make a scheme whereby county court judgments, or some
of them, may carry interest as well. These developments are considered further in Chapter 6.

1 Administration of Justice Act 1970, s 44.
2 Supreme Court Act 1981, Sch 3, para 11; see now the County Courts Act 1984, s 74.
The text is in Appendix A.

INTEREST ABROAD
1.13   Foreign judgments and foreign arbitration awards may
include orders for the payment of interest and, in addition, the sum
ordered to be paid may itself carry interest according to the law of
the country where interest was entered, or the law governing the
arbitration. Until 1977 the enforcement of a foreign judgment in this
country required the creditor first to convert his judgment into
sterling and then to enforce it as if it were a judgment given in our
High Court carrying interest at the rate provided by the Judgments
Act 1838. More recently, following the decision in the *Miliangos*
case[1] and consequential changes in legislation[2], it has become
possible for foreign judgments to be registered for enforcement in
the appropriate foreign currency. But they must still carry the
interest appropriate to an English judgment. Within the European
Economic Community, however, the Civil Jurisdiction and Judgments Act 1982 now provides for what might be called 'portable'
judgments which may be registered for enforcement in any part of
the Community (and in any of the United Kingdom's three law
districts) in the same terms as given by the original court and

carrying the same rate of interest. These developments are discussed further in Chapter 7.

1 *Miliangos v George Frank (Textiles) Ltd* [1976] AC 443, [1975] 3 All ER 801.
2 Administration of Justice Act 1977, s 4(2)(b).

1.14　The enforcement in this country of foreign arbitration awards has been the subject of a series of Conventions and statutes, noted in Chapter 8. These provide for the recovery in this jurisdiction of the interest accruing on the award as well as the award itself; but it has to be said that the various provisions regarding the recovery of such interest are not consistent with each other and that different results may sometimes be achieved depending whether the successful party seeks to enforce the award, as such, or sues instead on the failure to honour the award, as an independent cause of action.

NON-CONTENTIOUS BUSINESS

1.15　So far the recovery of interest has been considered as an aspect of compensation for actionable loss, in the general context of litigation. But interest has come to play an increasingly important role in fields of legal activity which are generally non-contentious such as (a) conveyancing, where completion may be delayed, and where questions may arise as to the allowance of interest on deposits held, and (b) the administration of the estate of a deceased person and settling questions as to what if any interest should be paid on legacies, funeral expenses and the like. Likewise proving for a debt in a bankruptcy or a company winding up can become extremely complicated if the creditor seeks to prove for interest as well: it is to be hoped that the Insolvency Act 1985 will provide simpler and more equitable solutions. The difficulties are examined further in the latter part of Chapter 3 and in Chapter 9.

MONEY IN COURT

1.16　Inflation, high interest rates and cash-flow problems have made litigants less willing to pay money into court than formerly, and have stimulated a greater concern to see that money in court is invested and that the interest accruing goes to the parties to the litigation, not to Her Majesty's Paymaster-General.[1] Recent developments are considered in Chapter 10.

1 See *Schroeder v Accountant General* [1980] 2 All ER 648, [1980] 1 WLR 1314.

TAX

1.17　Finally, it should not be forgotten that the recovery of interest is not simply a matter between creditor and debtor. The Commissioners of Inland Revenue have a watching brief as well. If interest was always required to be paid gross and was always taxable in the hands of the person entitled to it, the position would at least be simple. But not all interest counts as taxable income and, more serious, sometimes there is an obligation on the paying party, or on any intermediary, to deduct an amount equivalent to tax at the standard rate (or more) and to remit it direct to the Inland Revenue, paying the balance only to the ultimate recipient. These tricky areas are explored further in Chapter 11.

Chapter 2

The contractual right to charge interest

EXPRESS PROVISION
2.01   It is becoming increasingly common for contracts to provide expressly for the paying party to be charged interest on the principal debt. The motivation for including such a provision is not always the same: sometimes the charging of interest is the gist of the transaction, as in the case of a commercial loan, sometimes its inclusion is intended to stimulate prompt payment of the principal and sometimes it falls between the two, striking a balance between the supplier's need for cash and the customer's for credit. In times of economic stability when the pound kept its value and the cost of borrowing money was low a stipulation for the payment of interest was unusual and largely unnecessary in ordinary trading transactions. But it is now on its way to becoming the rule rather than the exception.

IMPLIED PROVISION
2.02   In addition to those cases where a right to interest is provided expressly by contract are cases where a contractual, or indeed quasi-contractual, right to charge interest is to be inferred from the course of dealing between the parties,[1] or from the custom of the trade, such as the customary charge of interest on a bank overdraft,[2] or from the circumstances of the particular transaction. In the last category belong such cases as that of the purchaser of land suing for the return of his deposit because of the vendor's inability to make title[3] and that of the surety who is required to pay the principal debt and looks to the debtor to reimburse him for the sum paid and interest on it down to repayment.[4]

1 *Re Marquis of Anglesey* [1901] 2 Ch 548.
2 *Gwyn v Godby* (1812) 4 Taunt 346.
3 *De Bernales v Wood* (1812) 3 Camp 258; *Babacomp Ltd v Rightside Properties Ltd* (1975) 234 Estates Gazette 201.
4 *Petre v Duncombe* (1851) 20 LJQB 242.

2.03 Another kind of indemnity arrangement involving the payment of interest is one which has come to prominence in the construction industry, as a means by which the builder may recoup his interest charges from the owner when progress of the work is delayed by circumstances outside the builder's control. For instance, the 1980 edition of the Standard Form of Building Contract provides for the building contractor to be indemnified against 'direct loss or expense' due to delays of a specified kind. It has been held[1] that interest payable on the capital outlaid on the venture by the building contractor qualifies as 'direct loss or expense' as regards interest accruing during a period of delay of the kind specified in the contract: the builder may charge the owner accordingly. Similarly worded provisions are to be found in the 1963 edition of the RIBA Standard Form of Building Contract (Local Authorities edition with quantities) and other standard forms of building contracts.[2] However, the results are not always the same because the pre-1980 forms of contract require items of 'direct loss or expense' to be claimed within a specified time and this means that a loss which, like interest, is constantly accruing[3] needs to be reasserted within intervals no longer than the time allowed for claim, otherwise the right to reimbursement under this head will be lost.

1 *F. G. Minter Ltd v Welsh Health Technical Services Organisation* (1980) 13 BLR 1, CA; *Rees and Kirby Ltd v Swansea City Council* (1984) 128 Sol Jo 46.
2 See the contracts considered in the cases cited in n 1, above.
3 Apportionment Act 1870, ss 2 and 5.

SIMPLE OR COMPOUND
2.04 A contractual provision for the payment of interest need not be limited to a requirement for interest to be paid at a specified rate on the principal. Subject to statutory restrictions considered later,[1] it may provide in addition, for compound interest.[2] Such additional provision needs to specify the periodicity of compounding, that is to say the interval at which each act of compounding is to take place or, which comes to the same thing, the interval at which the accrued interest is to be added to the principal and treated, for the purpose of future interest, as if it had been part of the principal all along. Liability to pay compound interest usually depends upon express provision to this effect in the contract; but such a term may

exceptionally be implied from the custom of the trade or from a course of dealing.[3]

1 See paras 2.07–2.16, below.
2 But see Dr F. A. Mann 'On Interest, Compound Interest and Damages'. (1985) 101 LQR at 43.
3 *Yourell v Hibernian Bank Ltd* [1918] AC 372.

VARIABLE RATES AND INDEX-LINKING

2.05   Variable interest rates may be allowed by contractual provision and interest may be recovered accordingly, so long as the provision is not so indefinite as to be void for uncertainty. The simplest way of achieving certainty, on the one hand, and the capacity to adjust to market conditions on the other, is to provide in the contract for the rate of interest to be linked directly to an external index. Such an index may itself be a rate of interest eg the rate prescribed from time to time under section 32 of the Land Compensation Act 1961.[1] Index-linking can protect the creditor in other ways too. For example, the obligation of payment in sterling may be linked to a domestic index such as the retail price index[2] or to the value of a specific foreign currency against the pound. There is no objection of public policy[3] to an index-linking provision which requires the money due, whether as principal or interest or both, to be ascertained by reference to such an index.[4]

1 See, for example, clause 1(b) of the Law Society's Contract for Sale (1984 Revision).
2 *Nationwide Building Society v Registry of Friendly Societies* [1983] 3 All ER 296, [1983] 1 WLR 1226.
3 But there are certain statutory restrictions: see paras. 2.10–2.12, below
4 *Multiservice Bookbinding Ltd v Marden* [1979] Ch 84; [1978] 2 All ER 489.

APPROPRIATION OF PAYMENTS

2.06   Where a payment is made generally on account of a debtor's liability to his creditor the creditor is free, subject to certain statutory restrictions, to appropriate it to the reduction of whichever of several liabilities he wishes to see reduced.[1] Likewise where the debtor is liable to pay interest as well as principal the creditor is generally free to apply it to the reduction of interest, rather than principal. Indeed, in the absence of clear evidence of how the payment has in fact been appropriated, the presumption is that it has been applied first to interest and then to principal.[2] The appropriation is of significance in determining the liability of the debtor to pay future interest, because this will be reduced, pro tanto, by a payment off the principal, but not by a payment off the interest already accrued due.

1 Hire Purchase Act 1965, s 5 and Consumer Credit Act 1974, s 81 place restrictions on the creditor's freedom at common law, as to which see *The Mecca* [1897] AC 286.
2 *Bower v Marris* (1841) 1 Cr & Ph 351; *Re Morris* [1922] 1 Ch 126, per Younger LJ.

Restrictions on the creditor and relief of the debtor

EQUITABLE RELIEF

2.07   The equitable jurisdiction to relieve against penalties extends to granting relief against provisions which impose a penal rate of interest: a reasonable rate of interest will be allowed instead.[1] Where provision is made for a contractual rate of interest and the contract provides in addition that interest will accrue at a specified higher rate in the case of default the latter provision will be struck down as a penalty.[2] There is, however, no objection to providing in the agreement (typically a mortgage agreement) for pre-default interest at a higher rate than that required and providing for it to be reduced in the event of punctual payment.[3]

1 *Bridge v Campbell Discount Co Ltd* [1962] AC 600, [1962] 1 All ER 385.
2 *Thompson v Hudson* (1869) LR 4 HL 1.
3 Ibid.

MONEYLENDERS ACTS

2.08   The Moneylenders Acts 1900 to 1927 are now repealed, but they still apply to transactions which were entered into before the repeal. The definition of 'moneylender' in section 6 of the 1900 Act applies to the 1927 Act as well[1] and includes 'every person whose business is that of moneylender, or who advertises or announces himself or holds himself out in any way as carrying on that business', but it makes various large exceptions, mainly for registered Friendly Societies and Building Societies and for any person bona fide carrying on the business of banking or insurance or any business not having for its primary object the lending of money, or in the course of which or for the purpose of which he lends money. In *Wills v Wood*[2] the Court of Appeal upheld a finding that a retired hotelier who over a period of four years made seven loans to different borrowers at 12% per annum was *not* carrying on the business of a moneylender.

1 Moneylenders Act 1927, s 29(2).
2 *Wills v Wood* (1984) 128 Sol Jo 222.

2.09   Section 1 of the 1900 Act enables any court of civil jurisdiction in which proceedings are, or may be, taken by a moneylender to recover money lent, or to enforce any agreement or security in respect of money lent, to reopen the transaction and, if satisfied that the interest rate is excessive or that its provisions are otherwise extortionate, to reopen the account as between lender and borrower, to make such adjustment in its provisions as may be reasonable and to strike a fresh balance. A rate in excess of 48% is presumed to be excessive.[1] If proceedings have been taken by the creditor to recover the loan or to have the debt admitted to bankruptcy the powers may be exercised in those proceedings. Otherwise the debtor may apply to the appropriate court for equivalent relief, such proceedings being by originating summons in the High Court and by originating application in the county court.[2] These facilities have been replaced, since 16 May 1977, by similar provisions in the Consumer Credit Act 1974[3] and the new provisions apply to transactions whenever made. But the old facilities are still available as regards transactions entered into before 16 May 1977 and they are in two respects wider than the new: first they apply to loans above the Consumer Credit Act limit[4] and secondly the relief may be granted to persons other than individuals, such as limited companies.[5]

1 Moneylenders Act 1927, s 10
2 RSC Ord5, r 3 App A, Form 8, CCR Ord 3, r 4, Form N393.
3 Consumer Credit Act 1974, ss 137 to 140, brought into operation on 16 May 1977 by the Consumer Credit Act 1974 (Commencement No 2) Order 1977 (SI 1977/1325).
4 £15,000: Consumer Credit Act 1974, s 8(2); Consumer Credit (Increase of Monetary Amounts) Order 1983 (SI 1983/1571).
5 By contrast the Consumer Credit Act 1974 applies only to consumer credit agreements and consumer credit is defined in s 8 as credit given to individuals. See Appendix A for the text.

2.10　　The provisions in the Moneylenders Act which had not already been repealed were repealed on 19 May 1985 by the Consumer Credit Act 1974 Commencement No 8 Order 1983[1] but they still apply to transactions entered into before that date. They protect the borrower in four important ways. First they require that the borrower should be given a memorandum of the contract and statutory particulars as to the rate of interest charged.[2] One result of this requirement of particularity is to prevent the creditor from providing for an adjustable rate, fixed to some external index.[3] Secondly, they invalidate any provision whereby a borrower is required to pay interest on a compound basis or at an increased rate if he defaults.[4] Thirdly, there is a special limitation period of 12 months from the date of the last payment becoming due, after which proceedings to recover the loan and interest are barred.[5] Finally, where proceedings are taken in respect of one or more unpaid instalments the court may determine the contract and order the payment of the unpaid balance together with such interest, if any, as the court may allow;[6] presumably the court will reduce the future interest where the effect of the order is to accelerate the return of the principal.

1 SI 1983/1551.
2 Moneylenders Act 1927, s 6 and First Schedule.
3 See para 2.05, above.
4 Moneylenders Act 1927, s 7.
5 Ibid, s 13(1).
6 Ibid, s 13(2).

HIRE-PURCHASE ACT 1965

2.11   The Hire-purchase Act 1965 has been repealed, as regards transactions entered into on or after 19 May 1985.[1] But it still applies to hire-purchase agreements, credit-sale agreements and conditional sale agreements[2] entered into before that date and on or after 1 January 1965 where the hirer, or buyer, is not a body corporate[3] and the price does not exceed the limit set by Section 2; the limit has gone up from £2,000 in 1965 to £7,500 in 1983.[4] The main thrust of the Act, which consolidated earlier measures, is to prescribe the form and contents[5] of such agreements and the procedure to be followed in making, cancelling or enforcing them.[6] The Act does not in terms restrict the charging of interest, either as an element in the total price to be paid or as an additional charge in the event of default, but the statutory framework is generally inhibiting. In particular, the requirement that the agreement should state the total purchase price, or hire-purchase price, seems to exclude the possibility of variable, or index-linked, interest charges in the main agreement.[7] This restriction does not necessarily apply to the charging of default interest on instalments which are in arrear; but the recovery of such interest presents other problems which are considered below.[8]

1 Consumer Credit Act 1974 (Commencement No 8) Order 1983, SI 1983/1551.
2 Hire-purchase Act 1965, s 1.
3 Ibid, s 4.
4 The limit was raised from £2,000 to £5,000, as from 1 June 1978, by an Order under s 3(SI 1978/461) and from £5,000 to £7,500, as from 1 June 1983 by a further Order (SI 1983/611).
5 s 7 and Schs 1 and 2 (forms and contents) and s 3 (legibility).
6 ss 8–10 (copies of agreement), ss 11–15 (cancellation), ss 25–26 (notices of default), ss 27–28 (rights of termination), s 29 (restrictions on contracting out) and ss 33–49 (recovery of possession and other remedies).
7 s 7(1)(a). The point is well made by Professor Goode in *Payment Obligations in Commercial and Financial Transactions* (1983), Part III.
8 See para 2.34, below.

CONSUMER CREDIT ACT 1974

2.12   The Consumer Credit Act 1974 applies to all consumer credit transactions made on or after 19 May 1985 and the provisions of the Hire-purchase Act 1965 and the Moneylenders Acts are repealed from that date, except as regards transactions already entered.[1] The new regime adopts features of the old but provides protection and relief on a more general plane for individuals (not corporations) who are granted credit of up to £15,000 on extortionate or oppressive terms. The theme of the Act is to regulate the execution of consumer credit agreements,[2] the supply of information[3] and the service of notices before enforcement.[4] As regards variable rates and index-linking, sections 90, 91 and 100 would seem to exclude such devices from regulated hire-purchase and regulated conditional sale, but to permit them in the case of regulated credit sale. The main sanction for non-compliance with the protective provisions of the Act is that it renders the the agreement unenforceable by the creditor,[5] but with the court having power to lift the sanction in certain circumstances, depending on the extent of the creditor's culpability and the prejudice, if any, to the debtor.[6] So far as concerns interest charges and their recovery, there are provisions, considered in the paragraphs immediately following, which deal expressly with (a) the debtor's right to remission of interest upon cancellation of the agreement (b) stipulations for default interest at a higher rate than the contractual rate, (c) rebate of interest on early settlement and (d) the reopening, by the court, of extortionate consumer bargains. The material parts of the Consumer Credit Act 1974 are set out in Appendix A.

1 See paras 2.10 and 2.11, above.
2 Consumer Credit Act 1974, ss 60–61 (making the agreement), 105 (securities) and 123–125 (negotiable instruments). 'Consumer credit agreement' is defined in s 8(2).
3 Ibid, ss 55, 62–64, 77–80, 97, 103 and 107–111.
4 Ibid, ss 76, 87–88 and 98.
5 Ibid, ss 65, 105(7), 111(2), 124(1) and (2). The fact that non-compliance may be a criminal defence under the Art does not enable the defendant to rely on a general defence of illegality, as in *Snell v Unity Finance Ltd* [1964] 2 QB [1963] 3 All ER 50, CA. See s 170.
6 Ibid, s 127.

(a) Remission of interest on cancellation
2.13   Part V of the Consumer Credit Act 1974 is concerned with entry into credit or hire agreements and provides, amongst other things, for certain kinds of regulated agreement[1] to be cancellable. The kinds of agreement to which this right applies are broadly those made on the customer's own premises.[2] The right is exercisable by the customer's serving a notice of cancellation within the statutory

17

period.[3] In the case of a straight loan the money has, of course, to be returned on cancellation and section 71 provides for the repayment of the money (the 'credit')[4] and interest. So long as the customer repays the loan in full within a month of cancellation or before the date for payment of the first instalment, no interest has to be paid.[5] Nor does interest have to be paid on any amount, less than the full loan, which is paid within the same period.[6] In the case where all, or some, of the loan remains outstanding after that period the liability for interest on the balance remains: as regards a straight loan the interest on the balance accrues under the terms of the cancelled agreement, but in the case of credit repayable by instalments the liability to repay the balance is conditional on the creditor making a signed request for repayment in the prescribed form,[7] which must state the amounts of the remaining instalments, recalculated in accordance with the agreement and without extending the payment period, but excluding any sum other than principal and interest.[8]

1 A consumer credit agreement for up to £15,000 which is not exempt under s 16.
2 Consumer Credit Act 1974, s 67 specifies agreements which are cancellable, provided that oral representations have been made. However, s 74 excludes any non-commercial agreements and, where the Director General of Fair Trading so determines, an agreement for an overdraft on a current account or to finance payments arising on, or connected with the death of a person which are prescribed by the Consumer Credit (Payments Arising on Death) Regulations 1983 (SI 1983/1554).
3 Consumer Credit Act 1974, s 68 defines the period.
4 Defined in s 9.
5 Consumer Credit Act 1974, s 71(2).
6 Ibid.
7 The Consumer Credit (Repayment of Credit on Cancellation) Regulations 1983 (SI 1983/1559) prescribes the form, with effect from 19 May 1985.
8 Consumer Credit Act 1974, s 71(3).

(b) Default interest at a higher rate than the contractual rate

2.14   A regulated consumer credit agreement[1] may require the customer to pay interest on sums which are not paid on the due date, but section 93 provides[2] that the rate of interest payable on default may not exceed the contractual rate ie the rate of interest specified in the credit charges, or where no such rate is specified, the rate of the total charge for credit if items included by virtue of section 20(2) are left out. The consequences of contravention are not clear: the effect may be to render the provision for interest wholly invalid or merely to restrict it to the maximum rate recoverable. As regards default interest rates in agreements to which section 93 does *not* apply, the equitable jurisdiction to relieve against penalties is relevant.[3]

1 A consumer credit agreement, defined in s 8(2), for up to £15,000 which is not exempt under s 16.

2 This section is in operation from 19 May 1985.
3 See para 2.07, above.

(c) Rebate of interest on early settlement

2.15   As regards a regulated customer credit agreement made on or after 19 May 1985[1] the customer is entitled, on notice to the creditor, to pay up in advance of the due date and, at the same time, to claim the statutory rebate.[2] The calculation of the rebate must accord with the Consumer Credit (Rebate on Early Settlement) Regulations 1983.[3] The early settlement of the customer's liability under the agreement discharges his liability, and that of any relative of his, under any linked transaction[4] which is not exempt from the operation of the provisions.[5]

1 Consumer Credit Act 1974, ss 94–96 came into operation on this date. A regulated consumer credit agreement is a consumer credit agreement defined in s 8(2) for up to £15,000 which is not exempt under s 16.
2 Consumer Credit Act 1974, ss 94 and 95.
3 SI 1983/1562.
4 'Linked transactions' are defined by s 19 and do not include agreements for the provisions of 'security' as defined in s 189(1).
5 The Consumer Credit (Linked Transactions) (Exemptions) Regulations 1983 (SI 1983/1560), made under s 96(3), exclude contracts of insurance, contracts which contain a guarantee of goods and contracts comprising or effected under agreements for the operation of deposit or current accounts.

(d) Re-opening extortionate consumer bargains

2.16   As from 16 May 1977, when sections 137–140 of the Consumer Credit Act 1974 came into operation,[1] the courts[2] have been empowered to re-open any credit agreement, made for any amount at any time with any individual (non-corporate) customer, which gives rise to an extortionate bargain. The procedure for seeking relief under these provisions, where there are no proceedings already on foot, is by originating summons to the High Court[3] or by originating application to the county court.[4] It should be noted that originating proceedings by the debtor, or surety, in respect of any regulated agreement[5] or agreement for either running-account credit[6] or fixed-sum credit[7] which does not exceed the county court limit[8] must be taken in the county court.[9] On the other hand, where the creditor has already started proceedings for the recovery of the debt the debtor, or surety, should seek the relief in those proceedings, by serving on the court and the other parties to the proceedings[10] notice of his desire to have the agreement re-opened.[11] The result of serving such a notice in High Court proceedings is to prevent the creditor from obtaining a default judgment without leave[12] and in county court proceedings is the equivalent of the delivery of a defence or answer so as to prevent a default judgment

19

being entered.[13] A bargain is extortionate if it requires payments which are 'grossly exorbitant' or otherwise 'grossly contravenes ordinary principles of fair dealings' and, in its approach to these issues, the court should have regard to certain considerations, particularly the debtor's age and experience, his state of health and the pressures on him and the interest rates prevailing at the time.[14] If the court determines that the bargain is extortionate[15] it may re-open the agreement and make various orders, including altering the terms of the agreement or any security instrument, directing accounts to be taken and ordering the resulting balance to be paid, or repaid.[16]

1 Consumer Credit Act 1974 (Commencement No.2) Order 1977 (SI 1977/325).
2 The High Court and the county courts.
3 RSC Ord 5 r3.
4 CCR Ord 49 r 4(14).
5 A consumer credit agreement or consumer hire agreement defined in ss 8(2) and 15(1) respectively, for up to £15,000, other than one which is exempt under s 16.
6 Consumer Credit Act 1974, s 10(1)(a).
7 Ibid, s 10(1)(b).
8 Currently £5,000, as provided by the County Courts Jurisdiction Order 1981 (SI 1981/1123); further increases may be made under the County Courts Act 1984, s 145.
9 Consumer Credit Act 1974, s 139(5).
10 RSC Ord 83, r 2, CCR Ord 49, r 4(15).
11 For a precedent see Appendix D6.
12 RSC Ord 83, r 3.
13 CCR Ord 49, r 4(15).
14 Consumer Credit Act 1974, s 138(1).
15 Ibid, s 138(2)–(5).
16 Ibid, s 139(1)–(4).

High Court proceedings for the recovery of contractual interest

INTEREST ACCRUING BEFORE AND AFTER ISSUE OF THE WRIT
2.17   Where the plaintiff has a contractual right to be paid interest he may sue for the interest according to substantially the same rules as apply to the recovery of any other sum of money which is due under a contract. In one respect, however, the law regarding the recovery of interest is more advantageous, from the creditor's point of view, than that regarding the recovery of other kinds of debt. This is in relation to money accruing due after the issue of the writ. The general rule is that a plaintiff may not proceed to judgment for any debt which was not owing at the date of issue of the writ. As regards any contractual right, or cause of action, accruing thereafter the plaintiff may not take it on board in those proceedings by amending his claim: he must start separate proceedings.[1] To this

inconvenient rule the recovery of interest is a well-established exception: the courts have always allowed a plaintiff to sue for contractual interest accruing after the writ and down to judgment;[2] indeed it is doubtful whether a plaintiff who recovers a judgment for a debt and contractual interest on it down to the date of issue may bring a second lot of proceedings in respect of any post-issue interest not claimed in the first set of proceedings.[3] It is therefore prudent, wherever contractual interest is still accruing at the date of issue, to include a claim for the interest accruing thereafter. The procedural implications of such a claim are considered in the paragraphs which follow.

1 *Eshelby v Federated European Bank* [1932] 1 KB 254; *Roban Jig and Tool Co v Taylor* (1979) FSR 130; *X v Y* (1984) 134 NLJ 724.
2 *Kidd v Walker* (1831) 2 B & Ad 705; *Practice Direction* 24 February 1983, para 2(e), [1983] 1 All ER 934, [1983] 1 WLR 377; see Appendix C.
3 *Florence v Jenings* (1857) 2 CBNS 454.

GENERAL INDORSEMENT OF THE WRIT
2.18   Before a writ is issued in any High Court action it must be indorsed with either a statement of claim or a concise statement of the nature of the claim made or the relief or remedy required (formerly called a 'general indorsement').[1] A general indorsement for a claim which is to include contractual interest until judgment or sooner payment must, at the very least, specify that such a claim is made. In addition it would be sensible to specify the rate and the amount owing at the date of issue; otherwise it may not be possible to obtain a default judgment for a liquidated sum: the amount owing by way of interest will first have to be assessed.[2]

1 RSC Ord 6, r 2(1)(a). See Appendix B for the text.
2 See Practice Direction, 23 February 1983, [1983] 1 All ER 934, [1983] 1 WLR 377, in Appendix C.

THE 'DEBT OR LIQUIDATED DEMAND' INDORSEMENT
2.19   Where a claim is made for a debt or liquidated demand only, the writ must be indorsed with a statement of the amount claimed in respect of the debt or demand and the defendant must be notified that if he pays this sum and the fixed costs within the time limited for acknowledging service further proceedings will be stayed.[1] In the case of a claim for contractual interest down to the date of issue only there can be no doubt that this counts as a liquidated demand and that the writ must be indorsed accordingly. On the other hand, where the plaintiff claims interest accruing after issue as well it is arguable that the claim is not for a debt or liquidated demand *only* and that no such indorsement is required. However this may be, the current practice[2] is to try for the best of

both worlds and to include a 'liquidated demand' indorsement for the interest accrued down to issue and, at the same time, to include a claim for interest thereafter down to judgment or sooner payment in either the general indorsement[3] or the specially indorsed statement of claim.[4] This can, however, lead to difficulties.[5]

1 RSC Ord 6, r 2(1)(b); see Appendix B.
2 *Practice Direction* 24 February 1983, para 2(b); [1983] 1 All ER 934, [1983] 1 WLR 377; see Appendix C.
3 See the preceding paragraph.
4 See para 2.20, below.
5 See para 2.23, below.

STATEMENT OF CLAIM

2.20   The statement of claim may be indorsed on the writ, or delivered separately.[1] In either event the claim for contractual interest must be dealt with in two ways. First, it must be pleaded in the main body of the statement of claim; the pleading must show how and when the right to interest has arisen and the rate at which it is accruing. This is merely a particular aspect of the general rule that a claim must be pleaded with sufficient particularity to enable the defendant to know what case he has to meet. It is reinforced, however, by RSC Order 18, rule 8(4). Second, the statement of claim must conclude with a statement of the remedy or relief which is sought[2] and the claim for interest must be specified in this statement and, for preference, broken down into (a) the interest accrued at the date of issue and (b) interest accruing thereafter at the same contractual rate. If the interest is not mentioned as part of the relief or remedy sought, there is a risk that the plaintiff may fail to obtain a judgment for it on the ground that he has not asked for it; or, again, if interest is claimed, but without specifying the rate and period, he may obtain a default judgment for interest to be assessed instead of obtaining final judgment straightaway for a liquidated sum.[3]

1 RSC Ord 6, r 2(1)(a), Ord 18, r 1.
2 RSC Ord 18, r 15(1). See Appendix B.
3 The problem is essentially the same as that considered in para 2.18, above.

PROCEEDINGS BEGUN OTHERWISE THAN BY WRIT

2.21   The requirement that a claim for contractual interest must be pleaded in the statement of claim applies only to actions begun by writ, since it is only in such proceedings that a statement of claim is required. In proceedings that are begun in other ways, however, by originating summons, originating motion or petition, the party starting the proceedings is required to state the remedy or relief claimed, just as he is in proceedings begun by writ.[1] The claim for interest should accordingly be specific, at least as to rate, although there is no practical advantage in separating the interest accrued at commencement from that accruing thereafter.

1 RSC Ord 7, r 3, Ord 8, r 3, Ord 9, r 2.

OBTAINING JUDGMENT

2.22   Provided that the claim for contractual interest has been properly framed there should be no difficulty about obtaining judgment for the amount of interest owing at that date, whether the judgment is obtained by default,[1] summarily[2] or after a hearing. But it is in any case advisable that the statement of claim should give sufficient information, including the amount of interest accruing daily, to enable the calculations to be made quickly.[3]

1 RSC Ord 13, r 1, Ord 19, r 2.
2 RSC Ord 14, Ord 86.
3 *Practice Direction* 24 February 1983, para 2(c), [1983] 1 All ER 934, [1983] 1 WLR 377; see Appendix C.

PAYMENT BEFORE JUDGMENT

2.23   If, after proceedings have been started but before judgment is obtained, the defendant pays up all that he owes, including interest down to the date of payment and costs, the plaintiff can have no reason for going on with the action and, if he does so, will not obtain a judgment.[1] Likewise, if the defendant pays everthing that he owes, including interest to date, into court, the plaintiff must accept it or pay the penalty in costs.[2] If however, the defendant pays the principal but not the interest, or not all of the interest, the plaintiff may accept the money as a payment on account and obtain judgment for the balance; and if the defendant pays a similarly insufficient sum into court the plaintiff will not be penalised in costs if he seeks judgment for the full amount.[2] Thus, as a general rule, the plaintiff is entitled to press his claim for interest down to the uttermost farthing. But to this general rule there is at least one exception.[3] It concerns the case where the plaintiff has claimed interest down to judgment or payment (whichever is the earlier) in his writ but has also indorsed his writ as a liquidated demand for the debt and interest due at issue.[4] Provided that the defendant meets that liquidated demand within the time for acknowledging service the action is automatically stayed and so the plaintiff cannot proceed to judgment for the interest accruing during the period between issue and payment, although it may be a period of several months, eg in the case of service of the writ abroad. One way out of the difficulty might be for the plaintiff to apply to lift the stay[5] and, if successful, then to proceed to judgment for the balance. Another might be to start proceedings for the balance. But the sum at stake would have to be very high to justify the obvious risks in pursuing either course.

1 *Hughes v Justin* [1894] 1 QB 667.
2 See para 10.03, below.
3 For another possible exception see para 10.04, below.
4 See para 2.19 above.
5 *Cooper v Williams* [1963] 2 QB 567, [1963] 2 All ER 282; *Buckland v Palmer* [1984] 3 All ER 554, [1984] 1 WLR 1109, CA.

County court proceedings for the recovery of contractual interest

PARTICULARS OF CLAIM

2.24   In the county court the procedure is similar to that of the High Court, but simpler. If the plaintiff is claiming contractual interest his particulars of claim must contain a statement to this effect,[1] giving particulars of the amount claimed down to the issue of the plaint, the period over which it is claimed and the rate.[2] If the plaintiff wishes to obtain interest at the same rate for the period after issue down to payment or judgment, this too should be stated in his particulars of claim; otherwise he will be unable to obtain a final judgment for the post-issue interest without having it assessed first.[3] Another point about quantifying the interest which has accrued down to issue is that it is taken into account in determining the fee payable[4] and the fixed costs recoverable[5] if the defendant pays up within 14 days of service and avoids a judgment; the interest accruing after issue is not liquidated at that date and is accordingly left out of account for these purposes.

1 CCR Ord 6, r 1A; see Appendix B.
2 CCR Ord 9, r 8(1)(a); see Appendix B.
3 CCR Ord 9, r 8(3); see Appendix B.
4 Item 1 of Sch 1 to the County Court Fees Order 1982 (SI 1982/1706).
5 CCR Ord 38, r 18, Appendix B, Part I.

DEFAULT JUDGMENT FOR CONTRACTUAL INTEREST

2.25   If he has followed the correct procedure, as above, and the defendant either admits the claim or fails to defend it, the plaintiff may request the entry of a judgment for the whole amount of the claim,[1] including contractual interest accruing down to the date of that request. But the request itself must state the amount of post-issue interest outstanding, after allowing for payments made since issue, and the rate and the period over which it is calculated;[2] the consequence of failing to do so is that the plaintiff will obtain no more than an interlocutory judgment for that interest which will not be made final until the interest down to that date has been assessed.[3]

1 CCR Ord 9, r 3(2) or r 6(1). See Appendix B.
2 CCR Ord 9, r 8(2); Prescribed Form N 14. See precedent D7 in Appendix D.
3 CCR Ord 9, r 8(3): see Appendix B.

PAYMENT OF THE CLAIM AFTER ISSUE AND BEFORE JUDGMENT

2.26 Where, after receiving the summons, the defendant makes a payment on account, whether through the court or otherwise, the plaintiff may take it and proceed to judgment for the balance. Where, on the other hand, a sum less than the whole claim is paid into court in satisfaction,[1] acceptance of it by the plaintiff has the consequence that the proceedings are stayed, except as regards the recovery of costs.[2] Where, finally, the defendant pays the whole amount of the claim into court within 14 days of service, the proceedings are stayed in the same way, except as regards the recovery of costs.[3] These three propositions are easy enough to apply in practice where the amount of the claim is no more than the amount claimed to be owing at the date of issue. But where the plaintiff claims interest for the period after issue the amount of the claim is growing all the time. The question then arises whether a defendant who wishes to stop the proceedings by paying the whole amount of the claim into court must pay the whole amount due at the date of payment or only the amount due at the date of issue. On a strict construction of the rules[4] it would seem that he must pay everything that is claimed as due at the date of payment and that the plaintiff may accordingly treat a payment of anything less (eg what was due at issue) as a payment on account. There is nothing in the prescribed form of summons[5] which is inconsistent with this interpretation but a defendant would have to read the particulars of claim as well as the summons in order to appreciate the point. In practice, however, an underpayment will probably do: a plaintiff who receives the money due down to issue within 14 days of service is unlikely to think it worth the trouble and expense of pursuing his claim for the interest accruing thereafter.

1 Unless accompanied by a notice that the payment is made in satisfaction, the payment into court of anything less than the whole amount due is treated as a payment on account: CCR Ord 11, r 1(2). See Appendix B.
2 CCR Ord 11, r 3. See Appendix B.
3 CCR Ord 11, r 2(1). See Appendix B.
4 CCR Ord 11, r 2(1) specifies the *whole* amount.
5 Prescribed Form N1.

Limitation periods

2.27 As mentioned earlier,[1] s 13(1) of the Moneylenders Act

25

1927 provides a special limitation period of 12 months from the last payment becoming due under the contract, after which time the right to take proceedings is, subject to certain exceptions, barred. This period applies to those moneylending transactions to which that Act applies which were entered into before 19 May 1985. In addition there are special provisions in the Limitation Act 1980 governing proceedings to recover interest secured by a mortgage or charge: these are considered below.[2] In other respects the recovery of contractual interest is subject to the same general law of limitations as the recovery of the principal debts, ie there is a 6-year period in the ordinary case[3] and a 12-year period in the case of a promise under seal.[4] But it should be noted, as regards unsecured loans, that if the agreement does not provide for repayment on or before a fixed or determinable day and does not effectively make the obligation to repay conditional on a demand for repayment, or on any other matter, the limitation period does not start to run until a demand in writing for repayment has been made.[5]

1 See para 2.10, above.
2 See paras 2.29, below.
3 Limitation Act 1980, s 5.
4 Ibid, s 8, an action on such a promise being an action on a specialty.
5 Ibid, s 6.

2.28   Where a contract, not under seal, provides for the payment of interest, it might be thought that the interest would continue to accrue after the expiry of the time for recovery of the principal and that the last six years' interest would always be recoverable. But the general rule is that principal and interest constitute one demand so that if the principal is barred so is the interest.[1] Conversely where there is an open-ended loan, without security,[2] the liability for agreed interest would seem to be open-ended too. Once a contractual right, whether to be paid principal or interest, is statute-barred it cannot be revived[3] but if while the limitation period is current, the debtor makes a payment in respect of the principal debt,[4] the limitation period starts afresh under section 29(5) of the Limitation Act 1980. A payment of interest is treated, by section 29(6), as a payment in respect of the principal debt, so the debt which might otherwise become barred is kept alive. As regards the unpaid interest, however, section 29(6) and (7) provide, in effect, that the recoverability of old interest is not sustained by a payment on account.

1 *Elder v Northcott* [1930] 2 Ch 422.
2 Limitation Act 1980, s 6.
3 Ibid, s 29(7).
4 See para 2.06, on appropriation of money paid.

Mortgage interest

2.29   Different considerations apply to the recovery of interest where payment is secured by a mortgage, typically but not necessarily a legal mortgage or charge on land. In most cases the mortgagee will sue not for the money, or to foreclose on the mortgage, but for possession, so that he may realise his security by exercising his statutory right of sale. The time limit for an action for possession or for the recovery of the principal or the proceeds of sale of land is 12 years[1] and the time limit for claiming arrears of mortgage interest is six years.[2] The 12-year limitation period for recovery of possession is extended by every payment made in respect of principal or interest,[3] whereas the six year period in respect of mortgage interest is not.[4]

1 Limitation Act 1980, ss 15(1) and 20(1).
2 Ibid, s 20(5).
3 Ibid, s 29(3).
4 Ibid, s 29(6) and (7); see para 2.28, above.

2.30   As regards the enforcement of the rights under the mortgage, the county court's jurisdiction, under section 21 of the County Courts Act 1984, to order possession of a mortgaged dwelling-house outside Greater London, is exclusive, and a claim for the repayment of the mortgage debt and interest may be included in those proceedings even though the sum involved may exceed the county court limit. The procedure for a mortgage action in the county court[1] is very similar to that in the Chancery Division of the High Court.[2] If, after recovery of possession and sale there is an unpaid balance of unsecured debt and interest this may be sued for like any other contract debt.

1 CCR Ord 6, r 5. See Appendix B.
2 RSC Ord 88.

Rent arrears

INTEREST ON ARREARS OF RENT AND INTEREST AS PART OF THE RENT
2.31   A lease, or tenancy agreement, may properly provide for the payment of interest at a specified rate in respect of any money obligation, including the obligation to pay rent, on which the tenant defaults. Such a provision is often found in business leases[1] and there seems to be no reason, in principle, why such a provision should not be included in a lease of residential premises, even where the rent is subject to statutory control.[2] The provision may be framed in one of two significantly different ways. One way is for it to be expressed as an independent monetary obligation, not as part of

the rent. This might be advantageous for the landlord in the case of a letting of premises within the protection of the Rent Act 1977, since such a provision would probably survive an application for the determination of a fair rent or a reference to a rent tribunal. Another way of providing for interest would be as part and parcel of the rent reserved under the lease, and this would be disadvantageous from the landlord's point of view if the amount of rent was, or became, subject to a statutory limit: any amount of interest, which took the tenant's monetary obligation over the rent limit, would not be recoverable.

1 Law Commission's Report No 88 on Interest (1978 Cmnd 7229), para 61.
2 See, for example, Parts III, IV and V of the Rent Act 1977.

FORFEITURE PROCEEDINGS
2.32 As regards forfeiture proceedings for non-payment of rent, a failure to pay interest might be a breach of a separate covenant, or it might merely be another aspect of the tenant's breach of his obligation to pay rent; it would depend on how the agreement was drawn. In the latter case if forfeiture proceedings were brought in the county court on the ground of non-payment of rent (including interest) the defaulting tenant would be able to save his lease by paying whatever he owed, plus costs, five clear days before the return day; the court would have no discretion in the matter.[1] If, on the other hand, the obligation to pay interest were separate from the obligation to pay rent and the lease provided a right of re-entry for breach of it, the court would have a discretion whether to order possession even if everything was paid up as soon as the proceedings were served.[2]

1 County Courts Act 1984, s 138(2).
2 Ibid, s 138(6) and (10).

DISTRESS
2.33 The same point comes up again in relation to distress for rent. Such slender authority as there is[1] suggests that the landord may distrain for interest where the obligation to pay it is part of the rent obligation reserved by the lease, but not where it arises from an independent undertaking.

1 *Skerry v Preston* (1813) 2 Chit 245.

Hire-purchase arrears

HIRE-PURCHASE ACT 1965
2.34 Notwithstanding its repeal by the Consumer Credit Act

1974, the Hire-purchase Act 1965 still applies to agreements made before 19 May 1985. The terms of those hire-purchase agreements and conditional sales to which the Act applies are somewhat circumscribed. However, a common characteristic of each is that the customer has the advantage of paying the cash price plus credit charges by instalments, usually one a month, instead of paying the cash price all at once; and, because the charge for the period of credit is worked out on the assumption that the instalments will be paid on time such agreements invariably provide for interest to be paid on any instalments which are in arrears. There is nothing in the Act to invalidate such a provision, or to impede its enforcement, and so long as the owner recovers his goods before going to court there is no difficulty about his obtaining judgment for the arrears of instalments and the interest that is due on them.[1] If however the hirer, or buyer, falls into arrears and the owner, after serving the necessary notices, takes proceedings for the recovery of his goods, the question of interest on the arrears tends to get overlooked. Unless it is claimed in the same proceedings as those in which he seeks a possession order, under section 35 of the Act, the creditor will find that he has to do without. If the possession order is suspended it will be on terms which require the payment of the balance of the hire-purchase price, but not anything on top.[2] If, on the other hand, the possession order is made and the goods are recovered the owner can come back to the court for arrears of instalments but not for interest on them.[3] Finally, if a possession order is made but later revoked[4] the hirer, or buyer, will be ordered to pay the balance of the price, and the court may indeed reduce this figure if the money has to be paid earlier than under the agreement,[5] but the Act makes no provision for the recovery of interest on top, if the money has to be spread over a longer period, as it usually has. The way out of all these problems would seem to be to sue for interest on the instalment arrears in the same action as that in which possession of the goods is sought and to obtain an order for its payment as an extra provision in the possession order. The prescribed forms of Hire-Purchase Act orders for possession[6] do not provide in terms, for judgment to be given at the same time for interest on instalment arrears; but so long as the claim for such is properly pleaded[7] there would seem to be no reason why the prescribed form of order should not be varied[8] to include a provision for such interests to be paid.

1 *Financing Ltd v Baldock* [1963] 2 QB 104, [1963] 1 All ER 443, CA; *Brady v St Margaret's Trust Ltd* [1963] 2 QB 494, [1963] 2 All ER 275, CA.
2 Hire-Purchase Act 1965, s 35(4)(b). See the definition of 'hire-purchase price' in s 58(1).

29

3 Ibid, s 44. Section 41 prevents the bringing of a separate action.
4 Ibid, s 42(3) and (4).
5 Ibid, s 42(6).
6 N 32(2)–(3).
7 CCR Ord 6, r 1A and 6(1)(xii). See Appendix B.
8 County Court (Forms) Rules 1982 (SI 1982/586) r 2(2).

CONSUMER CREDIT ACT 1974
2.35   A liability for interest on instalment arrears is clearly within
the contemplation of the Consumer Credit Act 1974, because section
93 limits the rate of interest that may be charged under a regulated
consumer agreement.[1] But in other respects the Act provides for the
recovery of interest on instalment arrears in a way which is, from the
creditor's point of view, more satisfactory than under the Hire-
Purchase Act 1965. In particular, a 'time order' under section 129
may apply to the payment of *'any* sum owed under a regulated
agreement', thereby including not only the rental instalment but
interest already accrued; and section 130 allows the court to provide
for sums which would become payable in the future as well, such as
future instalments and interest thereon. Moreover, in calculating the
balance to be paid where goods are not returned, section 133(2)
provides that a deduction made from the sum already paid is to be
made in respect of 'Any sum owed by the debtor in relation to the
goods (otherwise than as part of the total price)' which would seem
to cover interest accrued on arrears of instalments. On the other
hand there is a new restriction on the interest rate which may be
charged in respect of arrears of instalments: section 93 prohibits the
making of any contractual provision for interest on arrears at a rate
higher than the rate of interest charged for credit under the main
agreement.

1 See para 2.14, above and Appendix A for the text of the Act.

Chapter 3

Interest as damages at law and in equity

Interest as damages at law

3.01 The civil jury's power to award interest as damages for breach of contract was once seen as a very broad discretion, available in almost every case.[1] But the last time that such views received judicial support was in 1826 in *Arnott v Redfern*[2] when Best CJ said:

> Our law would not do what it professes to do, namely, provide a remedy for every act of injustice, if it did not allow damages to be given for interest where a creditor has been kept out of his debt (he using all proper means to recover it) by his debtor.

1 See para 1.06 above.
2 (1826) 3 Bing 353.

THE LONDON, CHATHAM AND DOVER RAILWAY CASE
3.02 But the force of Best CJ's observations was much diminished by the passing of the Lord Tenterden's Act in 1833. This Act empowered civil juries to award interest, but only in a narrowly drawn group of situations where the injustice would otherwise have been very great.[1] The question whether interest could be awarded in other situations, outside the Act, did not receive a definitive ruling until 1893, in *London, Chatham and Dover Rly Co v South Eastern Rly Co*[2] when the House of Lords decided that there was no general right to damages in the form of interest; it might only be awarded where there was an entitlement to interest pursuant to statute or contract or in the various situations in which a right to damages in the form of interest was established as a matter of mercantile usage. The

position was reluctantly confirmed by Lord Herschell in the following words:[3]

> I think that when money is owing from one party to another and that other is driven to have recourse to legal proceedings in order to recover the amount due to him, the party who is wrongfully withholding the money from the other ought not in justice to benefit by having that money in his possession and enjoying the use of it, when the money ought to be in the possession of the other party who is entitled to its use. Therefore, if I could see my way to do so, I should certainly be disposed to give the appellants, or anybody in a similar position, interest upon the amount withheld from the time of action brought at all events. But I have come to the conclusion, upon a consideration of the authorities, agreeing with the Court below, that it is not possible to do so, although no doubt in early times the view was expressed that interest might be given under such circumstances by way of damages.

1 See para 1.06, above.
2 [1893] AC 429.
3 Ibid, at p 437.

3.03   In 1966 the Lord Chancellor, Lord Gardiner, cleared the way for a fresh look at old precedents by announcing, in the form of a *Practice Note*,[1] that the House of Lords would not necessarily regard itself as bound by its earlier decisions if it seemed right in any particular case to depart from them. In 1984 the point which had been decided in the *London, Chatham and Dover Railway* case came before the House of Lords again; it arose directly for decision in *President of India v La Pintada Cia Navegacion SA*.[2] But, notwithstanding their evident dissatisfaction with the existing state of the law,[3] their Lordships decided that the common law position was as stated in the *London, Chatham and Dover Railway* case. Interestingly the reasoning which led Lord Brandon, at least, to this conclusion was very similar to that which had weighed with Lord Herschell nearly a hundred years before: it was that Parliament had intervened in 1982 (as in 1833) to confer a modicum of statutory relief on the assumption that no broader relief was to be had at common law and that it was therefore too late to take a more generous view of the common law position. Thus the right to seek interest as damages for breach of contract, where there is no contractual provision in this regard, must now be seen as wholly exceptional, the main exceptions being based on mercantile usage.

1 [1966] 3 All ER 77, [1966] 1 WLR 1234.
2 [1984] 2 All ER 773, [1984] 3 WLR 10, HL.
3 See in particular the speeches of Lord Roskill and Lord Scarman.

MERCANTILE USAGE: BILLS OF EXCHANGE
3.04   The clearest, and possibly the only genuine example of a
common law right to claim interest as damages, based on mercantile
usage, is in relation to the dishonour of bills of exchange. The right
to such damages was one of the features of the Law Merchant which
Lord Mansfield succeeded in having incorporated into the common
law of England and in 1807 Lord Ellenborough, although generally
opposed to awards of interest as damages,[1] conceded that the right
to interest as damages for dishonour of a bill was well established.[2]
Indeed, the right to such damages still exists today[3] although
creditors normally prefer to sue instead for statutory interest under
section 57 of the Bills of Exchange Act 1882.

1 See para 1.06, above.
2 *De Havilland v Bowerbank* (1807) 1 Camp 50, at 57.
3 *Re Gillespie, ex Robarts* (1885) 16 QBD 702.

BILLS OF EXCHANGE ACT 1882
3.05   The recoverability of interest as damages at common law
was, and still is, a valuable remedy for the holder of a dishonoured
bill. But the drawback was that such damages had to be assessed, by
a jury, before a judgment could be entered which the creditor could
enforce. This meant extra time and extra costs—and a real risk that
the pursuit of interest, as an enforceable award, would mean
throwing good money after bad. A way round this difficulty was
provided by section 57 of the Bills of Exchange Act 1882.[1] By the
provisions of this section the redress for the dishonour of the bill,
including interest, is deemed to be liquidated damages and the
creditor may accordingly sue for the following sums, as liquidated
debts (a) the amount of the bill, (b) interest thereon from the time of
presentment for payment, if the bill is payable on demand, and from
maturity of the bill in any other case, and (c) the expenses of noting
or, where protest is necessary and the protest has been extended, the
expenses of protest. This might seem to enable the creditor to write
his own award for interest at whatever rate he likes. But a safeguard
is provided by subsection (3), whereby the claim for interest may, if
justice require it, be disallowed wholly or in part and, where a bill is
expressed to be payable with interest at a given rate, interest as
damages may or may not be given at the same rate as interest proper.
Current practice is to plead, as the rate claimed for interest on a
dishonoured bill, the rate payable on the Short Term Investment
Account[2] or, at least, not to venture much higher than the base rate
charged by banks for lending money.[3] The claim for interest under
the statute must, of course, be pleaded and the relief sought in the

pleading (and in the writ) should include a claim for interest down to judgment or sooner payment, as well as for the interest accrued at issue of the writ, shown as a liquidated debt.[4]

1 See Appendix A for the text of the section.
2 See para 10.13 and Appendix E.
3 *Practice Direction*, 23 February 1983, [1983] 1 All ER 934, [1983] 1 WLR 377; see Appendix C.
4 Ibid.

REIMBURSEMENT OF INTEREST CHARGES AS AN ITEM OF SPECIAL DAMAGES

3.06 Another exception, which might be said to derive from mercantile usage, was opened up by the Court of Appeal in *Trans Trust SPRL v Danubian Trading Co Ltd*[1] by allowing that a head of loss that was within the contemplation of the parties might be recovered as special damages for breach of contract *even if it took the form of interest*. This has been exploited at least twice recently.[2] First, in *Ozalid Group (Export) Ltd v African Continental Bank Ltd*,[3] Donaldson J, as he then was, held that the late payment of money payable in a depreciating currency entitled the plaintiff to recover, as special damages for breach of contract, (a) the difference between the sterling equivalent of the currency at the date when it should have been paid and when it was paid and (b) interest on the difference, from the date when payment was due. Next in *Wadsworth v Lydall*[4] the Court of Appeal held that the interest charges incurred by the plaintiff farmer in borrowing money to buy a new home as a result of the defendant's breach of contract, in failing to pay the full price of the farm, constituted special damages which were within the contemplation of the parties and recoverable accordingly. On the other hand, it was held by Neill J in *Alsabah Maritime Services Co Ltd v Philippine International Shipping Corpn*[5] that interest charges could not be recovered as special damages where the contract provided expressly that further charges would not arise under it unless agreed between the parties, and where the charging of interest was illegal in the jurisdiction in which the contract sum should have been paid.

1 [1952] 2 QB 297, [1952] 1 All ER 970.
2 See too *Bushwall Properties Ltd v Vortex Properties Ltd* [1976] 2 All ER 214, [1975] 1 WLR 1649, which was reversed on another point: [1976] 1 WLR 591, CA.
3 [1979] 2 Lloyd's Rep 231.
4 [1981] 2 All ER 401 [1981] 1 WLR 598, CA.
5 (1983) Times, 8 December.

ADMIRALTY

3.07 The Admiralty jurisdiction to award interest as damages, or as an addition to the damages, still exists and may be invoked. These circumstances include claims for damage to property and for salvage. Interest was described in the old cases[1] as the *entitlement* of the plaintiff, but in more recent times it has taken the form of a discretionary award,[2] and the courts have shown some flexibility over the rate of interest to be applied; the Short Term Investment Account was used in *The Funabashi*.[3] As regards the period, the starting-date is often taken as the date of the collision, but the date of paying the repair bill may be the more appropriate starting-date in the case of a vessel that was damaged but not sunk.[4] But, unlike contractual interest, the interest element in an Admiralty claim may not be pursued in isolation, once the substantive damages have been paid.[5]

1 *The Dundee* (1827) 2 Hag Adm 137 *Kong Magnus* [1891] P 223.
2 *The Berwickshire* [1950] P 204, 208.
3 [1972] 1 WLR 666. For rates see Appendix E.
4 *The Hebe* (1847) 2 Wm Rob 530.
5 *The Medina Princess* [1962] 2 Lloyd's Rep 17; *President of India v La Pintada Compania Navigacion SA* [1984] 2 All ER 773, [1984] 3 WLR 10, HL.

Interest in equity

3.08   It has been held that a defendant who has obtained and retained money by fraud may be ordered to pay interest on it.[1] This liability for interest can be based in quasi-contract (as money had and received) or as breach of fiduciary duty. As regards the latter, the equitable jurisdiction to order someone in breach of duty to pay interest as ancillary relief in an action for damages or rescission or for the taking of an account awarded is well-established. Indeed the jurisdiction includes power to order the interest to be compounded with periodic rests, say, yearly. Compound interest might well be appropriate in the case of a flagrant breach of fiduciary duty by someone who invested trust money on his own account.[2] Interest may also be awarded in an administration action.[3]

1 *Johnson v R* [1904] AC 817.
2 *Burdick v Garrick* (1870) 5 Ch App 233; *Wallersteiner v Moir (No 2)* [1975] QB 373, [1975] 1 All ER 849, CA.
3 See paras 9.05–9.10, below.

SPECIFIC PERFORMANCES
3.09   Interest may be awarded on the purchase price where a decree of specific performance is ordered against a purchaser,[1] but not in the case of a purchase of shares ordered by the court under section 75 of the Companies Act 1980.[2]

3.10 *Interest as damages at law and in equity*

1 *Re Hewitt's Contract* [1963] 3All ER 419; *Harvela Investments Ltd v Royal Trust Co of Canada* [1984] 2 All ER 65 (reversed on appeal, on a different point: [1985] 1 All ER 261, CA).
2 *Re a Company (No 003420 of 1981)* (1983) Times, 30 November.

SECRET PROFITS
3.10   It is a general principle of trust law that where a person receives money from someone with whom there is a fiduciary relationship he is a trustee for the depositor of any interest made by the investment of that money.[1] This applies wherever a fiduciary relationship exists between the client and the professional adviser, be he solicitor, stockbroker or accountant. The object of the rule is to prevent the expert from abusing his position of confidence in order to make a secret profit with his client's money. But so long as the profit is disclosed there is no reason why he and the client should not agree how it is to be applied and, indeed, that it, or part of it, should be kept by the depositee as remuneration for professional services.

1 *Brown v IRC* [1965] AC 244, [1964] 3 All ER 119.

SOLICITORS
3.11   The duties owed to a client by his solicitor, regarding interest accruing on money deposited with him, are now regulated by statute and by rules.[1] By section 33(1) of the Solicitors Act 1974, rules may be made regarding the solicitor's duty to account to his client for interest on the client's money and the Solicitors' Account (Deposit Interest) Rules 1975 have been made in exercise of these powers. Rule 2(1) makes it a general rule that when a solicitor holds or receives money for a client on which, having regard to all the circumstances (including the amount and the length of time for which the money is likely to be held) interest ought in fairness to the client to be earned for him, the solicitor should either (a) deposit the money in a designated account and pay him the interest accruing, or (b) pay the client, out of his own money, a sum equivalent to the interest which would have accrued for the benefit of the client if it had been so deposited.[2] This general rule is glossed by rule 3 which deems the requirement to pay interest to be satisfied wherever the solicitor receives £500 or more of which at least £50 is likely to be left at the end of two months.

1 For the effect on these rules of the composite rate of tax scheme for interest on bank deposits, see the Law Society's statement (1985) 82 Law Society's Gazette pp 738–740, the material parts of which are set out in G2 in Appendix G.

3.12   The rules just described, in outline, replace the fiduciary duty of a solicitor to account to his client for deposit interest on the client's money.[1] Furthermore, nothing in section 33 of the Solicitors Act 1974 is to affect any agreement *in writing* between the solicitor and his client as to the application of the client's money or interest on it;[1] nor is anything in the section to apply to money received by a solicitor which is money subject to a trust of which the solicitor is a trustee.[2]

1 Solicitors Act 1974 s 4(a). Part II of the Administration of Justice Bill makes similar provisions for licensed conveyancers.
2 Ibid, s 4(b).

ESTATE AGENTS AND STAKEHOLDERS
3.13   Whereas the right to claim interest in equity may well arise in a contractual context, it arises out of the relationship, not out of the contract. At law, on the other hand, it is for the contracting parties to provide, either expressly or impliedly, for the payment of interest on a deposit, otherwise none is due. Thus at common law the stakeholder, say an auctioneer, who holds money paid by a prospective buyer, is entitled to keep for himself any interest that accrues on the money while deposited in his bank account.[1] The same applies in the case of a solicitor, as where the vendor's solicitor receives the purchaser's deposit and holds it in the capacity of a stakeholder. Money so held is not client's money and is accordingly outside the scope of the Solicitor's Accounts (Deposit Interest) Rules 1975.[2] Before the coming into operation of the Estate Agents Act 1979, estate agents used to keep the interest accruing on money deposited with them as stakeholders, as they were entitled to do at common law. But that Act made two important changes. First it made the estate agent a trustee of money received on behalf of a client, *or in the capacity as stakeholder.*[3] Second, it provided for regulations to be made for interest to be paid on money so received; and regulation 7 of the Estate Agents (Accounts) Regulations 1981[4] requires interest to be paid on any amount of client's money in excess of £500 on which interest exceeding £10 has accrued or would have accrued if deposited.[5] However, as in the case of solicitors, different arrangements for the payment of interest will prevail if made in writing. It has been suggested that the legislation affecting estate agents ought, in the consumer interest, to be applied to solicitors as well.[6]

1 *Potters v Loppert* [1973] Ch 399, [1973] 1 All ER 658.
2 See para 3.12, above.
3 Estate Agents Act 1979, s 13(1).
4 SI 1981/1520.
5 As regards accounting to the client for interest which is paid less the composite rate of tax (CRT) the position of estate agents is broadly the same as that of solicitors, as set out in the Law Society's statement in G2 in Appendix G. See, too, para 11.14, below.
6 National Consumer Council's discussion Paper 'Whose Interest?' (1984).

Chapter 4

Statutory interest

Statutory entitlement

4.01   There are many statutory provisions which create entitlement to interest. The most important of them are those concerned with interest on judgments and awards, on debts admitted to proof in an insolvency and on overdue tax. These are dealt with in the chapters which follow. Of the rest the following are representative of the many different situations in which a statutory right to interest may arise:

(a) Statutory Form of Conditions of Sale, condition 4;[1]
(b) Housing Act 1957, s 10(3), Housing Act 1961, s 18(3) and Housing Act 1974, s 94(3);
(c) Land Compensation Act 1961 s 32(1) and the Acquisition of Land (Rate of Interest after Entry) Regulations which are made thereunder;[2]
(d) Carriage of Goods by Road Act 1965, Sch, art 27;
(e) Solicitors' Remuneration Order 1972, art 5(1).[3]

1 S R & O 1925/779.
2 The rate fixed by these Regulations has been adopted as the contract rate, if no other rate is expressly agreed, under the National Conditions of Sale and the Law Society's Conditions of Sale.
3 SI 1972/1139.

ENFORCEMENT OF STATUTORY ENTITLEMENT TO INTEREST
4.02   In some of the instances just given the statutory entitlement merely supplements the contractual arrangements made between the parties,[1] in which case the interest may be recovered by court proceedings in the same way as if it were contractual interest, except

that the statutory basis of the claim must, of course, be pleaded.[2] With others the entitlement to interest is a freestanding right, independent of any contractual arrangement.[3] Here again it may be recovered through the courts like contractual interest except that the statutory basis of the entitlement must be pleaded. Where the statute provides for interest to accrue 'until payment' the plaintiff who sues to recover the charges, expenses and interest to which he is statutorily entitled may obtain an order for interest on the charges and expenses to accrue after judgment at the rate provided by that statute instead of the judgment rate (if any).[4] Some statutory rights to interest, typically those under the various Housing Acts, are enforceable by methods other than suing the defaulter to judgment: other possibilities include the enforcement of a statutory charge,[5] seeking a local authority charging order[6] and obtaining a county court order for the money to be paid by the person who has had the benefit of the expenditure in question.[7]

1 See, for example (a), (d) and (e) in the preceding paragraph.
2 *Sheba Gold Mining Co Ltd v Trubshaw* [1892] 1 QB 674.
3 See the examples in (b) and (c).
4 *Ealing v El Isaac* [1980] 2 All ER 548, [1980] 1WLR 932, CA. See paras 6.06, 6.07 and 6.17, below.
5 Housing Act, s 10(3), s 14; Housing Act 1961, s 18(5).
6 Housing Act 1957, ss 14 and 15; Housing Act 1974, s 95.
7 Housing Act 1961, s 18(6).

Discretionary awards pursuant to statute

4.03   The other main category of statutory interest is the discretionary award of interest made pursuant to statute. The interest recoverable under section 57 of the Bills of Exchange Act 1882 could be classed under this head, because the interest so recovered is not absolute entitlement but subject to a judicial discretion.[1] A further example, which is considered in Chapter 6, concerns the award under section 66(a) of the Solicitors Act 1974 of interest on disbursement items in a taxed bill of costs.[2] But the most widely and frequently invoked statutory discretion is that which empowers the courts to award interest on debts and damages. This head of statutory interest started with sections 28 and 29 of Lord Tenterden's Act,[3] was developed and extended by section 3(1) of the Law Reform (Miscellaneous Provisions) Act 1934 ('the 1934 Act') and is now to be seen at full stretch in section 33A of the Supreme Court Act 1971 and section 69 of the County Courts Act 1984, as a result of the reforms made by the Administration of Justice Act 1982. Awards of statutory interest in relation to damages for personal

39

injury are treated separately in the next chapter: the remainder of
this chapter is about statutory interest on debts and on damages,
outside personal injury litigation.

1 See para 3.05 above.
2 See para 6.04, below.
3 Civil Procedure Act 1833. See para 1.06, above.

STATUTORY INTEREST UNDER THE 1934 ACT

4.04 Powers to award interest on debts and damages were given
to all courts of record by section 3(1) of the Law Reform (Miscella-
neous Provisions) Act 1934 ('the 1934 Act'). The text of this
provision, including the four subsections added by section 22 of the
Administration of Justice Act 1969, is set out in Appendix A.
However, by section 15(4) and (5) of the Administration of Justice
Act 1982, these provisions ceased to have effect in relation to the
High Court and the county courts as from 1 April 1983 when section
15 was brought into operation by the Administration of Justice
(Commencement No 1) Order 1983 (SI 1983/236). As regards the
High Court and the county courts new powers to award interest
have been inserted in the Supreme Court Act 1981 and the County
Courts Act 1959 (since consolidated) by Parts I and II of Schedule 1
to the Administration of Justice Act 1982. The relevant provisions,
namely section 35A of the Supreme Court Act 1981 and section 69
of the County Courts Act 1984 are set out in Appendix A.
Consequential amendments have been made to the Crown Proceedings Act 1947 and section 375A of the Income and Corporation
Taxes Act 1970 (interest on damages for personal injuries or death
not income for tax purposes) by Part III of Schedule I and section
74, respectively, of the Administration of Justice Act 1982. Accordingly the old law now applies to no more than a few miscellaneous
courts of record before which applications for interest must be very
rare; they include the Restrictive Practices Court,[1] election courts,[2]
the Transport Tribunal,[3] the Barmote Courts of the High Peak[4]
and the Employment Appeal Tribunal[5] (but not industrial tribunals). There is no decided case law on the practice of these courts in
relation to awards of interest and the subject is not discussed further
in this book. However, the Court of Appeal deserves a special
mention since it is a superior court of record[6] on which no powers
are conferred by section 15(1) and (2) of the Administration of
Justice Act 1982. It might therefore be argued that such powers as it
was able to exercise under section 3(1) of the 1934 Act remain and
might be exercised. But in the case of an appeal from the High Court
or county court the Court of Appeal would possess the interest-

awarding powers of the court of first instance, by virtue of section 15(3) of the Supreme Court Act 1981, so the need to resort to the 1934 Act would not arise except, perhaps, as a basis for awarding interest for the period between the judgment at first instance and the decision of the Court of Appeal.[7]

1 Restrictive Trade Practices Act 1956, s 112(3).
2 Representation of the People Act 1983, s 123(2).
3 Transport Act 1962, Sch 10, para 1.
4 High Peak Mining Customs and Mineral Courts Act 1851, s 15.
5 Employment Protection (Consolidation) Act 1978, Sch 11, para 12.
6 Supreme Court Act 1981, s 15(1).
7 See, for example, the somewhat dubious award of interest made by the Court of Appeal in *Cook v J Kier & Co Ltd* [1970] 2 All ER 513, [1970] 1 WLR 774.

DEFECTS IN THE 1934 ACT AND SUBSEQUENT REFORMS
4.05   The changes in the powers of the High Court and the county courts implement in part the recommendations of the Law Commission in their Report No. 88 on Interest.[1] Part II of the Report points to defects in the 1934 Act and considers two main options for reform: (1) the introduction of a statutory *entitlement* to interest at a prescribed rate on all contract debts, save to the extent that the parties may otherwise agree and (2) the conferment on courts of record of a wider *discretion* to award interest than that arising under the 1934 Act. The first option has not been taken up, notwithstanding the Law Commission's recommendations in this regard, but the second one has, subject to some important modifications.

1 (1978) Cmnd 7229; see paras 236–239 and cll 10 and 11 of the draft Bill annexed to the Report.

(a) Debts or damages paid before the issue of proceedings
4.06   One defect in the 1934 Act which was identified by the Law Commission but which has been carried over into the new law is that it gives the courts no power to award interest in respect of debts or damages which are paid late but before the commencement of proceedings. The failure to include a remedy for this defect in the reforms of 1982 attracted critical comment from the House of Lords in the *President of India v La Pintada Compania Navigacion SA*.[1] The other defects, considered below, have been treated, although not exactly in the ways recommended by the Law Commission.

1 [1984] 2 All ER 773, [1984] 3 WLR 10, HL.

(b) Debts or damages paid after issue but before judgment
4.07   A serious weakness in the 1934 Act was that it did not enable the court to award interest in respect of a debt or damages

paid after the issue of proceedings and before judgment. In the *Techno-Impex* case Lord Denning MR observed that 'Many astute debtors take advantage of this. They delay for months before writ is issued. They delay many more months till the action is about to come to trial. Then they pay the principal at the last moment before judgment. And thus get out of paying interest.'[1] The ploy so described is no longer available since the new law empowers the High Court and county courts to award interest in the case of any sum paid after the start of proceedings and before judgment.[2]

1 *Techno-Impex v Gebr Van Weelde Scheepraartkantoor BV* [1981] QB 648 at 661, [1981] 2 All ER 669 at 674.
2 Supreme Court Act 1981, s 35A(1)(a); County Courts Act 1984, s 69(1)(a): see Appendix A.

(c) Judgment without trial

4.08   Another weakness in the 1934 Act was that its operation was limited to proceedings which were 'tried'. The requirement of a 'trial' may suggest a trial on the merits rather than summary judgment or a default judgment. But the Court of Appeal held, in *Gardner Steel Limited v Sheffield Bros (Profiles) Ltd*,[1] that proceedings under RSC Order 14 amount to a trial for the purpose of enabling the court to award interest under section 3(1) of the 1934 Act. This decision would seem to apply with equal force to a judgment under CCR Order 9 rule 14 in the county court. As regards a default judgment the position is not so clear. Before the decision of Drake J in *Alex Lawrie Factors Ltd v Modern Injection Moulds Ltd*[2] it was thought by some that section 3(1) could *not* be invoked in the case of a default judgment.[3] Drake J held the contrary but, there being no Court of Appeal decision on the point, it remained open to some doubt, particularly as regards judgments obtained by default, or on an admission, in the county court. This doubt has now been removed: there is no requirement in the new provisions that the proceedings have to be 'tried' before the power to award interest may be invoked, so interest may now be included in any judgment whether obtained by default or on an admission or after a contest.

1 [1978] 3 All ER 399, [1978] 1 WLR 916, CA.
2 [1981] 3 All ER 658.
3 See the dicta of Fisher J in *Waite v Redpath Dorman Long Ltd* [1971] 1 QB 294 at 299, [1971] 1 All ER 513 at 516.

(d) Uncertainty as to what, if any, interest might be awarded

4.09   Under the 1934 Act the award of interest was entirely at the discretion of the court. General principles regarding the exercise of that discretion were propounded as the case law developed, and were glossed by the amendments to section 3(1), which were made by section 22 of the Administration of Justice Act 1969, but nothing touched the decision in *Riches v Westminster Bank Ltd*[1] that interest could be sought and awarded without the applicant's having either to stipulate for it in his pleadings or to give his opponent prior notice of his intention to apply. This was supportable so long as the defendant was not expected to include anything on account of discretionary interest when he made a payment into court,[2] but on 1 October 1980 the law in this respect was changed by amendments to the rules on payment into court, as recommended by the Law Commission in their Report.[3] As a result, a payment into court which does not include something on account of discretionary interest may now turn out to be inadequate in this respect. On the other hand separate amendments to the rules now require the plaintiff to include any claim for interest in his pleadings, even if it is only a claim for a discretionary award under the new provisions.[4] The power to impose this important procedural condition was created by the insertion of the words 'subject to rules of court' in section 35A(1) of the Supreme Court Act 1981 and the insertion of an equivalent phrase in the county court provisions. Thus the new law, by requiring the plaintiff, if he wants discretionary interest, to stipulate for it in his pleadings has, pro tanto, reduced the uncertainty as to whether an application is to be made and whether interest should be included in any payment into court.

1 [1943] 2 All ER 725.
2 *Jefford v Gee* [1970] 2 QB 130, at 149 and 150, [1970] 1 All ER 1202, at 1211.
3 See now RSC Ord 22, r 1(8), and CCR Ord 11, r 1(8); para 243 of the Law Commission's Report No 88. See Appendix B for the text.
4 RSC Ord 18, r 8(4), CCR Ord 6, r 1A; see Appendix B.

4.10 The uncertainty about the sum to be awarded by way of discretionary interest has been reduced in another way as well. Whereas under the old law the fixing of the rate and period for a discretionary award required an assessment by the court, the new law allows discretionary interest to be included 'at such rate as the court thinks fit *or as rules of court may provide*'.[1] The additional words, in italics, have made it possible for discretionary interest on debts to be included in a default judgment without an assesment, so long as the claim for discretionary interest is made in the proper form at a rate authorised by rules of court. The authorised rate is now fixed, by RSC Order 13, rule 1(2) and CCR Order 9, rule 8, as *no higher than the rate payable on judgment debts in the High Court at the date of commencement of proceedings*. The linkage of the

Supreme Court rules to the rate specified in section 17 of the Judgments Act 1838, as that section has effect from time to time, is permitted by section 35A(5) of the Supreme Court Act 1981; by section 75(2) of the County Courts Act 1984 the same linkage is permitted in respect of the County Court Rules. The result overall is to reduce the area of uncertainty which surrounded discretionary awards under the 1934 Act, although the greater certainty has not been achieved in the way recommended by the Law Commission which was by creating a statutory *entitlement* to interest as a prescribed rate in respect of contract debts.

1 Supreme Court Act 1981, s 35A(1), County Courts Act 1984, s 69(1); see Appendix A.

THE NEW REGIME FOR THE HIGH COURT AND COUNTY COURTS; DEBTS AND DAMAGES TO WHICH IT APPLIES

4.11   The new regime is not radically different from the old; it is basically the same model as before, but with improvements. Like the old it empowers the High Court or, as the case may be, a county court, to award simple interest in 'proceedings for the recovery of a debt or damages', a phrase which has been carried over from the 1934 Act. As regards proceedings for the recovery of *a debt*, these are not limited to proceedings for the recovery of a contract debt but would seem to include any proceedings for the recovery of a liquidated sum to which the plaintiff may be entitled. For example, the phrase has been held to cover an action for salvage[1] and, in another case,[2] an action for the value of work done under a contract which had been frustrated. On the other hand, an application for a maintenance order is not a proceeding for the recovery of a debt. This is because the question what, if anything, should be paid by way of maintenance is essentially a matter for the court's discretion; before the order is made there is no entitlement which may be characterised as a liquidated debt. By the same reasoning, however, arrears of maintenance due under a separation agreement or other contractual arrangements, are contract debts which are recoverable as such, and so interest may be awarded. Property disputes which are determined under section 17 of the Married Women's Property Act 1882, typically proceedings for a declaration as to the beneficial interests in the home, will not normally be, or include, proceedings for a debt or damages. Arguably, however, a claim to all or part of the proceeds of sale of the disputed property is a proceeding for the recovery of a quasi-contractual debt on which a discretionary award of interest might in some circumstances be appropriate.[3]

1 *The Aldora* [1975] QB 748, [1975] 2 All ER 69.

2 *BP Exploration Co (Libya) Ltd v Hunt (No 2)* [1983] 2 AC 352.
3 See *Harrison v Harrison* (1975) 5 Fam Law 15, CA for a situation where an award of interest on a share of a matrimonial home was held *not* to be appropriate.

4.12   Whereas the proceedings to which the new regime applies are substantially the same as under the old, some of the restrictions on the award of interest in such proceedings have been eased a little. In particular, section 3(1) of the 1934 Act qualified the interest-awarding powers by provisos that nothing in the section should (a) authorise the giving of interest upon interest or (b) apply in relation to any debt on which interest was payable as of right. By contrast, the corresponding qualifications in the new regime are that the court's powers (a) are limited to awarding simple interest and (b) may not be exercised in respect of a debt, as regards a period during which interest on the debt already runs.[1] Accordingly, an award may be made under the new provisions in respect of a debt which comprises contractual interest and also in respect of a debt which carries interest for a period other than the period for which an award of interest is sought. For example, where goods are sold on the terms that simple interest shall run at a specified rate from 28 days after the delivery of a statement of account, the unpaid seller not only may sue for the debt and contractual interest but also, under the new regime but not the old, may seek an award of interest (a) on the principal debt in respect of the initial period of 28 days and (b) on the contractual interest in respect of the subsequent period. However, the new power to make such awards would only be exercised in exceptional circumstances, the normal practice being not to make discretionary award of interest which would run contrary to the arrangements for the payment of interest which have been agreed expressly.[2] Moreover it is doubtful whether a claim for discretionary interest in respect of the sum accruing as contractual interest can properly be formulated as a claim for a liquidated debt for the purpose of obtaining a default judgment without an assessment. The objection is that the calculation of such an award involves more than the application of a certain rate to a certain sum over a certain period: in addition the court would need to investigate and determine the periodicity of the act of moving accrued interest over to the principal. As regards proceedings for the recovery of *damages*, the only exclusion made by the new regime is the one made by the old, namely that nothing in it is to affect the damages recoverable by way of interest upon the dishonour of a bill of exchange.[3]

1 Compare Supreme Court Act 1981, s 35A(1) and (4) and County Courts Act 1984, s 69(1) and (4), with Law Reform (Miscellaneous Provisions) Act 1934, s 1(1)(a) and (b). The text of all three is in Appendix A.

2 *Harvela Investments Ltd v Royal Trust Co of Canada* [1984] 2 All ER 65, (reversed by the Court of Appeal on another point: [1985] 1 All ER 261).
3 Supreme Court Act 1981, s 35A (7) and County Courts Act 1984, s 69(7); Law Reform (Miscellaneous Provisions) Act 1934, s 3(1)(c). See Appendix A.

STATUTORY INTEREST AND THE COUNTY COURT LIMIT

4.13   The rest of this chapter is concerned with the recovery of interest under section 35A of the Supreme Court Act 1981 and section 69 of the County Courts Act 1984 by means of proceedings in the High Court and county courts respectively; references here-after to 'statutory interest' should be construed accordingly. Before considering the procedure and practice in the two jurisdictions, High Court and county court, it is convenient to examine the relevance of statutory interest to the county court limit and to the various tariffs for costs and court fees which are fixed by reference to the monetary value of the claim. Section 69(8) of the County Courts Act 1984 is to the same effect as section 3(1C) of the 1934 Act, and provides that, in determining whether an amount exceeds the county court limit, or an amount specified in any provision of the County Courts Act 1984, no account is to be taken of the provision of section 69 or of anything done under it. Thus an action for debt or damage that is just within the county court jurisdictional limit for contract and tort (currently £5,000) will not be put beyond it by the addition of statutory interest, although the addition of contractual interest would have such an effect. So too with section 20, which fixes the monetary bands between which a High Court judgment carries only county court costs and the monetary minimum below which a High Court judgment carries no costs at all: the effect of section 69(8), as was confirmed recently by the Court of Appeal in *Matarazzo v Kent Area Health Authority*,[1] is to require that an amount awarded by way of statutory interest should be left entirely out of account. The same principle applies in county court litigation when determining the size of the claim for the purpose of applying the appropriate scale to the costs involved. With fees, however, the principle does *not* apply. For the purpose of determining the amount of court fees payable on issue the Court Fees Order, made under what is now section 128 of the County Courts Act 1984, requires that money claimed by way of interest should be treated in the same way as any other sum of money.[2] Likewise with the issue of a warrant to enforce a judgment the fee is calculated by reference to the amount for which it issues, without distinguishing between amounts due pursuant to section 69 and other amounts.[3]

1 (1983) Times 25 March.

2 County Court Fees Order 1982 (SI 1982/1706), item 1 of Sch. 1.
3 Ibid., Sch. 1, item 4, col. 2.

Pleading a claim for statutory interest as a liquidated debt

4.14   A creditor who is owed a liquidated sum under a contract which does not provide for contractual interest and who takes proceedings in the High Court or a county court to recover the debt should consider whether to claim statutory interest as well. A failure to pursue the question of interest might be an actionable breach of duty on the part of a plaintiff trustee (vis-à-vis the beneficiaries) or on the part of the legal advisers (vis-à-vis the plaintiff client). But, quite apart from these considerations, it is generally advisable to include a claim for statutory interest wherever the creditor goes to court over the substantive debt. Otherwise he may find that the satisfaction of his legal claim leaves him seriously under-compensated. As regards the formulation of the claim for statutory interest, where the debt itself is liquidated, and does not involve the taking of an account, it would seem better to present the claim for statutory interest as a claim for a liquidated sum, down to the date of issue and continuing thereafter until judgment or sooner payment, rather than to claim statutory interest at large. The obvious advantage in turning the claim for statutory interest into a liquidated sum is that it avoids the need for an assessment by the court and thus speeds the process by which a final judgment for the interest is obtained.

THE PERIOD OVER WHICH STATUTORY INTEREST MAY BE CLAIMED AND THE RATE

4.15   The two variables in a liquidated claim for interest pursuant to section 35A of the Supreme Court Act 1981 or section 69 of the County Courts Act 1984 are the period over which such interest is claimed and the rate. As to period, the earliest point from which interest can be claimed on a debt is the date on which the cause of action arose and the latest date to which it can be claimed is the date of the judgment for that debt. But the proper date from which statutory interest should be awarded is not necessarily the date when the debt fell due, although this would no doubt be appropriate if the parties had agreed on a specific date for payment. Where, on the other hand, a date for payment has not been agreed beforehand, the case law suggests that the award of interest should be from the date when payment could reasonably have been expected in the ordinary way of business, which would normally be shortly after the creditor delivered his bill.[1] As to rate, one or possibly two per cent over base lending rate would probably be adjudged reasonable, at least as regards a debt arising in a commercial context between one business enterprise and another.[2] However, if such a rate would exceed the rate payable on High Court judgments at the date of issue, a choice of the higher rate would have one serious disadvantage, namely that if a default judgment were obtained the interest element would have to be assessed.[3] Thus the advantage of obtaining a default judgment that could be enforced more speedily, without an assessment, would have to be weighed against the disadvantage of a sum less than might be awarded on an assessment. The disadvantage might prove serious if the discrepancy in rate was significant, the debt itself was large and the case took a long time coming to trial.

1 *Kemp v Tolland* [1956] 2 Lloyd's Rep 681; *The Rosarino* [1973] 1 Lloyd's Rep 21; *General Tire & Rubber Co v Firestone Tyre & Rubber Co Ltd* [1975] 2 All ER 173, at 188, [1975] 1 WLR 819, at 936–837, per Lord Wilberforece.
2 *FMC (Meat) Ltd v Fairfield Cold Stores Ltd* [1971] 2 Lloyd's Rep 221.
3 Because a default judgment for liquidated interest would not meet the requirements of RSC Ord 13 r 1(2), or, in the county court, CCR Ord 9, r 8. See Appendix B for the text.

INDORSEMENT OF THE WRIT

4.16   A generally indorsed writ for the recovery of a debt and interest on it pursuant to section 35A of the Supreme Court Act 1981 should state that interest is claimed pursuant to that section. In addition, where the interest claim is presented as a liquidated sum the indorsement should specify the rate and quantify the amount due at the date of issue of the writ; it should also state that interest is claimed at the same rate thereafter (but expressed as a daily rate, ie so much money per day) until judgment or sooner payment.[1] In addition the writ should bear a 'debt or liquidated demand' indorsement[2] covering not only the substantive debt but also the interest quantified down to the issue of the writ.[3]

1 *Practice Direction*, 23 February 1983 [1983] 1 All ER 934, [1983] 1 WLR 377; see Appendix C.
2 Ibid and see, too, RSC Ord 6, r2(1)(b), set out in Appendix B, and para 2.19, above.
3 See Appendix D for precedents.

STATEMENT OF CLAIM

4.17   The statement of claim may be indorsed on the writ[1] or served separately.[2] In either case the claim for interest pursuant to section 35A must be pleaded[3] and the prayer at the end of the pleading must include the claim for interest as part of the relief or remedy which is sought.[4] Views differ as to how best to meet the requirements that the claim for interest should be 'pleaded'. Some precedents[5] suggest including a paragraph, 'Further, pursuant to section 35A of the Supreme Court Act 1981 the Plaintiff is entitled to recover interest at the rate of ..... from .....'; others[6] suggest a paragraph, 'Further, the Plaintiff claims interest pursuant to section 35A of the Supreme Court Act 1981 on the said sum of ..... at the rate of ..... from .....'. Against these, it may be said that, so long as the prayer for relief particularises the claim for interest in the manner recommended for a general indorsement,[7] all that is needed in the body of the pleading is a statement of the date when the debt was due to be paid and that it is a debt to which section 35A of the Supreme Court Act 1981 applies. But since the current Practice Direction requires the claim under the Act, the rate and the amount accrued at issue to be 'pleaded',[8] the prudent course is to provide for such matters in the main body of the pleading and to cover them, by reference, in the prayer for relief at the end.[9]

1 RSC Ord 6, r 2(1)(a); text in Appendix B.
2 RSC Ord 18, r 1.
3 RSC Ord 18, r 8(4); text in Appendix B.
4 RSC Ord 18, r 5(1).
5 *Atkin's Court Forms* under 'Actions'.
6 NLJ Precedent 3/1984, (1984) 134 NLJ 181–182.
7 See the preceding paragraph.
8 *Practice Direction*, 23 February 1983. [1983] 1 All ER 934, [1983] 1 WLR 377; see Appendix C.
9 See Appendix D for precedents.

PROCEEDINGS BEGUN OTHERWISE THAN BY WRIT
4.18 With proceedings begun in the High Court otherwise than by writ, the party starting the proceedings is required to state the remedy or relief claimed, just as in proceedings begun by writ.[1] If interest is claimed pursuant to section 35A of the Supreme Court Act 1981 this should be stated expressly and the claim should specify the rate; but, as with contractual interest,[2] there is no practical advantage in separating the interest for the period down to commencement from that for the period thereafter.

1 RSC Ord 7, r 3, Ord 8, r 3, Ord 9, r 2.
2 See para 2.21, above.

PROCEEDINGS IN THE COUNTY COURT
4.19 The procedure for recovering interest in the county court pursuant to section 69 of the County Court Act 1984 is almost exactly the same as for recovering contractual interest.[1] The particulars of claim must contain a statement to the effect that such interest is claimed;[2] this statement could as well appear in the words of claim at the end of the pleading as in a paragraph in the main body of it.

4.20 *Statutory interest*

More important are the requirements of CCR Order 9, rule 8(1) since, unless his particulars of claim meet them, the plaintiff may not obtain a default judgment for the interest under Order 9 rule 3(2) or rule 6(1). The requirements are that the amount of interest claimed down to issue, the rate and the period must all be set out in the particulars of claim[3] and that the rate must not exceed that payable on judgments debts in the High Court at the date of issue.[4] All such statutory interest is left out of account when determining whether the claim is within the jurisdiction of the county court but *is* taken into account for the purpose of calculating the fees to be paid.[5]

1 See para 2.24, above.
2 CCR Ord 6 r 1A; text in Appendix B.
3 CCR Ord 9, r 8(1)(a); text in Appendix B.
4 CCR Ord 9, r 8(1)(b); text in Appendix B.
5 See para 4.13, above.

JUDGMENT FOR STATUTORY INTEREST

4.20 A judgment for statutory interest may be in one of two forms: a final judgment for a liquidated sum, or an interlocutory judgment for interest to be assessed (followed by a final judgment when the assessment has been made).[1] In the case of a liquidated claim for statutory interest at a rate no higher than that payable on High Court judgments, a plaintiff who is entitled to sign judgment in default[2] may have judgment entered for the interest as a liquidated debt. The procedure is the same as in the case of contractual interest: thus in the High Court the plaintiff may obtain judgment for the interest right up to the date of entering judgment,[3] whereas in the county court he may have it only up to the date of his request for judgment to be entered, and the request must state the amount of post-issue interest and the rate and the period over which it is calculated.[4] In either jurisdiction, the plaintiff must give proper credit for payments made by the defendant between issue and judgment.[5] For reasons mentioned later[6] such payments may not be appropriated to costs or statutory interest until the principal debt has been discharged. Accordingly, in a case where payments have been made on account between issue and judgment the claim for statutory interest will need to be broken up into several periods, starting a fresh period with every payment, so that the interest is calculated on the reduced balance.[7]

1 See Appendix D, 4 and 5 for High Court precedents and, in the county court, Prescribed Forms N 17, 30 and 34 (substituting 'interest' for 'damages').
2 RSC Ord 13, r 1, Ord 19, r 2; CCR Ord 9, r 3(2), r 6(1).
3 See para 2.22, above.
4 CCR Ord 9, r 8(2), Prescribed Form N14. See para 2.25, above and precedent 7 in Appendix D.

5 *Hughes v Justin* [1894] 1 QB 667.
6 See para 4.22, below.
7 Prescribed Form N14 (county court) may need considerable elaboration: see Appendix D7.

4.21 The preceding paragraph is concerned with bare money claims and applies, in this context, to the recovery of rent or rentals and statutory interest thereon, as it applies to other classes of debt. But a failure to pay rent or rentals may give rise to more than a bare money claim: the owner may claim, in addition, a possession order in respect of the land or goods. In such a situation the defendant may succeed in redeeming his forfeited lease by paying off the arrears or, as the case may be, in obtaining a suspension of the order of possession on terms that the arrears are paid off in a certain way. The question then arises whether the payment of statutory interest is, or may be, a condition of the relief against forfeiture or of the suspension of the order for possession. In the case of forfeiture proceedings in the county court, based on non-payment of rent, section 138(2) of the County Courts Act 1984 gives the tenant an unqualified right, not less than 5 clear days before the return day, to pay all the rent in arrears and the costs of the action, whereupon the action ceases and the tenant gets back his lease. This makes no provision for the payment of statutory interest and seems to rule out the possibility of the landlord's proceedings on his claim in this respect since the whole action has 'ceased'. In the case of other kinds of proceedings for possession of land, for example under section 146 of the Law of Property Act 1925 or Part VII of the Rent Act 1977 or Part I of the Housing Act 1980, the court has a discretion as to the terms on which an order for possession may be suspended and the payment of statutory interest, where awarded, may or may not be made a condition of suspension, depending on the circumstances of the particular case. It would seem appropriate for the payment of statutory interest, where ordered, to be a condition of the suspension as a general rule. As regards suspended orders for the delivery up of goods, under section 35 of the Hire Purchase Act 1965 or section 135 of the Consumer Credit Act 1974, the court has a similar discretion to make the payment of statutory interest, where awarded, a condition of the suspension. But, of course, statutory interest may not be awarded on arrears which carry a right to interest by contract, as will usually be the case in a consumer credit transaction.[1]

1 Supreme Court Act 1981, s 35A(4), County Courts Act 1984, s 69(4), text in Appendix A; as regards the recovery of the contractual interest in such circumstances see paras 2.34, 2.35, above.

LIMITATION PERIODS, PAYMENTS ON ACCOUNT AND APPROPRIATION

4.22   The procedure and practice regarding the recovery of statutory interest as a liquidated debt is as nearly as possible the same as in the case of contractual interest. There are, however, differences which stem from the fact that there is no *right* to be paid statutory interest until it is ordered by a court: there is no earlier entitlement as there is in the case of contractual interest. One consequence is that the Limitation Act 1980 has no application to statutory interest; since there is no cause of action for such interest there is no question of its being applied for out of time. On the other hand, if the proceedings for the principal debt, or damages, are themselves statute-barred and the plaintiff accordingly fails to obtain either a judgment or payment, the application for statutory interest must fail as well. Another practical difference between statutory interest and contractual interest is that since the creditor has no accrued right to statutory interest (until ordered by the court) he may not appropriate a debtor's payment on account to the reduction of statutory interest except where it is clear that this is the debtor's intention; for instance, if, after proceedings are started, he pays a sum 'on account' which exceeds the principal he may be taken to have intended the extra to be applied in respect of the claim for statutory interest. The discharge, by payment, of the principal debt, does not prejudice the plaintiff's claim to statutory interest on it, so long as proceedings to recover the debt, and statutory interest on it, had already begun.[1]

1 Supreme Court Act 1981, s 35A(1)(a); County Courts Act 1984, s 69(1)(a), text in Appendix A.

The assessment of statutory interest

4.23   Whereas judgment may be entered for statutory interest as a liquidated sum in the circumstances described in paragraph 4.21, there are other situations where the quantification of the sum recoverable as statutory interest has to be undertaken by the court; that is to say, there has to be an assessment. The most obvious such situations are:

(1) where the claim for interest is defended;

(2) where the interest is claimed not as a liquidated sum but in general terms, eg 'such interest, pursuant to section 35A of the Supreme Court Act 1981, as the Court may see fit to award';

(3) where statutory interest is claimed in respect of damages or some other unliquidated amount;

(4) where the rate at which statutory interest is claimed exceeds the High Court judgment rate.

In a case where the claim for statutory interest is defended the issues as to whether any and if so what interest should be awarded are litigated and decided in the same way as any other issues before the court. In the other instances, where the case is uncontested, statutory interest is assessed according to much the same procedure as damages are assessed in a case where judgment has already been obtained by default on the question of liability. For example, if the claim is for a liquidated debt together with statutory interest at a rate higher than the High Court judgment rate at the date of issue of proceedings, the appropriate course would be to apply for a default judgment in respect of the debt and for interest to be assessed and to seek an appointment thereafter for the assessment, with notice of the appointment being given to the defendant as in the case of an appointment to assess damages.[1] The plaintiff will thereby obtain a judgment for the debt which will be enforceable without having to wait for the assessment of the interest. The assessment, when it takes place will, however, be for statutory interest down to the date of the earlier judgment, not down to the date of the assessment, since a different kind of interest accrues during the intervening period by virtue of section 17 of the Judgments Act 1838.[2]

1 RSC Ord 37, r 1, CCR Ord 22, r 6.
2 *Borthwick v Elderslie Co Ltd (No 2)* [1905] 2 KB 516, CA, approved in *Erven Warnink BV v J Townsend & Sons (No 2)* [1982] 3 All ER 312, CA. The decision by Whitford J in *Fablaine Ltd v Leggill Ltd* [1982] Com LR 162 that interest may be awarded down to the date of the assessment seems to be of questionable authority.

GENERAL PRINCIPLES
4.24   From the decided cases on awards of statutory interest certain principles emerge, some of wider application than others. Statutory interest on awards of damages in personal injury litigation has special peculiarities which are considered in the next chapter. On the preliminary question whether an award of statutory interest should be made at all the broadest and clearest statement of principle is that of Lord Denning MR in *Harbutt's Plasticine Ltd v Wayne Tank and Pump Co Ltd* [1970] 1 QB 447, [1970] 1 All ER 225:

> It seems to me that the basis of an award of interest is that the defendant has kept the plaintiff out of his money; and the defendant has had the use of it himself. So he ought to compensate the plaintiff accordingly.

If only it were always as simple as that! But it is not. For instance where the defendant has a valid counterclaim or cross-action for a larger sum than he owes but which he is, for technical reasons, unable to set off in extinction of the plaintiff's claim, an award of statutory interest might well be refused.[1] Likewise where the court's disapproval of the plaintiff's conduct is marked by the refusal of an order for his costs,[2] the same circumstances might well justify a refusal of a discretionary award of statutory interest. Factors such as the plaintiff's culpable delay or the refusal of a reasonable offer of settlement would be material.[3]

1 *Business Computers Ltd v Anglo-African Leasing Ltd* [1977] 2 All ER 741, [1977] 1 WLR 578.
2 Supreme Court Practice (1985) 62/2/10–12.
3 See paras 4.30 and 5.12, below.

4.25   As regards the period which an award may cover, it cannot pre-date the cause of action even where the loss or expenditure goes back further; conversely it cannot post-date the assessment or, where the assessment follows a judgment, the judgment.[1] Within this span interest may not be awarded on a debt in respect of a period for which interest is already running[2] but it may be awarded on the rest; for example, where the agreement provides for contractual interest to accrue 28 days after delivery of a statement, statutory interest may theoreticaly be awarded in respect of the earlier period. But in the ordinary way a claim for statutory interest is unlikely to succeed where there is contractual provision for interest and the award of statutory interest is almost invariably made over a single period running right up to the date of the assessment or judgment. So the crucial question regarding the period for which there should be statutory interest is not when it is to end but when it is to start.

1\ See para 4.23, above, and notes.
2 Supreme Court Act 1981, s 35A(4), County Courts Act 1984, s 69(4); text in Appendix A.

4.26   The general rule regarding statutory interest on a debt is that it should be awarded (if awarded at all) from the date by which, in a commercial setting, persons acting honestly and reasonably would be expected to have paid the debt.[1] Accordingly where a date for payment has been settled by agreement this should be the starting point; otherwise it should be shortly after the delivery of a bill, allowing the debtor a reasonable interval to make the necessary financial arrangements but no more. The question whether the debtor should be sent an itemised bill and allowed time to consider it point by point must depend, for an answer, on the circumstances of the particular case, including the usages of the particular trade and the terms, if any, that were agreed. As regards the liability of an assignor of a lease for the assignee's failure to pay the rent, it would be proper to order the assignor to pay interest on the arrears from the date when he was informed of the landlord's service of a forfeiture notice on the assignee.[2]

1 See the cases noted at n 1 to para 4.15, above.
2 *Allied London Investments Ltd v Hambro Life Assurance* (1985) 135 NLJ 184.

4.27 Where the claim is for damages or quantum merit or money had and received, the same general approach is adopted as in the case of contract debt. Thus where the nature and size of the plaintiff's claim is apparent at the moment the cause of action accrues, as for example in the case of salvage, interest may properly be claimed for the full period back to the date of the cause of action.[1] Where on the other hand a contract is frustrated and the plaintiff does not intimate the intention to claim straightaway, interest may properly be awarded but only from the date that the defendant is first apprised on the claim.[2] Three other situations are worth mentioning, because they are covered by reported decisions. First, in an action for damages for infringement of a patent it has been held that an award of interest should ordinarily be ordered to run from the date of the grant of a patent.[3] Second, in a wrongful dismissal case where the plaintiff has a contractual right to be employed at an agreed salary for a certain number of years the starting point for the assessment of his damages might be the cost of an annuity to buy equivalent income from the date of dismissal together with interest on that sum down to the assessment (or judgment) at a commercial rate.[4] Third, in *Re FB & CH Matthews Ltd* (in liquidation)[5] the Court of Appeal declared that a bank had been fraudulently preferred in a liquidation and ordered the bank to pay statutory interest on the sum involved from the date of the members' voluntary liquidation.

1 *The Aldora* [1975] QB 748, [1975] 2 All ER 69.
2 *BP Exploration (Libya) Ltd v Hunt (No 2)* [1983] 2 AC 352. [1982] 1 All ER 125.
3 *General Tire & Rubber Co v Firestone Tyre & Rubber Co Ltd* [1975] 2 All ER 173, [1975] 1 WLR 819 HL.
4 *Bold v Brough Nicholson & Hall* [1963] 3 All ER 849 [1964] 1 WLR 201.
5 [1982] Ch 257, [1982] 1 All ER 338.

RATE OF INTEREST: JUDGMENT RATE AND THE RATE OBTAINABLE ON
THE SHORT TERM INVESTMENT ACCOUNT

4.28 In a commercial context, that is to say in litigation between businessmen, an award of statutory interest ought, on the face of it, to be fixed at a commercial rate, this being the rate at which a commercial enterprise may ordinarily be expected to borrow money to bridge the gap in income caused by the unjustified withholding of the payment in question. One, or possibly two, per cent annum over base lending rate has been held appropriate in commercial cases.[1] In a non-commercial context, there are at least two rates of interest which are fixed by statute which could not be stigmatised as excessively high (or low) whatever their relationship at any given date to base lending rate. One is the rate payable on High Court judgments;[2] this is the rate to choose if the plaintiff wishes to obtain the maximum rate of statutory interest recoverable as a liquidated debt. The other is the rate payable on the short term investment of money paid into court.[3]

1 *FMC (Meat) Ltd v Fairfield Cold Stores Ltd Greater London Council* [1971] 2 Lloyd's Rep 221; *Tate & Lyle Food and Distribution Ltd* [1981] 3 All ER 716, [1982] 1 WLR 149; *International Military Services Ltd v Capital and Counties Bank Plc* [1982] 2 All ER 20, [1982] 1 WLR 575.
2 Judgments Act 1838, s 17; Administration of Justice Act 1970, s 44(1). See Appendix A for statutory text and Appendix E for rates.
3 See para 10.13, below. For rates see Appendix E.

SPECIAL FACTORS TO BE TAKEN INTO ACCOUNT
4.29   In deciding whether to award any, and if so what, interest to the plaintiff the Court should not have particular regard to the borrowing facilities at his disposal or the particular uses to which the money might have been put if paid on time. But there is one special factor that should be taken into account in a commercial context, namely the extent to which the plaintiff has been saved from paying income or corporation tax by claiming as tax-deductible expenses the expenses which he seeks to recover from the defendant as damages. In *Tate and Lyle Industries v Greater London Council*[1] it was held that the interest on expenses should be calculated at a commercial rate from the date that the expenses were incurred but that there should be deducted from that award interest at roughly the same rate on the continuing tax advantage for the time that it was enjoyed: the difference was awarded.

1 [1981] 3 All ER 716, [1982] 1 WLR 149.

4.30   Another special circumstance which needs to be taken into account, at least in personal injury litigation, is that the plaintiff is not literally deprived of the use of his money for any period during which the loss is made good not by the defendant but by the plaintiff's own insurers.[1] On the other hand, where those insurers

have rights of subrogation in respect of the interest over the period
concerned, their indemnity should be left out of account.[2] The list of
special circumstances which should be taken into account cannot be
regarded as closed: culpable delay on the part of the plaintiff may be
such a circumstance,[3] as may an unscrupulous use by the defendant
of the plaintiff's money to finance his own speculative ventures.[4]

1 See para 5.14, below.
2 *H. Cousins & Co Ltd v D & C Carriers Ltd* [1971] 2 QB 230, [1971] 1 All ER 55, CA,
  Aliter, if the insurers have no subrogation rights in respect of the interest.
3 *Birkett v Hayes* [1982] 2 All ER 710, [1982] 1 WLR 816, CA.
4 *Wallersteiner v Moir (No 2)* [1975] QB 373, [1975] 1 All ER 849, CA.

Chapter 5

Personal injury litigation

5.01 The idea that compensation for injury is incomplete unless it includes interest for the time that the injured person has been kept waiting for his money is comparatively new. Indeed it is only in regard to compensation claims that are, or may be, litigated in the High Court or county court that the question of interest arises. Compensation for injuries may be ordered in the Magistrates' Courts under the provision of the Criminal Justice Act 1982,[1] but there is no provision for ordering the payment of interest as a separate item. The Crown Court has equivalent powers and it is just arguable that, since it is a court of record,[2] it may award interest under the 1934 Act[3] in respect of compensation which is ordered in the nature of damages. But even if the power to award interest exists, or if interest may be taken into account even if not awarded, the practice is to award compensation at a level lower than that obtainable as damages in the civil courts or indeed through the Criminal Injuries Compensation Board,[4] and that Board has no power to award anything in respect of interest.[5] Accordingly it is only in the High Court and county courts that an injured person may expect to recover interest on the compensation which he may be awarded; the jurisdiction to award it dates from the 1934 Act but it was not invoked on anything but the rarest occasion until 1970 when *Jefford v Gee*[6] reached the Court of Appeal.

1 Section 67 of that Act substitutes wider powers of compensation for those contained in s 35(1) of the Powers of Criminal Courts Act 1973.
2 Courts Act 1971, s 4(1).
3 See Appendix A for the relevant text, and also para 4.04, above.
4 See the article 'Compensation orders in cases of violence' by Mr Michael Ogden QC, chairman of the Criminal Injuries Compensation Board; *The Magistrate* (1985) 41 pp 5–6.

5 The terms of the Revised 1979 Scheme are in Appendix C to the Board's Twentieth Report (1984) Cmnd 9399.
6 [1970] 2 QB 130, [1970] 1 All ER 1202; counsel for Mr Gee said that only one reported case had been found where interest was awarded in a personal injury case in this country.

THE WINN REPORT AND SECTION 22 OF THE ADMINISTRATION OF JUSTICE ACT 1969

5.02   The Committee on Personal Injuries Litigation made a report in 1968 (The Winn Report)[1] which recommended among other things that interest should be added to damages in respect of personal injury or death whether applied for or not. The purpose was to give a stimulus to plaintiffs not to delay the issue of proceedings and a stimulus to defendants, and their insurers, to carry proceedings, once started, to a speedy conclusion. It may be doubted whether the implementation of these recommendations has in fact made any significant difference to the pace of personal injury litigation[2] but the new practice of awarding interest as the general rule rather than as the exception has certainly meant an increase in the amount of money recovered by plaintiffs. The change in practice stems from section 22 of the Administration of Justice Act 1969, which added subsections (1A), (1B), (1C) and (1D) to section 3(1) of the 1934 Act.[3] These changes were inspired by the Winn Report although not exactly what was recommended. The substance of subsections (1A), (1B) and (1D) is now contained in section 35A(2) and (7) of the Supreme Court Act 1981 and section 69(2) and (6) of the County Courts Act 1984. The effect is that, subject to rules of court, where damages for personal injuries or death exceed £200, an award of interest *must* be made unless the court is satisfied that there are special reasons to the contrary. One minor difference may be noted between the old statute and the new: whereas a mandatory award under subsections (1A) and (1B) was called for if a judgment for over £200 represented *or included* damages in respect of personal injuries or death, the new subsections only apply where the damages for personal injuries or death exceed £200; they do not apply, as the earlier law did, to a judgment for, say, £300 for damage to the plaintiff's car and £50 for bruises and shock. But the point may be of little more than academic interest having regard to the decline in the value of £200 since 1969 when the threshold was set and the growing practice of claiming interest on damages whatever the nature of the litigation.

1 Cmnd 3091.
2 See Law Commission Report No 56 on Personal Injury Litigation—Assessment of Damages (1973) HC 373, paras 271–272.

3 The amended text is set out in Appendix A, along with the other relevant statutory provisions.

5.03   There are no special rules of court in the High Court or in the county courts regarding the pleading of a claim for interest in a personal injuries case, except that the claim for interest should be pleaded in accordance with RSC Order 18 rule 8(4) and CCR Order 6, rule 1A,[1] and that a plaintiff contending for more by way of interest than that normally awarded under the guidelines (considered below) should bring the material matters to the defendant's notice, preferably by pleading them in the Statement (or Particulars) of Claim.[2]

1 See Appendix B for the text.
2 *Dexter v Courtaulds Ltd* [1984] 1 All ER 70, [1984] 1 WLR 372, CA.

The guidelines

5.04   More important perhaps than the rules of court are the guidelines for awards of interest in personal injury litigation, as laid down in a run of cases beginning with *Jefford v Gee.*[1]

1 [1970] 2 QB 130, [1970] 1 All ER 1202, CA.

5.05   The guide-lines on awards of interest in respect of special damage are still those laid down in *Jefford v Gee,*[1] namely that, in principle, an award of interest should be made in respect of each and every item of special damage from the date that the relevent loss was incurred and that the rate should be the average rate obtainable on the Short Term Investment Account from the date of the loss to the date of judgment. This rate is described in succeeding paragraphs as 'the appropriate rate'. On the other hand, in the normal case where special damages consist of, or include, loss of earnings which accrue periodically over a long space of time the better approach is to take the whole period, right back to the date of the accident but to allow interest at only half the appropriate rate.[2]

1 [1970] 2 QB 130, at 146–147, [1970] 1 All ER 1202, at 1208; followed in *Dexter v Courtaulds Ltd* [1984] 1 All ER 70, [1984] 1 WLR 372, CA.
2 For details of the rates obtainable in recent years, see Appendix E

THE LIVING PLAINTIFF'S FUTURE LOSS OF EARNINGS

5.06   The guide-line on interest in respect of a living plaintiff's future loss of earnings is simple and, again, it remains that laid down in *Jefford v Gee*,[1] namely that no interest should be awarded, the reason being that, as regards future loss, the plaintiff has not been kept out of his money.

1 [1970] 2 QB 130, 147, [1970] 1 All ER 1202, 1209.

PAIN, SUFFERING AND LOSS OF AMENITY

5.07   The guide-lines applicable to awards of general damages for pain, suffering and loss of amenity have changed significantly over the years. In *Jefford v Gee* the Court of Appeal favoured taking as the starting point the date of service of the writ,[1] or other relevant process,[2] and making an award of interest at the appropriate rate. But in *Wright v British Railways Board*[3] the House of Lords decided that, so long as inflation was a feature of the economic scene, the award of interest in respect of general damages for pain, suffering and loss of amenity should be at a 'conventional' rate of 2% per annum, this sum being roughly the net yield (after allowing for inflation) which may be obtained in inflationary times by investing in index-linked savings or securities. The main justification for this conclusion is that the awards of damages tend to drift upwards as the purchasing power of the pound falls and inflation-proofing is already taken care of; so anything more than 2% would lead to over compensation.

1 [1970] 2 QB 130, at 147, [1970] 1 All ER 1202, at 1209.
2 In third party proceedings the starting date is that of service of the notice: *Slater v Hughes* [1971] 3 All ER 1287, [1971] 1 WLR 1438, CA.
3 [1983] 2 AC 773, [1983]2 All ER 698, adopting to a large extent the reasoning of the Court of Appeal in *Birkett v Hayes* [1982] 2 All ER 710, [1982] 1 WLR 816.

LOSS OF DEPENDENCY

5.08   As regards claims for loss of dependency under the Fatal Accidents Act 1976, the Court of Appeal said in *Jefford v Gee* that interest should be awarded on the whole dependency award at the appropriate rate from the service of the writ to the date of the award.[1] But in *Cookson v Knowles*[2] the Court of Appeal acknowledged that this led to over-compensation in two respects: (1) the interest award covered economic loss in the future as well as in the past, contrary to the guide-lines affecting injured plaintiffs who were still alive, and (2) the economic loss down to the date of the award did not accrue all at once at the date of the service of the writ but gradually built up like a loss of earnings claim. Accordingly the

Court of Appeal ruled that the plaintiff should have interest on no more than that part of the dependency damages which represented economic losses down to the date of the award and at half the appropriate rate from the date of the service of the writ to the date of the award. It should be noted, incidentally, that the guide-lines governing the rate at which interest should be awarded on damages are not the same as the principles governing the rate at which money payable in the future should be discounted on account of its accelerated receipt. In *Auty v National Coal Board*[3] the Court of Appeal upheld the judge's decision to discount at 5% per annum, notwithstanding actuarial evidence (held inadmissible) that the probability of inflation made that rate unrealistically high.

1 [1970]2 QB 130, at 148, [1970] 1 All ER, 1202, at 1209–1210.
2 [1979] AC 556, [1978] 2 All ER 604.
3 [1985] 1 All ER 930.

LOSS OF EARNINGS OF PLAINTIFF WHO DIES

5.09   As for the future loss of earnings of a plaintiff who dies and whose claim is pursued for the benefit of his estate under section 1 of the Law Reform (Miscellaneous Provisions) Act 1934, the law was changed by section 4 of the Administration of Justice Act 1982 as regards causes of action accruing after 1 January 1983 and also as regards causes of action accruing before, where the plaintiff dies after.[1] In these two situations the claim for earnings in the 'lost years' is no longer maintainable, but any claim for loss of income and other special damage down to the date of the death and any items of general damages for pain, suffering, and loss of amenity should presumably be dealt with in the same way as in the case of a living plaintiff.[2] On the other hand, where the plaintiff has died before 1 January 1983 the estate may still pursue a claim for the income he would have received but for his untimely death.[3] In such a case the award of interest ought, according to the principles applied in *Cookson v Knowles*, to be calculated on that part of the award for loss of earnings down to the date of the award, at half the appropriate rate for the period from service of the writ down to the date of the award. However, in *Goodall v Hall*,[4] 2% was awarded on the whole sum, as if the substantive claim were for pain and suffering.

1 Administration of Justice Act 1982, sections 4(2) and 73(3) and (4).
2 See paras 5.05 and 5.07, above.
3 *Pickett v British Rail Engineering Ltd* [1980] AC 136; [1979] 1 All ER 774; *Gammell v Wilson* [1982] AC 27, [1981] 1 All ER 578.
4 (1982) Times, 1 April, a decision of a Deputy High Court Judge.

BEREAVEMENT
5.10 The Administration of Justice Act 1982 made another major change in the law relating to claims arising out of death. It gave the surviving spouse or the parent a right to damages for bereavement in respect of the wrongful death of the other spouse or child. The terms of the new remedy are set out in section 1A of the Fatal Accidents Act 1976[1] and they apply to deaths on or after 1 January 1983, but not to deaths before. The bereavement damages are a fixed sum of £3,500, which the Lord Chancellor has power to vary by order, but has not varied yet. Since the damages are in the form of a 'conventional' award for general damages for pain and grief it may be contended that the reasoning in *Wright v British Railways Board*[2] should apply and the award of interest should accordingly be at 2%, over the period from the date of the service of the writ to the date of the award. Alternatively, since the sum is not at large but has been liquidated by statute, it may be argued that interest should be awarded on it from the date of the death at the appropriate rate, or, perhaps, at the rate payable on High Court judgments.[3]

1 Inserted by Administration of Justice Act 1982, s 1.
2 See n 3 to para 5.07, also *Ichard v Frangoulis* [1977] 2 All ER 461, [1977] 1 WLR 556.
3 See para 5.13, below, for further possibilities.

Departure from the guidelines

5.11 The guidelines do not provide a complete code. For instance, they do not cater expressly for the case where an interim payment has been made which ought in the ordinary way to reduce the amount of interest for which the defendant would otherwise be liable.[1] On the other hand they do contemplate a departure from the usual practice in exceptional situations, three of which are considered below.

1 See paras 5.15–5.17, below.

DELAY BY THE PLAINTIFF AND OTHER CONSIDERATIONS
5.12 The guide-lines assume that the plaintiff will pursue his claim with reasonable diligence. If, therefore, there is unreasonable or culpable delay in the prosecution of the proceedings it may be appropriate to make a reduction in either the period over of which or rate at which the interest is awarded.[1] Conversely where the issue of the writ, or its service, is postponed at the request of the

defendant, the postponement may be accompanied by an undertaking by the defendant to accept liability for interest as from the date of the postponement. Even where no such undertaking is given it may be appropriate for the starting date for the interest to be backdated, if the defendant has acted in bad faith in getting the issue or service of the writ deferred.[2] Any special circumstances justifying a backdated award should normally be set out in the claim for interest so that the defendant is put on notice and able to take account of them when paying into court.[3]

1 *Birkett v Hayes* [1982] 2 All ER 710, [1982] 1 WLR 816, CA.
2 See *Chadwick v Parsons* [1971] 2 Lloyd's Rep 49.
3 *Dexter v Courtaulds* [1984] 1 All ER 70, [1984] 1 WLR 372.

THE STRAIGHTFORWARD CASE

5.13   Although the date of service of the writ provides a reasonable starting point for interest on general damages where they are still at large it may be appropriate to take an earlier starting date[1] in the straightforward case where quantum presents no particular difficulty, for instance where the only claim is for bereavement or for the recently abolished claim for 'loss of future happiness'.[2]

1 Such as the letter before action: *Jefford v Gee* [1970] 2QB 130, at 147; [1970] 1 All ER, 1202, at 1209.
2 The latter was sustainable under the Law Reform (Miscellaneous Provisions) Act 1934, s 1 until abolished by the Administration of Justice Act 1982, s 1.

INSURED LOSSES

5.14   The question of interest in respect of insured losses remains open. In *Jefford v Gee* it was said that, in principle, the plaintiff should not be awarded interest in respect of items of special damage for which he was indemnified by first party insurance or receive an interest free loan from an outside source.[1] As a statement of principle this seems to be wrong, at least where the plaintiff is indemnified by insurers with rights of subrogation[2] but in the usual personal injury case the point does not arise for consideration because of the very wide application of the 'half-rate' rule.[3]

1 [1970] 2 QB 130, at 146, [1970] 1 All ER 1202, at 1208.
2 *H. Cousins & Co Ltd v D & C Carriers Ltd* [1971] 2 QB 230, [1971] 1 All ER 55, CA.
3 See para 5.05, above.

Interim orders and payments on account

5.15   The power to order payments on account was recommended by the Winn Committee,[1] in the context of personal injury litigation. It has been given effect by section 20 of the Administration of Justice Act 1969, which enables a scheme for ordering payments on account of 'damages, debt or other sum (excluding any costs)' to be made by rules of court. A series of rules have been made. The first such rules were those added to RSC Order 29 in 1970 to allow interim payments to be ordered in personal injury cases, and it is for this reason that the topic is included in this chapter. But in 1977 further rules were added to allow the ordering interim payments for the use and occupation of land of which a possession order is sought. Finally RSC (Amendment No 2) Rules 1980[2] substituted a new and enlarged Part II (Interim Payments) RSC Order 29, which now take up in full the rule-making powers conferred by section 20 of the 1969 Act. Order 29 rule 9 defines 'interim payment' as a payment on account of *any damages, debt or other sum (excluding costs)* which he may be held liable to pay to or for the benefit of the plaintiff. These rules have been applied, with minor modifications, to equivalent proceedings in the county court by CCR Order 13, rule 12, thus making good the deficiency in county court procedure which was exposed in *Felix v Shiva*.[3]

1 Committee on Personal Injuries Litigation (1968), Cmnd 3691, Part IV.
2 SI 1980/1010.
3 [1983] QB 82, [1982] 3 All ER 263, CA. For the text of RSC Ord 29, Part II, see Appendix B.

5.16   Interim payments may be ordered by the court as payments on account of any damages, debt or other sum. Contractual interest would no doubt rank as a debt for these purposes. Discretionary interest under section 35A of the Supreme Court Act 1981 and section 69 of the County Courts Act 1984 would not, although it might very well count as an 'other sum'. But the practice of leaving discretionary interest out of account when ordering interim payments grew up when such interest did not have to be paid into court[1] and it seems likely that the old practice will continue, at least in personal injury litigation. This practice requires all questions of discretionary interests to be left over to the trial, assuming that the case is not settled in the meantime. The making of an interim payment, whether voluntarily or pursuant to an order, must not be disclosed to the court until all questions of liability and amount have been determined, except with the consent of the paying party.[2] Arguably the question whether an award of discretionary interest should be made is a 'question of liability'[3] so a defendant who wishes to pray in aid a payment on account as going in reduction of the interest to be awarded should see that that fact is disclosed to the court before that question is determined. The nature of the adjustment in the award that should then be made to take account of the interim payment remains unclear. But it is suggested that the simplest and fairest method would be for the court to determine, first, the amount of interest which would have been awarded if there had been no payment on account and, next, to determine and deduct therefrom the sums actually accruing to the plaintiff as interest while the money has been in court (if paid into court at all) together with a fair sum in respect of interest for any period in which the payment, or any part of it, was at the plaintiff's free disposal following a payment out of court or a direct payment to him by the defendant. In the latter regard the fairest rate would probably be the rate that might have been obtained over the relevant period if the money had been invested in court on the Short Term Investment Account; but a higher rate might be right in a commercial case, where interest is awarded on the substantive claim at a rate in excess of base lending rate.

1 See para 10.04, below.
2 RSC Ord 29, r 15.
3 On the other hand the awarding of costs has been held not to be a 'question of liability': *Millensted v Grosvenor House (Park Lane) Ltd* [1937] 1 KB 717, [1937] 1 All ER 736, per Scott LJ.

OVERPAYMENT ON ACCOUNT

5.17 The preceding paragraphs assume that the payment on account is less than the amount found due at the trial. But there may have been an overpayment, in which case the court may order a repayment of the difference under RSC Order 19 rule 17.[1] The question may then arise as to whether the overpaying party should recover interest in respect of the overpayment. If the money has been in court and invested there is no problem about directing the payment out to him of an appropriate part of the interest which has accrued. If however the money was paid direct to the other party a question arises as to the court's power, under section 35A(1) of the Supreme Court Act 1981 (and its county court equivalent) to 'include in any sum for which judgment is given simple interest . . . . on all or any part of the debt or damages in respect of which judgment is given or payment is made before judgment'. If the words 'the debt or damages' mean the debt or damages for which the main proceedings are brought, then the overpayment is not part of them, and so there is no power to award interest on the order for repayment. On the other hand an award of interest on the overpayment might be justified on the ground that the application for repayment is itself a proceeding for the recovery of a debt.

1 See Appendix B for the text.

Provisional damages

5.18   Section 6 of the Administration of Justice Act 1982 has
inserted a new section 32A in the Supreme Court Act 1981,[1]
whereby the High Court may award provisional damages in any
personal injuries case in which there is proved or admitted to be a
chance that at some definite or indefinite time in the future the
plaintiff will develop some serious disease, or suffer some serious
deterioration in his physical or mental condition. The idea is that, in
such a case, there should not be a premature valuation of the chance,
which would necessarily be too high if the disease or detorioration
never came about, or too low if it did. Instead, if the plaintiff so
frames his claim, the Court should award damages on the assumption that there will be no such disease or deterioration, but should
grant him liberty to apply for damages on this account later if the
assumption proves false.

1 County Courts Act 1984, s 51 makes equivalent provision for the county court.

INTEREST IN RESPECT OF THE DISEASE OR INJURY ESTABLISHED AT THE
TRIAL
5.19   The details of the scheme are not yet clear.[1] Presumably,
however, the Court will make its provisional award of damages for
the injuries that are already manifest in the same way as if it were a
final award and will order the payment of interest thereon in the
normal way.[2]

1 Neither Rules of Court nor Commencement Order have been made at the date of
   going to print.
2 See paras 5.05–5.07, above.

INTEREST IN RESPECT OF THE SUBSEQUENT DISEASE OR DETERIORATION
5.20   Assuming that, after a provisional award has been made,
the plaintiff suffers the disease or deterioration which was contemplated as a possibility (or 'chance') at that time, the plaintiff may
then apply to the court for a further award and, provided that the
application is procedurally in order and the material facts are
proved, a further award will be made. Presumably this further award
will be treated as a free-standing award, not merely an assessment in
fulfilment of the original judgment; otherwise whatever is awarded
on the second occasion will automatically attract interest under the
Judgments Act 1838, backdated to the first.[1] A more satisfactory
position would be for the second decision to have the status of a
separate judgment, so as to enable the court to award interest on it
under section 35A of the Supreme Court Act 1981. On the other

hand, the plaintiff's case for an award of interest cannot be regarded as having much merit, he having elected to forgo an early assessment on the merits in favour of a nil assessment, with liberty to apply later. He cannot make much of the argument that he has been kept out of his money and if interest is to be awarded at all in such cases it ought to be for only a very short period, one would think.

1 *Borthwick v Elderslie SS Co Ltd* (No 2) [1905], 2 KB 516; *Erven Warnink v Townend (No 2)* [1982] 3 All ER 312.

Chapter 6

Interest after judgment

The High Court

HIGH COURT JUDGMENTS

6.01   High Court judgments carry interest at the statutory rate in force at the time of entering the judgment. This is provided by section 17 of the Judgments Act 1838.[1] The rate may be changed by an order made by the Lord Chancellor under section 44 of the Administration of Justice Act 1970 and the judgment carries interest at the rate then applicable; it is not affected by any subsequent changes in the rate.[2] Orders of the High Court for the payment of money carry interest in the same way as judgments and this applies to orders made in any Division, including the Family Division.[3]

1 See Appendix A for the text.
2 cf *Rocco Giuseppe v Tradax SA* [1984] 1 WLR742: changes in the rate are set out in Appendix E.
3 This seems to be the effect of s 18 of the Judgments Act 1838: *K v K* [1977] Fam 39, [1977] 1 All ER 576.

TIME FROM WHICH INTEREST ACCRUES

6.02   The operative time for interest to start accruing on the judgment is, according to section 17 of the Judgments Act 1838, 'the time of entering up the judgment'. Where there is a time-lag between the giving of the judgment and the completion of the formalities of entry, the question arises whether section 17 is referring to the earlier or the later date. It is clear, from *Parsons v Mather & Platt Ltd*[1] and RSC Order 42 rule 3, that where judgment is given for the payment of a liquidated sum the operative date is when judgment is given rather than the later date when it is formally entered. In the case of a judgment for damages to be assessed, the better view would seem to be that interest does not start with the date of the assessment, but is backdated to the date when judgment was given.[2] On the other hand where judgment is given for money to be paid at some future date

69

interest will not start to accrue until that date arrives.[3] The same applies where the judgment is for the money to be paid by instalments: since the judgment is for the payment of periodic instalments the interest starts to accrue on each instalment as it falls due.[4] However, an instalment order may not be made in the High Court, except by consent or in bankruptcy or in the case of lump sum payments ordered to be paid by instalments.[5] A judgment for an instalment order should not be confused with a stay of execution on terms that the judgment debt is paid off by specified instalments: this stays execution but does not prevent interest from running even where the specified instalments are paid in accordance with the terms of the stay.

1 [1977] 2 All ER 715, [1977] 1 WLR 855.
2 *Borthwick v Elderslie SS Co Ltd (No2)* [1905] 2 KB 516 and *Erven Warnink BV v J Townend & Sons (Hull) Ltd (No 2)* [1982] 3 All ER 312 provide clear Court of Appeal authority for this conclusion. On the other hand where an action was compromised on the terms that the defendant would pay whatever damages were found by a referee to be due, the interest ran from the court's adoption of the referee's report: *Ashover Fluor Spar Mines Ltd v Jackson* [1911] 2 Ch 355. Further, in *Fablaine Ltd v Leygill Ltd* [1982] Com LR 162, Whitford J reversed a Master's decision that interest on damages once assessed should be backdated to the date of judgment for the purpose of s 17 of the Judgments Act 1838 and awarded interest on the damages for the period from judgment to assessment under the 1934 Act instead.
3 *Erven Warnink BV v J Townend & Sons Hull Ltd (No 2)* [1982] 3 All ER 312, CA.
4 *Caudery v Finnerty* (1892) 66 LT 684; *Morse v Muir* [1939] 2 KB 106, [1939] 2 All ER 40.
5 Matrimonial Causes Act 1973, s 23; see the succeeding paragraph.

MAINTENANCE ORDERS

6.03 The question whether High Court maintenance orders carry interest under the Judgments Act 1838 seems not to have been put to the test. As regards periodical payments, the recovery of interest on arrears must usually be of little more than academic interest, having regard to the following factors:

(a) the amount of the order may be varied upwards or downwards, and, to some extent, retrospectively

(b) arrears may be remitted,[1] and

(c) it would be very difficult, in a case where irregular payments were made on account of a maintenance liability, to determine whether they were, or should be, appropriated to principal or interest and what balance was owing at any given date.

Not surprisingly interest is, for practical as well as theoretical reasons, left out of account. However, it can be of real significance in relation to an order for a High Court order for a lump sum payment,[2] which has all the usual characteristics of a judgment debt.

There is no doubt that any order for the payment of a lump sum carries interest from the date when payment is ordered to be made, and if ordered to be paid by instalments from the date each instalment is due.[3] Moreover, as regards the period between the date of the order and the date for payment of each instalment, the court may order that interest is to accrue at a specified rate.[4]

1 Matrimonial Causes Act 1973, s 31(2A).
2 Ibid, s 23(1) (c) and (f) and (3).
3 *Erven Warnink BV v J Townend & Sons (Hull) Ltd (No 2)* [1982] 3 All ER 312, CA.
4 Matrimonial Causes Act 1973, s 23(6).

COSTS

6.04 As a qualification to the general rule that interest on a judgment debt runs from judgment, the courts have held that an order for the payment of costs to be taxed takes effect, for the purpose of starting interest running, from the date of the taxation certificate.[1] Presumably if the costs are agreed without a taxation interest starts to run from the date of the agreement. There is no general power to award interest on costs for any earlier period except that interest may be allowed on disbursements as between solicitor and client;[2] but the trustees of an estate who incur legal costs as an expense of its administration may recover interest for the time that they are out of pocket pursuant to RSC Order 44, rule 9.

1 *K v K* [1977] Fam 39, [1977] 1 All ER 576; *Erven Warnink BV v J Townend & Sons (Hull) Ltd (No 2)* [1982] 3 All ER 312.
2 Solicitors Act 1974, s 66(a).

SUCCESSFUL APPEALS

6.05 A plaintiff who appeals successfully against a dismissal of his claim will be entitled to interest on the judgment from the date of the order of the Court of Appeal (or House of Lords) allowing the appeal, or such earlier date as it may specify.[1] If damages are directed to be reassessed the interest will run from the date of the original judgment.[2]

1 *Nitrate Producers SS Co Ltd v Short Bros Ltd* (1922) 127 LT 726, HL.
2 *Macbeth & Co Ltd v Maritime Insurance Co Ltd* (1908) 24 TLR 559.

MERGER

6.06 In the leading case on merger, *in re Sneyd, ex Fewings*,[1] Lindley LJ said:

> Now it may be technical, but it is well settled, that, if there is a debt secured by a covenant, and judgment is recovered on the covenant, the debt on the covenant merges in the judgment debt ... [the principal sum] is no longer payable under the covenant, it is payable under the judgment;

the covenant to pay interest is gone, and the judgment bears interest only at [the judgment rate].

1 (1883) 25 Ch D 338.

6.07 Thus the legal consequence of the merger of a debt on the covenant into a judgment debt is that instead of interest on the covenant the creditor gets interest on the judgment at a rate which may very well be lower. But the doctrine of merger is by no means as broad as might appear from the decision just cited. It does not apply where the covenant to pay interest is in a form which negatives merger; and merger may be negatived by separating the covenant to pay interest from the covenant to pay the principal. This is indeed the way in which a building society mortgage is normally drawn, so that the building society may rely on an independent covenant to pay the interest when suing the debtor for the outstanding balance. In such a case the High Court may order the payment of the balance outstanding at the date of judgment together with a specified sum per day thereafter by way of interest at the contractual rate.[1] The plaintiff should, of course, take care that his pleaded claim is for interest down to *payment*, not 'judgment or sooner payment'.[2]

1 *Ealing London Borough Council v El Isaac* [1980] 2 All ER 548, [1980] 1 WLR 932. CA.
2 This is the exceptional case alluded to in the concluding words of the *Practice Direction* of 24 February 1983: [1983] 1 All ER 934, [1983] 1 WLR 377; see Appendix C.

Recovery of judgment interest

WRITS OF EXECUTION

6.08 A writ of fieri facias, if issued in the form prescribed by RSC Appendix A, Form 53, or in one of the prescribed variations, requires execution to be levied to satisfy the judgment debt and interest accruing thereon. The interest is not yearly interest, for the purposes of the tax legislation, so no question of deducting tax arises.[1] Moreover, the execution is not limited to the interest due at the issue of the writ; the levy should be for interest right down to the date of payment. Presumably in a case where goods are seized and sold the date of payment is the date when the price of the goods is received.

1 *Re Cooper* [1911] 2 KB 550; see para 11.10, below.

GARNISHEE PROCEEDINGS

6.09　A judgment creditor may bring proceedings against the judgment debtor's debtor (the garnishee) under RSC Order 49 as a means of recovering what is due to him under the judgment, including interest accruing thereon. Rule 2(a) of Order 49 requires the judgment creditor to state the balance due under the judgment at the time of his application. But this does not mean that judgment interest crystallises at this date and that nothing can be done regarding the interest accruing thereafter. On the contrary, the garnishee order (be it nisi or absolute)[1] attaches the whole of the sum owing to the judgment debtor or 'so much thereof as may be sufficient to satisfy the said judgment'. Accordingly the sum which is entered in the order absolute as the balance due under the judgment should not be limited to the figure stated in the affidavit, as required by rule 2(a); it should include as well the interest accruing in the intervening period.

1 See RSC Appendix A, Forms 72 and 73.

CHARGING ORDERS

6.10　There is no doubt that a judgment creditor who seeks a charging order in the High Court[1] to secure payment of a judgment which carries interest is entitled to have the interest secured as well as the judgment debt.[2] However, where a High Court judgment is obtained for a sum within the county court limit, proceedings to obtain a charging order may have to be taken in the county court[3] even though the judgment is a High Court one which carries interest under the Judgments Act 1838. The County Court Rules and Forms[4] provide for the making of a charging order to secure the payment of a High Court judgment but do not provide explicitly for interest which is accruing on the judgment. There is no obvious reason in logic or justice why the creditor should be deprived of his right to interest or be given less complete security through the county court than through the High Court. It is accordingly suggested that wherever the creditor applies to the county court for a charging order to secure the payment of a High Court judgment debt he should apply to the court for the inclusion of the words 'and interest at the statutory rate' before the words 'together with the costs' in both the order nisi and the order absolute.[5]

1 RSC Ord 50.
2 See RSC Appendix A, Forms 75 and 76.
3 Charging Orders Act 1979, s 1.
4 CCR Ord 31, Prescribed Forms N86 and N87.
5 By r 2(2) of the County Court (Forms) Rules 1982 (SI 1982/586) the Prescribed Forms may be used 'with such variations as the circumstances may require'.

ATTACHMENT OF EARNINGS ORDER

6.11   A High Court judgment may be enforced through the county court by means of an attachment of earnings order.[1] The procedure requires the applicant to file, amongst other things, an office copy of the High Court judgment and an affidavit of the amount due under it, in support of the application,[2] and, if an order is made, a copy of it must be sent to the proper officer of the High Court,[3] the judgment itself remaining a judgment of the High Court throughout. All of these considerations raise the expectation that the attachment of earnings order, when made, will secure the payment of all the money due under the relevant judgment, including interest accruing after the making of the order; and the definition of 'judgment debt' in the Act[4] is certainly wide enough to include interest. But the payment of subsequent interest is not mentioned expressly in County Court Prescribed Form No 60. It is accordingly suggested that where an order is sought to enforce recovery of money due under a High Court judgment the creditor should apply for the form to be varied to include, after the words 'the amount payable under the judgment', the words 'together with interest at the statutory rate', on the same basis as recommended in the preceding paragraph in respect of charging orders.

1 Attachment of Earnings Act 1971, ss 1(2)(b) and 2(c).
2 CCR Ord 27, r 4(1)
3 CCR Ord 27, r 10(3).
4 Attachment of Earnings Act 1971, s 2(c).

EXECUTION OF HIGH COURT JUDGMENT AS IF OBTAINED IN THE COUNTY COURT

6.12   A judgment or order of the High Court for the payment of money, including any award etc that has become enforceable as such, may be enforced in the county court 'as if it were a judgment of that court'. This facility is separate from, and additional to, the jurisdiction of the county court, considered in the preceding paragraphs, to enforce recovery of a High Court judgment by charging the debtor's property and by attaching his earnings. It exists by virtue of section 105(1) of the County Courts Act 1984 which was brought into force on 1 September 1984[1] in place of the slightly narrower facility that existed under section 139 of the County Courts Act 159, as enacted. The procedure for enforcing through the county court is set out in CCR Order 25, rule 11, paragraph (1)(b) of which requires an affidavit in support 'verifying the amount due under the judgment, order, decree or award'. Thus the High Court creditor may enforce through the county court as regards not only the judgment debt but also interest accruing on it. However since the High Court debt becomes recoverable as if it were a judgment of the county court, the creditor must take the county court processes of enforcement as they are. Accordingly interest accruing under the Judgments Act 1838 in respect of the period after the process of county court enforcement has been put in motion may not be recovered in that proceeding, under the existing law. Perhaps this defect will be remedied as an incidental feature of a scheme for interest on county court judgments under section 74 of the County Courts Act. 1984.

1 Administration of Justice Act 1982 (Commencement No 2) Order 1984, SI 1984/1142. See Appendix A for the text of the section.

RECOVERY OUTSIDE ENGLAND AND WALES

(a) Judgment debts

6.13   Pending the bringing into force of the material provisions of the Civil Jurisdiction and Judgments Act 1982, the creditor with a High Court judgment in his favour may register it in other parts of the United Kingdom and in other countries in the world in accordance with the procedure required by the court of registration. The procedure for registering abroad under the Administration of Justice Act 1920 or under the Foreign Judgments (Reciprocal Enforcement) Act 1933 involves the production of a certified copy of the judgment which is to be registered and the procedure for obtaining such a certified copy is laid down in RSC Order 71, rule 13. The effect of such registration is to give the creditor the equivalent of a judgment given in that country for the amount outstanding on the judgment, but whereas under the 1920 Act it is as if the original judgment were given on registration[1] (thus losing any interest accruing in between), under the 1933 Act the registration covers the judgment debt and any interest which accrued on it prior to registration, as well as the costs of registration and of the application for a certified copy.[2] Whether the judgment, as registered, will carry further interest and, if so, at what rate, will be determined according to the law of the country concerned. Registration and enforcement in Scotland and in Northern Ireland follow more or less the same pattern[3] with the same effect that interest accruing between judgment and registration is lost.

1 Administration of Justice Act 1920, s 9(3)(a).
2 Foreign Judgments (Reciprocal Enforcement) Act 1933, s 2(2) and (6).
3 Judgments Extension Act 1868, s 1 and Sch.

(b) Maintenance orders
6.14   A High Court maintenance order, including an order for a lump sum payment, may be registered in another part of the United Kingdom pursuant to Part II of the Maintenance Orders Act 1950 and the effect of registration is for the order to be treated as if made in the place of registration:[1] the question whether it carries interest after registration must be determined accordingly. As regards the enforcement outside the United Kingdom of a High Court order for a lump sum payment, it would seem that the same procedure is to be followed as for any other kind of judgment debt and that the facilities and conditions set out in the preceding paragraph will apply. Orders for periodical payments may be enforced abroad in accordance with the provisions of the Maintenance Orders Act 1972, but that Act does not provide for the recovery of interest on arrears.

1 Maintenance Orders Act 1950, s 18(1).

(c) Civil Jurisdiction and Judgments Act 1982
6.15   When section 18 and Schedule 6 of the Civil Jurisdiction and Judgments Act 1982 come into operation the High Court Judgments which require money to be paid will become enforceable in other parts of the United Kingdom according to a new regime which is, for all practicable purposes, the same as the regime introduced by sections 4, 7 and 12 of the Act for enforcing High Court judgments in the other Member States. Presumably both will be brought into operation at the same time. The key features of the new regime are for the judgment to be registered in the appropriate court in the other law district[1] or Member State[2] on the basis of a certificate of the judgment of the High Court, obtained in accordance with RSC Order 71.[3] The registered judgment takes effect in accordance with the terms of the original judgment and interest continues to run at the same rate.[4] The reasonable costs or expenses of and incidental to the registration are recoverable as if they were sums recoverable under the judgment and carry interest accordingly.[5] A similar regime exists for the enforcement of maintenance orders in other Member States.[6]

1 Civil Jurisdiction and Judgments Act 1982, s 18, Sch 6.
2 Ibid, s 4(1).
3 Ibid, Sch 6, paras 2–4 and RSC App A, Form 111 (for registration intra UK); RSC Order 71, rr 25–39 and Form 110 (for registration in another Member State).
4 Ibid, Sch 6, paras 6 and 8 (for registration intra UK) and ss 4(3) and 7 (for registration in another Member State).
5 Ibid, Sch 6, paras 7 and 8(3) (for registration intra UK) and ss 4(2) and 7(3) (for registration in another Member State).
6 Ibid, ss 5 and 7. Registration intra UK is still dealt with under part II of the Maintenance Orders Act 1950.

The county courts

JUDGMENTS ACT 1838

6.16   Sections 17 and 18 of the Judgments Act 1838 provide for judgment debts and orders for the payment of money to carry interest. They are not expressly limited in their ambit to judgments and orders of superior courts and might be thought to include those of the county courts. But in *R v Essex County Court Judge*[1] it was decided that county court judgments and orders are outside the scope of these provisions. More recently that decision has been doubted[2] and reforms have been urged[3] and, as a result of changes made by the Supreme Court Act 1981,[4] the Lord Chancellor now has power to provide, by order, for certain judgments and orders of the county court to carry interest. The enabling provision is now contained in section 74 of the County Courts Act 1984[5] but no order has yet been made. The probable effects of such an order are considered later in this chapter.[6] As for the existing law, it is appropriate to mention briefly the exceptional circumstances in which county court judgment debts may carry interest under the existing law and other situations in which interest may be ordered to run for a period or periods after judgment.

1 (1887) 18 QBD 704.
2 *K v K* [1977] Fam 39, [1977] 1 All ER 576, CA.
3 Ibid; *Sewing Machine Rentals Ltd v Wilson* [1975] 3 All ER 553, [1976] 1 WLR 37; *Ealing London Borough v El Isaac* [1980] 2 All ER 548, [1980] 1 WLR 932, CA.
4 Sch 3, para 11.
5 See Appendix A.
6 See para 6.23, below.

RECOVERY OF INTEREST THAT IS NOT MERGED IN JUDGMENT

6.17   The doctrine of merger has already been considered in the context of High Court judgments.[1] But the most recent decision on the subject, *Ealing London Borough v El Isaac*[2] was an appeal from a county court decision that the local housing authority's right to recover interest on the cost of certain expenses under section 6(4) of the Housing Act 1969 was merged in the county court judgment and was, in effect, irrecoverable thereafter although the statutory provision was that interest should run until payment. Templeman LJ gave the leading judgment allowing the appeal. He observed that the doctrine of merger was nowadays of very restricted application and concluded that it could not override a statutory provision that the creditor was entitled to statutory interest at a prescribed rate until he was paid.[3] He also made comments on the practice, regarding the recovery of mortgage interest, which are of particular relevance to the county court jurisdiction. He said:[4]

The High Court, and the county court for that matter, make similar orders in mortgage actions as a matter of course, for every standard mortgage contains a covenant in a form which negatives merger. There is also no difficulty, if the county court thinks fit, in providing for payment by equal periodical instalments of capital and interest over a specified period of years, whether five years or any other period of years. Every repayment building society mortgage contains provision of a specified amount for the repayment of capital and interest over a particular period.

1 Para 6.06, above.
2 *Ealing London Borough v El Isaac* [1980] 2 All ER 548, [1980] 1 WLR 932, CA.
3 Provided, of course, that the claim is properly pleaded: see para 6.07, above.
4 *Ealing London Borough v El Isaac* [1980] 2 All ER 548 at 552, [1980] 1 WLR 932 at 938.

6.18   In the circumstances just described, where a county court judgment or order is expressed as carrying interest at a particular rate, the creditor may enforce the judgment as to both principal and interest. Accordingly when requesting the issue of a warrant or execution the creditor should apply for the prescribed form[1] to be modified by the inclusion, after the word 'costs' of the words 'together with interest at the rate . . . per cent per annum'. He should apply for such a phrase to be inserted, in a similar fashion, in the appropriate prescribed forms for attachment of earnings orders[2] and for garnishee orders[3] and for charging orders.[4] The power to vary the forms is provided by the County Court (Forms) Rules 1982.[5]

1 N 44.
2 N 55, 58, 60, 64, 66.
3 N 84, 85, 85(1).
4 N 86, 87.
5 SI 1982/586, r 2(2).

MAINTENANCE ORDERS
6.19   Interest does not run on maintenance orders which are made in the county court,[1] although the main proceedings may have been heard in the High Court. However, where a lump sum is ordered to be paid at some future date, or by instalments, the court may direct that the payment, or instalments, so ordered should carry interest down to the date when the money should be paid over.[2] This power is exercisable by a divorce county court.[3]

1 For reasons given in para 16.6, above.
2 Matrimonial Causes Act 1973, s 23(6).
3 Matrimonial Causes Act 1967, s 2(1), as amended by the Matrimonial Causes Act 1973.

COSTS
6.20   A county court order for costs does not carry interest any

more than a county court judgment debt does. But the costs of county court litigation are not necessarily always interest-free. If, for any reason, the costs incurred in such proceedings are taxed in the High Court then the amount ordered to be paid carries interest under the Judgments Act 1838.[1] Also, on a taxation, in any court, of costs in respect of any contentious business, the taxing officer may allow interest at such rate and from such time as he thinks fit on money disbursed by the solicitor for the client and on money of the client in the hands of, and improperly retained by, the solicitor.[2]

1 *K v K* [1977] Fam 39, [1977] 1 All ER 576, CA.
2 Solicitors Act 1974, s 66(a). But this provision seems to apply only to a taxation as between a solicitor and his own client: *Hartland v Murrell* (1873) LR16 Eq 285.

HIGH COURT EXECUTION TO ENFORCE COUNTY COURT JUDGMENTS
6.21   Although a county court judgment does not carry interest, procedure now exists for the enforcement of a county court judgment debt of over £2,000[1] through the High Court 'as if it were a judgment or order of that court'.[2] The procedure for transferring the county court judgment up, for enforcement, is set out in CCR Order 25, rule 13 and the practice for enforcement is set out in Queen's Bench Practice Directions.[3] Each of the relevant prescribed forms of the writ of fieri facias has been revised[4] so as to be suitable for enforcing either a High Court judgment or a transferred county court judgment, with interest under the Judgments Act 1838 running in the one instance from the date of the judgment and in the other from the date of the transfer up.

1 The sum of £2,000 is specified by the Transfer of County Court Judgments (Specified Amount) Order 1984, SI 1984/1141.
2 County Courts Act 1984, s 106(2): for the text see Appendix A.
3 *Practice Direction 20A*, dated August 1984 and also *Practice Direction* dated 15 November 1984. For the text of each see Appendix C.
4 See forms 53, 54 and 56 in Appendix A to the Rules of the Supreme Court as substituted by RSC (Amendment) 1984, SI 1984/1051.

CHARGING ORDERS IN THE HIGH COURT TO ENFORCE COUNTY COURT JUDGMENTS
6.22   There are a variety of situations in which a judgment creditor may seek a charging order in the High Court to enforce a county court judgment debt. One instance is where the property to be charged is a fund in the High Court.[1] Another is where the sum involved exceeds the county court limit.[2] A third is where a charging order is properly sought in the High Court as regards one debt, or order, and a county court judgment debt owed between the same

parties is enforced by means of the same proceedings.[3] In all these cases the question arises whether the High Court charging order may be expressed to secure the payment not only of the county court debt, but also statutory interest on it at the rate prescribed by the Judgments Act 1838. The creditor has no right to such interest apart from the charging order, but it is arguable that the jurisdiction of the High Court to give security to the creditor and relief, for the present, to the debtor includes the power to provide for interest in the charging order. An obligation to pay interest is implicit in any charge on land[4] and it may be argued from this that a charge which is ordered by the court, at least in respect of land, should carry a right to interest on the debt so secured unless the prescribed form indicates, as County Court Forms N 86 and 87 do, that interest is not to be charged in the normal way.[5]

1 Charging Orders Act 1979, s 1(2)(a).
2 Ibid, s 1(2)(c).
3 Ibid, s 1(4).
4 *Re Drax* [1903] 1 Ch 781.
5 The converse situation of a county court charging order to secure a High Court debt is considered in para 6.10, above.

LORD CHANCELLOR'S ORDER FOR INTEREST TO RUN ON COUNTY
COURT JUDGMENTS AND ORDERS

6.23   The Lord Chancellor has power to provide by order for county court judgments and orders to carry interest[1] and has had this power since 1 January 1982 when the Supreme Court Act 1981 came into force. But it has obviously not been easy to devise a system to match the High Court procedure, which has the obvious advantage of speed and economical use of court staff, within the county court's unenviable role as the bank through which the debtor's payments must pass[2] and by which the state of his indebtedness must be recorded.[3] The Lord Chancellor's Department published a first consultation paper in October 1981 and a second, quite different, one on 24 August 1983. From the terms of the second, which is set out as an Appendix to this book,[4] it appears that the proposals in the first paper have now been discarded and that what emerges eventually will be something much closer to the High Court procedure, the key feature of which is that the calculation of interest is primarily a matter for the creditor, not the court. Points to look for in the new scheme are:

(a) whether the county court creditor will be allowed to appropriate payments to interest before principal, as he can in the High Court;

(b) whether there will be a line, at say the limit for small claims procedure,[5] below which judgment debts will not carry interest;

(c) whether, in the case of an instalment order, interest will run on the whole debt from judgment or only on instalments as and when they fall due;[6]

(d) how High Court interest and county court interest will fit together in cases which are transferred either up or down for enforcement;[7]

(e) whether processes of enforcement will operate on interest down to the date of payment, as in the High Court,[8] or only down to the date of applying for the process in question.[9]

1 County Courts Act, 1984, s 74. See Appendix A for the text.
2 County Courts Act 1959, s 99(3), the repeal of which by the Administration of Justice Act 1982 is not yet in force.
3 County Courts Act 1984, s 73; Register of County Court Judgments Regulations 1936, SR & O 1936/1311.
4 See Appendix F.
5 Currently £500; CCR Ord. 19, r 2(3).
6 See para 6.02, above.
7 See paras 6.12 and 6.21, above.
8 See paras 6.08–6.10, above.
9 See para 6.18, above

RECOVERY OUTSIDE ENGLAND AND WALES

6.24   Since county court judgments do not carry interest automatically the question how such interest might be recovered outside England and Wales is of little more than academic interest. However, in those rare cases where interest may be ordered to run after judgment,[1] a certificate of the judgment in question may be granted by the home court and registered in a Scottish sheriff court, as if made by that court, under the Inferior Courts Judgments Extension Act 1882.[2] At present there is no procedure for taking a county court judgment further afield for enforcement (except as regards maintenance orders). However, when the Civil Jurisdiction and Judgments Act 1982 comes into force the judgment creditor will be able to enforce his county court judgment not only in any other law district within the United Kingdom, according to the same regime as for High Court judgments,[3] but also will be able to take it abroad for enforcement in any other Member State within the European Economic Community, by presenting the certificate to the court specified in Article 32 of the Convention, the text of which is set out in Schedule 1 to the Act. If by the time all this comes to pass, the Lord Chancellor has made an order for county court judgments and orders to carry interest, the creditor will then be able to recover such interest at the rate provided, not only at home but in any other law district or Member State within the Community.

1 See para 6.17, above.
2 CCR Ord 35 provides for the procedure to be phased.
3 See para 6.15, above. Note that a certificate of a county court judgment is registered in the *superior* court of the other law district, in accordance with para 5 of Sch 6 to the Act, not, as might have been expected, in a court of equivalent status.

Other courts and tribunals

6.25   With other courts of civil jurisdiction, such as magistrates courts and tribunals, the general rule is that orders, or awards, for the payment of money do not carry interest automatically in their own right. One significant exception, although not yet effective, is in relation to awards made by industrial tribunals. The Employment Act 1982 inserted a provision in Schedule 9 to the Employment Protection (Consolidation) Act 1978, enabling the Secretary of State, by Order, to provide for tribunal awards to carry interest.[1] But no such order has been made so far. Other statutory tribunals, such as the Lands Tribunal, may be invested with the power to award interest under section 19A of the Arbitration Act 1950;[2] but much depends on the terms of the legislation by which the tribunal is constituted.[3]

1 Para 64 of Sch 9 to that Act.
2 See para 8.02, below.
3 See, for example, Lands Tribunal Act 1949, s 3(8).

Chapter 7

Interest in respect of foreign money liabilities and interest on foreign judgments

Foreign money liabilities

7.01 In the case of a claim which contains a foreign element questions may arise whether a plaintiff, suing in England and Wales, is entitled to any and, if so, what interest before judgment. They fall to be determined, as regards contractual interest, by the proper law of the contract[1] and, as regards interest on damages in tort, by the law, or laws, governing tortious liability,[2] although arguably the lex fori is, or ought to be, applied in fixing the rate of interest in either situation.[3] It is clear, however, that, where there is no entitlement to interest under the appropriate law, an award may be made under section 35A of the Supreme Court Act 1981, or, as the case may be, section 69 of the County Courts Act 1984. If, in such a case, a judgment is sought in a foreign currency and interest falls to be assessed, the assessment is likely to be made at the rate applicable to that currency.[4] However, the need for an assessment may be avoided in the case of a default judgment so long as the plaintiff has pleaded his claim for interest as a liquidated claim at the rate payable on High Court judgments.

1 *Graham v Keble* (1820) 2 Bli 126; *Société des Hôtels Le Touquet Paris-Plage v Cummings* [1922] 1 KB 451, at 460; *Miliangos v George Frank (Textiles) Ltd (No 2)* [1977] QB 489, at 496–497.
2 *Ekins v East India Co* (1717) 1 P Wms 395, 24 ER 141.
3 See Law Commission's Report No 124 on Foreign Money Liabilities (1983) Cmnd 9064) paras 2.27–2.33 for a detailed and critical analysis of this branch of the law.

4 *Miliangos v George Frank (Textiles) Ltd (No 2)*, above; *The Pacific Colocotronis* [1981] 2 Lloyd's Rep 40, at 45–47. But note also the different approach taken in *Helmsing Schiffahrts GmbH & Co KG v Malta Drydocks Corpn* [1977] 2 Lloyd's Rep 444.

INTEREST AFTER JUDGMENT

7.02 Where the plaintiff is owed a contract debt which the contract provides is to be measured and paid in a foreign currency, the judgment should be expressed in that currency followed by the words 'or the sterling equivalent at the time of payment' (a *Miliangos* judgment). Before the House of Lords decision in *Miliangos v George Frank (Textiles) Ltd*[1] judgments in England and Wales were always expressed in sterling. Since that date the *Miliangos* principle has been developed by a number of decisions on the circumstances in which the plaintiff's judgment should be expressed in a foreign currency.[2] In order to enforce a *Miliangos* judgment it will normally be necessary to convert the judgment into sterling because this is the currency in which execution is levied and in which the judgment is most conveniently enforced.[3] Judgment interest is then calculated on the sterling into which the currency is converted, as if this were the sum for which judgment had been given originally. A notional conversion is also needed for other purposes, such as to determine the scale on which the plaintiff's costs should be paid. All these points, about converting a foreign currency judgment into sterling, are covered in a comprehensive practice direction[4] which is, however, analysed critically by the Law Commission in Part V of their Report No 124 on Foreign Money Liabilities.[5] The Report contends, in particular, that it is unjust that a judgment in a foreign currency should carry interest at the rate provided by section 17 of the Judgments Act 1838 for the period prior to its conversion into sterling in a case where the foreign currency is much stronger or weaker than sterling: in such a case a lower (or, as the case may be, higher) rate of interest would be more appropriate. The Report accordingly recommends that courts and arbitrators should be empowered to direct that a judgment or award which is expressed in a foreign currency should carry interest at such fixed or variable rate of interest as the court thinks fit instead of at the English judgment rate which would otherwise apply. Until the law is changed, however, judgments in England and Wales carry the same rate of interest throughout whether expressed in sterling or in a foreign currency.

1 [1976] AC 443.
2 The *Miliangos* principle has been applied in a foreign money judgment for damages for breach of contract (*The Folias* [1979] AC 685) and in a judgment on a claim in tort for damage to property (*The Despina R* [1979] AC 685) and has been accepted as applicable in personal injury litigation (*Hoffman v Sofaer* [1983] 1 WLR 1350).

3 But see *Choice Investments Ltd v Jeromnimon* [1981] QB 149, [1981] 1 All ER 225, CA.
4 The Senior Master's Practice Direction (Judgment: Foreign Currency) [1976] 1 All ER 669, [1976] 1 WLR 83, as amended [1977] 1 All ER 544, [1977] 1 WLR 197, is set out in Appendix C.
5 (1983) Cmnd 9064.

Interest on judgments obtained outside England and Wales

7.03   The question what, if any, interest is carried by a judgment obtained outside England and Wales is determined by the law of the country where the judgment was entered. The interest rate for judgments in England and Wales comes into play, however, when the plaintiff either registers the foreign judgment here or sues on it and obtains a judgment in England and Wales based on the cause of action arising from the foreign judgment. The Civil Jurisdiction and Judgments Act 1982 changes the law regarding interest on judgment obtained within the European Economic Community, but these changes are not yet in force. It is therefore necessary to consider first the law as it is now and next the changes which will take place when the relevant provisions of the 1982 Act come into operation.

THE PRESENT LAW, IGNORING CHANGES MADE BY THE CIVIL
JURISDICTION AND JUDGMENTS ACT 1982
7.04   Under the present law, ignoring changes made by the Civil Jurisdiction and Judgments Act 1982, a plaintiff who has obtained a judgment outside England and Wales may sue on it and obtain a judgment in this country in respect of the foreign judgment debt and interest accruing thereunder. The judgment thus obtained carries interest in the normal way. The date of the accrual of the cause of action, on which the English action is based, is the date of the debtor's failure to honour the foreign judgment.[1]

1 *Grant v Easton* (1883) 13 QBD 302; *Re Flynn (No 2) Flynn v Flynn* [1969] 2 Ch 403, [1969] 2 All ER 557.

7.05   As regards those foreign judgments which may be enforced in this country by registration here, registration is the preferred method of obtaining a locus standi for enforcing it, and from the moment of registration the registered judgment carries interest under section 17 of the Judgments Act 1838 as if it were a judgment obtained in the court of registration. This applies to (a) judgments obtained in Scotland or Northern Ireland[1] (b) Commonwealth judgments to which Part II of the Administration of Justice Act 1920 applies[2] (c) foreign judgments for which reciprocal arrangements have been made for enforcement under the Foreign Judgments (Reciprocal Enforcement) Act 1933 and (d) European Community Judgments.[3] The former rule against registering judgments in a foreign currency was abrogated by section 4(2)(b)(i) of the Administration of Justice Act 1977, so a foreign judgment in a foreign currency ought normally to be registered in that currency, but with the same effect as if in the usual *Miliangos* form.[4] Remarkably, of the various kinds of judgments just described, it is only in the case of a foreign judgment registered under the Foreign Judgments (Reciprocal Enforcement) Act 1933 that the judgment creditor is entitled to include in the sum registered the interest which has accrued on the foreign judgment down to that date.[5] This is one of the factors to be taken into account in deciding whether to enforce a judgment by registration, or by suing on the original judgment and claiming the interest on that judgment in those proceedings.[6]

1 Crown Debts Act 1801, Judgments Extension Act 1868 and inferior Courts Judgments Extension Act 1882.
2 See the Judgments (Administration of Justice Act 1920, Part II) (Consolidation) Order 1984 (SI 1984/129), for a list of the countries specified at the date of the consolidation.
3 European Communities (Enforcement of Community Judgments) Order 1972 (SI 1972/1590).
4 See para 7.02, above.
5 Foreign Judgments (Reciprocal Enforcement) Act 1933, s 2(6).
6 Other factors are that, except under the 1933 Act, the facility for registration is only available for one year from the original judgment and that a plaintiff who opts for a civil action rather than registration may be penalised in costs under s 6 of the 1868 Act, s 8 of the 1882 Act and s 9(5) of the 1920 Act. Section 6 of the 1933 Act bars proceedings to enforce the foreign judgment except by registration.

CHANGES MADE BY THE CIVIL JURISDICTION AND JUDGMENTS ACT 1982

7.06   When section 7 of the Civil Jurisdiction and Judgments Act 1982 comes into operation any judgment which has been obtained in another Member State and which is registered for enforcement in England and Wales will be subject to a new regime as regards judgment interest. If, in accordance with the law of that State, interest is recoverable under the judgment from a particular date or time the rate of interest and the date or time from which it is so recoverable are to be registered with the judgment and the judgment so registered must provide for future interest accordingly. This is provided by subsection (1). Subsection (5) states that registered judgments are not to carry interest except under that section; so a judgment which is obtained in a Member State and which does not carry interest there will not carry interest when registered here. On the other hand, subsection (3) provides for the reasonable costs of registration to carry interest as if an order for the payment of the costs were made on registration by the registering court. An equivalent regime is instituted, by section 18(1)(a) and paras 6, 7 and 8 of Schedule 6, for the enforcement in England and Wales of judgments obtained in Scotland or Northern Ireland and interest thereunder and, by Part II of Schedule 11, for the recovery in England and Wales of interest on arrears under maintenance order made in Scotland or Northern Ireland.

Chapter 8

Arbitration

Arbitrator's power to award interest

THE OLD LAW
8.01   Statutory arbitrators have the powers with which they are invested by statute whereas arbitrators who are appointed pursuant to an arbitration agreement have such powers as are bestowed upon them, expressly or impliedly, by the parties. In *Chandris v Isbrandt-sen-Moller*[1] the Court of Appeal decided that a submission of a dispute to an arbitrator, in accordance with an arbitration agreement, empowered the arbitrator to include in his determination an award of interest to the same extent as if he were a court of record. The rationale is that the parties to an arbitration agreement are assumed to have intended the arbitrator to be equipped to do justice between them just as if he were a civil court of record. However, the *Chandris* principle does not mean that all arbitrators can award interest wherever the justice of the case requires it. To start with, the *Chandris* principle does not apply to statutory arbitrators: they have no power to award interest unless so empowered by the statute in question. Then again, the power to award interest may be excluded by the terms of the arbitration agreement and even where such an exclusion would be unfair and unreasonable it cannot be struck down by the Unfair Contract Terms Act 1977, since such terms are outside the scope of that Act.[2] Thirdly, the powers of courts of record to award interest under the 1934 Act may not be exercised as regards a disputed debt which is paid during the course of the proceedings.[3] Fourthly the *Chandris* principle may have been undermined by the removal of the High Court and the county courts from the 'courts of record' to which the 1934 Act applies.[4]

1 [1951] 1 KB 240, [1950] 1 All ER 768; *The Finix* [1978] 1 Lloyds Rep 16.

2 Unfair Contract Terms Act 1977, ss 14(2), 25(3).
3 See para 4.07, above.
4 See para 4.04, above.

THE NEW LAW

8.02 For these and no doubt other reasons the Arbitration Act 1950 has been amended, by section 15 and Part IV of Schedule 1 to the Administration of Justice Act 1982, with effect from 1 April 1983, by the insertion of a new provision, section 19A, which confers on arbitrators the same general powers to award interest as the other provisions in Schedule 1 confer on the High Court and county courts.[1] It should be noted that these powers allow interest to be awarded down to the date of the award, but not beyond. Section 19A applies to statutory arbitrators as well as to those appointed pursuant to an arbitration agreement. There is, however, one statutory arbitration which is excluded from the benefit of section 19A, namely county court arbitrations conducted pursuant to section 64 of the County Courts Act 1984 and rules of court. By section 7(3) of the Arbitration Act 1979 county court arbitrations are put outside the provisions of the Arbitration Act 1950. But this is not to say that the county court arbitrator has no power to consider a claim for discretionary interest. On the contrary, county court disputes are referred for him to decide by making an award which is as binding and effectual to all intents as if given by the judge. A claim for interest under section 69 of the County Courts Act 1984 will have to be pleaded if it is to be entertained at all[2] and will therefore be on the pleadings as a 'matter in dispute' (to use the language of section 64) which the arbitrator is required by the court to determine. He must therefore decide it in accordance with the relevant law, ie s 69 of the County Courts Act 1984, and determine whether the judgment which is to be entered to give effect to his award should include any and if so how much interest under that section.

1 The text is included in Appendix A.
2 CCR Ord 6, r 1A, the text of which is in Appendix B.

SUMS WHICH ARE NOT THE SUBJECT OF THE REFERENCE

8.03 One problem remains, however, notwithstanding the amendment to the Arbitration Act 1950. It concerns the one defect in the 1934 Act which was not put right by the Administration of Justice Act 1982, namely the problem of the debtor who withholds payments for an unreasonable period but pays up before the proceedings have been started whether before a court of record or an arbitrator.[1] Section 19A(1) empowers the arbitrator to award interest on any sum which is the subject of the reference, but which is paid before the award, but not to award interest on a sum which is not the subject of the reference because, for example, it is paid before the arbitration proceedings are started. On the other hand, section 19A(2) makes it clear that the powers under subsection (1) are without prejudice to any other power of an arbitrator or umpire to award interest and it might be argued that a commercial arbitrator appointed to decide a dispute about, say, demurrage may be impliedly empowered by the parties to award interest in such a situation, eg where the demurrage is disputed and delayed but eventually paid before the arbitration is on foot. This argument was put in the *Tehno-Impex* case[2] and Lord Denning MR concluded that City of London arbitrators did have such powers as a matter of custom or usage. Furthermore he and Watkins LJ concluded that the power could be exercised by an arbitrator of a maritime dispute if the Court of Admiralty could have exercised it in an equivalent situation. This approach, which is the *Chandris* approach in another guise, was upheld by the House of Lords, in *President of India v La Pintada Compania Navigacion SA*.[3] However Lord Brandon, with whose speech the others concurred, firmly rejected the argument that the Court of Admiralty, or indeed of Chancery, ever had power to award interest except on a sum that was itself the subject of a judgment or order. Moreover, their Lordships unanimously rejected the view of Lord Denning MR that City of London arbitrators were empowered to award interest on sums that had already been paid. Lord Roskill and Lord Scarman expressed concern at the failure of Parliament to deal with this particular problem but, for good or ill, it is now clear that an arbitrator cannot exercise any greater power to award interest than that which is conferred by section 19A of the Arbitration Act 1950 unless some additional power is conferred upon him expressly by the parties.

1 See para 4.06 above.
2 [1981] QB 648, [1981] 2 All ER 669, CA.
3 [1984] 2 All ER 773, [1984] 3 WLR 10.

Interest accruing after the award

INTEREST UNDER SECTION 20 OF THE ARBITRATION ACT 1950

8.04 Ever since 1934[1] arbitration awards have carried interest. Section 20 of the Arbitration Act 1950 now provides that

A sum directed to be paid by an award shall, unless the award otherwise directs, carry interest as from the date of the award and at the same rate as a judgment debt.

The words 'unless the award otherwise directs' do not give the arbitrator a statutory discretion as to the rate and period for which interest should run after the award: his statutory discretion is limited to directing that interest under that section should not run. This was the conclusion of a majority of the House of Lords in *Timber Shipping Co SA v London & Overseas Freighters Ltd.*[2] In *Rocco Giuseppe v Tradax SA*[3] Parker J arrived at the same conclusion and rejected the argument of the successful party in the arbitration that the interest rate on an award would fluctuate if the judgment rate were subsequently changed[4] and also the alternative argument that the arbitrator had a discretion, under section 20, to direct that it should so fluctuate.

1 Arbitration Act 1934, s 11.
2 [1972] AC 1, [1971] 2 All ER 399.
3 [1984] 1 WLR 742.
4 Administration of Justice Act 1970, s 44(1).

8.05   Section 20 of the Arbitration Act 1950 is expressed in very general terms and appears to apply to all awards, those made pursuant to statute as well as those made pursuant to arbitration agreements, and foreign as well as English.[1] There is, however, one kind of award to which it does *not* apply and that is the award made by a county court arbitrator to whom a county claim is referred under section 64 of the County Courts Act 1984. Section 7(3) of the Arbitration Act 1979 disapplies section 20 of the Arbitration Act 1950 in relation to county court arbitration. However, county court awards take effect as judgments under section 64(3) of the County Courts Act 1984 and may therefore qualify for interest under the Lord Chancellor's scheme under section 74 of that Act.[2]

1 But see *Dalmia Dairy Industries Ltd v National Bank of Pakistan* [1978] 2 Lloyd's Rep 223.
2 See para 6.23, above.

INTEREST ARISING OTHERWISE
8.06   In the case of a reference to arbitration which arises not from statute but from the contractual arrangements of the parties, they have a limited freedom to confer jurisdiction on the arbitrator as to how he should deal with questions of interest. They might, for instance, agree in advance that whatever sum should be awarded by the arbitrator should carry interest at a predetermined rate until payment. In such a case the arbitrator would no doubt direct that

section 20 of the Arbitration Act 1950 was not to apply; the award would then carry interest at the predetermined rate, just as judgment debts may carry interest at the predetermined contractual rate in those cases where the doctrine of merger does not apply.[1] The parties might go further and agree, as one of the terms of the reference, that the arbitrator should have a discretion to fix the rate of interest which his award should carry down to payment. Here again the arbitrator would seem to have power to direct that the statutory rate should not apply and to fix the post-award rate himself in exercise of the jurisdiction conferred upon him at common law. But it might be argued that the common law jurisdiction has been supplanted by section 20 of the Arbitration Act 1950 and that since the decision in the *Timber Shipping* case,[2] an award of interest for the period down to payment cannot be made in an English arbitration although it may properly be made in a foreign one, if permissible under the law governing the arbitration.[3]

1 See paras 6.06–6.07, above.
2 [1972] AC 1, [1972] 1 All ER 399.
3 *Dalma Dairy Industries Ltd v National Bank of Pakistan* [1978] 2 Lloyd's Rep 223.

Recovery of interest

8.07   Where an arbitral award includes an award of interest the processes by which that interest may be recovered are the processes by which the award itself may be enforced. These are considered in turn, below, and in none of them does any point of difficulty arise regarding interest down to the date of the award. But interest in respect of the period after the award receives different treatment depending on the process invoked.

RECIPROCAL ENFORCEMENT OF FOREIGN AWARDS
8.08   Where an arbitral award has, under the law of the country where it was made, become enforceable as a judgment of the foreign court and where reciprocal arrangements have been made pursuant to Part II of the Administration of Justice Act 1920 or the Foreign Judgments (Reciprocal Enforcement) Act 1933, the award may be enforced in this country by registration.[1] This means that interest accruing between the award and the registration may be included in a registration under the 1933 Act, but not under the 1920 Act.[2]

1 Administration of Justice Act 1920, s 12(1), Foreign Judgments (Reciprocal Enforcement) Act 1933, s 10A; RSC Ord 73, r 8.
2 See para 7.05, above.

ARBITRATION (INTERNATIONAL INVESTMENT DISPUTES) ACT 1966
8.09   In the relatively uncommon case of an arbitral award to
which the Arbitration (International Investment Disputes) Act 1966
applies, a special facility for enforcement exists. By section 2(1) the
award may be registered in the High Court[1] as a judgment backdated to the date of the award, so that interest under section 17 of
the Judgments Act 1938 accrues on it from the date of the award,
not just from the date of the registration.

1 RSC Ord 73, r 9.

SECTION 26 OF THE ARBITRATION ACT 1950

(a) Enforcement through the High Court
8.10   The usual way of enforcing an English award is by means
of section 26 of the Arbitration Act 1950 which provides that the
court may give leave for enforcement through the processes of the
High Court if the amount sought to be recovered exceeds the county
court limit (currently £5,000),[1] and through the processes of the
county court if it does not.[2] High Court enforcement is a possibility
for any English award on an arbitration agreement or pursuant to
statute[3] or for any New York Convention award to which section
3(1)(a) of the Arbitration Act 1975 applies. It is also a possibility for
any foreign award to which section 35 of the Arbitration Act 1950
applies[4] and for any other foreign award on an arbitration agreement, although the court may exercise its discretion to refuse the
facility in the case of a foreign award which is in terms which cannot
be enforced as a High Court judgment.[5] Moreover an award on an
arbitration agreement means an award on a *written* agreement;[6] so
an oral agreement to go to arbitration is not sufficient to found an
application to the High Court. The procedure for making an
application to the High Court for leave to enforce is as set out in
RSC Order 73, rule 10. Once the leave has been obtained the usual
methods of enforcement may be invoked. In addition the award may
be entered as a High Court judgment 'to the same effect'[7] which
presumably means that an award which carries interest under
section 20 of the Arbitration 1950 will be given the same sort of
back-dating as an award under the Arbitration (International
Investment Disputes) Act 1966.[8] If the award carries interest down
to payment at a rate different from that arising under section 20 of
the Arbitration Act 1950,[9] the registration will involve not only
backdating but also the insertion of a non-statutory rate of interest.

1 Arbitration Act 1950, s 26; the county court limit may be raised from £5,000 by an
  order under s 145 of the County Courts Act 1984.

2 Arbitration Act 1950, s 26(2). The text of the relevant provisions is set out in Appendix A.
3 Ibid, s 31.
4 Ibid, s 36(1).
5 *Dalmia Cement Ltd v National Bank of Pakistan* [1975] QB 9, [1974] 3 All ER 189.
6 Arbitration Act 1950, s 32.
7 Ibid, s 26(1).
8 See the preceding paragraph.
9 See para 8.06, above.

(b) Enforcement through the county court
8.11   As regards awards where the amount sought to be reco-vered does not exceed the county court limit, the same general considerations apply and the procedure for seeking leave to enforce is provided by CCR Order 25, rule 12. Where leave is given the enforcement may proceed in respect of interest on the award as well as the award itself, as in the High Court. But unlike the provision for the High Court, the provision for the county courts does not allow the award to be entered as a county court judgment. County court arbitrations, on the other hand, are outside the scope of section 26; but an award is entered as, and takes effect as, a judgment of the court.[1]

1 See para 8.05 above.

ACTION ON THE AWARD
8.12   Finally, any arbitral award may be enforced by a civil action in the High Court or county court, depending on the amount involved. Where there is an arbitration agreement the cause of action is contractual, the non-performance of the award being a breach of the agreement under which the arbitration took place.[1] Where the arbitration is a statutory one the award may be sued on as a civil debt. In all cases the limitation period runs from the non-performance of the award, not the date on which any antecedent agreement was made.[2] The interest accruing on the award may be recovered in such proceedings down to the date of judgment into which the cause of action becomes merged: thereafter statutory interest accrues on the judgment if it would accrue in the case of any other kind of monetary judgment of that court.[3] If the entitlement to interest at a certain rate has already been decided by the arbitrator, or accrues under statute, the court has no power to increase the rate or award additional interest.[4]

1 *Bremer Oeltransport GmbH v Drewry* [1933] 1 KB 753.
2 *Agromet Motoimport v Maulden Engineering Company (Beds) Ltd* (1984) Times, 17 April.
3 *Dalmia Dairy Industries Ltd v National Bank of Pakistan* [1978] 2 Lloyd's Rep 223.
4 Ibid.

Chapter 9

Winding up of partnerships, estates and companies

9.01   This chapter is concerned with the recovery of interest in a winding up where the affairs that are being wound are (a) a partnership (b) an estate of a deceased person (c) the estate of a bankrupt and (d) a company. Other provisions concerning the recovery of interest are dealt with incidentally.

PARTNERSHIPS
9.02   Section 24(3) of the Partnership Act 1890 provides that:

A partner making, for the purpose of the partnership, any actual payment or advance beyond the amount of capital which he has agreed to subscribe, is entitled to interest at the rate of five per cent per annum from the date of the payment or advance.

9.03   The rate of 5% per annum was fixed by statute at a time when the cost of borrowing money was lower than it is today. However, a partner who advances more capital than his agreed contribution is not bound to accept 5%. All the subsections of section 24 are 'subject to any agreement express or implied between the partners'; he may therefore seek his partners' agreement to the payment of a higher rate of interest in respect of capital advance in excess of the agreed contribution. Indeed the partners may agree to the payment of interest on the capital subscribed as well, but in the absence of any such agreement subsection (4) rules out the right to interest in this respect.

9.04   Section 24 is not directly concerned with the winding up of a partnership, but it lays down rules which, unless otherwise agreed,

95

provide a matrix of rights and duties from which the final accounts on dissolution take their shape. Section 42, on the other hand, comes into play on dissolution and not before. It concerns the situation where a member of a firm has died or otherwise ceased to be a partner and the surviving or continuing partners carry on the business without any final statement of accounts as between the firm and the outgoing partner or his estate. Section 42(1) provides that, in such a case, the outgoing partner or his estate is entitled, in the absence of any agreement to the contrary, to interest on his share of the partnership assets at 5% per annum. Further, the subsection allows an option to stipulate instead for 'such shares of the profits made since the dissolution as the Court may find to be attributable to the use of his share of the partnership assets'. These provisions may be ousted by an agreement to the contrary, but if the effect of such an agreement is to confer an option on the surviving or continuing partners to purchase the interest of the deceased or outgoing partner and that option is exercised, there must be full compliance with all the material terms of the option: otherwise subsection (2) provides that the outgoing partner or his estate has the same rights as are provided in the absence of agreement by subsection (1).

THE ESTATE OF A DECEASED PERSON

9.05   RSC Order 44 regulates the winding up of an estate where there is a court order for its administration; the same provisions have been adopted by CCR Order 23 rule 2(1) for county court administrations. The number of estates administered pursuant to court order is small in proportion to those administered without such an order but the prudent course for trustees of the estate is to apply the same rules to an administration out of court and this is what normally happens.

9.06   RSC Order 44 rule 9 establishes a general right in the creditor of a solvent estate to be paid interest at the contractual or statutory rate wherever there is a contractual or statutory rate to it and, in other cases, to be paid interest from the date of the judgment in the administration action at the rate payable on High Court judgments at that date. Paragraph (2) of rule 9 provides that the entitlement to interest under the rule is to be met out of any assets which may remain after satisfying the costs of the cause or matter, the debts which have been established and the interest payable on such of those debts as by law carry interest. Paragraph (3) adds that funeral, testamentary and administrative expenses are to be treated as debts of the estate for the purpose of the rule but that where they are incurred after the judgment in the administration action interest at the rate payable on High Court judgments does not start to run until the expenses become payable. These provisions apply subject to the Court's power, under paragraph (1), to order otherwise.

9.07   As regards interest on legacies, rule 10 of Order 44 provides that, subject to any directions in the will or codicil, interest should be allowed at the rate of 6% per annum from one year after the testator's death, thus allowing the executors a full year in which to pay out the legacies interest-free. As with rule 9 the provisions of rule 10 are subject to a discretion in the Court to order otherwise.

9.08   Where a minor is left a contingent legacy by a parent, provision may be made for the maintenance of the minor out of income from the legacy at the rate of 5% per annum. This is provided by section 31(3) of the Trustee Act 1925.

9.09   The money payable to a widow on her husband's dying intestate carries interest from the date of his death at the rate fixed by the Lord Chancellor under section 28 of the Administration of Justice Act 1977, which enables him to vary the rate originally fixed at 4% per annum by section 46(1)(i) of the Administration of Estates Act 1925. The rate was set at 7% in 1977 and lowered to 6% by the Intestate Succession (Interest and Capitalisation) Order 1977 (Amendment) Order 1983.[1]

1 SI 1983/1374.

9.10   Finally, as regards estates of deceased persons, reference should be made to the apportionment of income and capital between tenant for life and remaindermen where the nature of the relevant investments operates unfairly as between them. As regards unauthorised investments which the trustees are under a duty to sell, whether under the rule in *Howe v Earl of Dartmouth*[1] or under an express direction to sell, the income has to be adjusted so that the tenant for life receives a fair yield, income in excess being treated as capital. Four per cent has, in the past, been regarded as a fair yield[2] but the Court might well take a higher figure today, possibly the rate payable on the Short Term Investment Account.[3]

1 (1802) 7 Ves 137 ER
2 *Re Parry, Brown v Parry* [1974] Ch 23.
3 See *Bartlett v Barclays Bank Trust Co Ltd (No 2)* [1980] Ch 515, [1980] 2 All ER 92. See, too, para 10.13, below and Appendix E.

INSOLVENCY LAW BEFORE THE INSOLVENCY ACT 1985 COMES INTO
FORCE

(a) Bankruptcy and insolvent estates
9.11   Before the Insolvency Act 1985 comes into operation the
law regarding the creditor's recovery of interest in the debtor's
bankruptcy is as provided by the Bankruptcy Act 1914. By section
30(3) of that Act a creditor who is entitled to be paid interest on his
debt may prove in the bankruptcy for the interest outstanding at the
date of the receiving order. However, where, before the date of the
receiving order, payments have been made, or the creditor has
realised his security for the debt, the amounts which are admissible
to proof (a) as interest, and (b) as principal are arrived at by
apportioning the receipts to principal and interest in the proportion
that the principal bears to the sum payable as interest at the agreed
rate.[1] The interest is admissible to proof at a rate not exceeding 5%
per annum, but the excess over 5% may be paid out of the estate
once the provable debts have been paid in full.[2] As regards debts
which do not carry interest as a matter of entitlement the creditor
may prove in the estate at a rate not exceeding 4% per annum, down
to the date of the receiving order; however the interest only runs
from the date when the debt was due if a date for payment has been
set by a written instrument; otherwise it runs from the giving of a
notice that interest will be claimed from the date of demand until
payment.[3] As for debts payable at a future date, the creditor may
prove subject to a rebate of 5% per annum for the period by which
payment has been accelerated.[4]

1 Bankruptcy Act 1914, s 66(2)(b); *In Re Amalgamated Property Co Ltd* [1984] 3 All
  ER 272, [1984] 3 WLR 1101.
2 Bankruptcy Act 1914, s 66(1).
3 Ibid, Sch 2, r 21.
4 Ibid, Sch 2, r 22.

9.12   The question of paying interest for the period *after* the date
of the receiving order does not arise until all proving creditors have
been paid in full as regards debts and interest down to that date. If
there is a sufficient surplus, interest at 4% is payable for the period
from the receiving order down to the date of payment; if it is not
sufficient all debts proved other than deferred debts, rank pari
passu.[1]

1 Bankruptcy Act 1914, s 33(8).

9.13   By section 34 and Schedule 1 to the Administration of

Estates Act 1925 the rules in bankruptcy apply to the administration of insolvent estates of deceased persons.

(b) Winding up a company

9.14   As regards proving in a winding up for interest on a debt which is already due, the same rules apply in the case of a company as in the case of a bankrupt,[1] except that the date down to which pre-liquidation interest may be claimed is the date of the petition in the case of a compulsory winding up[2] and the date of the resolution in the case of a voluntary winding up.[3] However, where the company has sufficient assets to pay off all the debts proved in the liquidation it is no longer to be regarded as insolvent.[4] Accordingly the creditor who has a right to contractual or statutory interest is remitted to his contractual rights:[5] there is no bar to his recovery of the interest accruing after the presentation of the winding-up petition.[6] The creditor who has no such right is likewise in the same position as if there had been no winding-up proceedings.[7] That is to say he cannot recover interest in the winding up. So long as he has been paid his debt without having to sue for it he cannot recover discretionary interest on it under section 35A of the Supreme Court Act 1981 either.[8] But if proceedings have been taken in the High Court or a county court to recover the debt, he may obtain an award of interest in those proceedings by the procedure outlined in Chapter 4.

1 Companies Act 1948 s 317 as interpreted in *In Re Theo Garvin Ltd* [1969] 1 Ch 624. See too, Companies Winding Up Rules 1949 (SI 1949/330), rr 100, 101. See now Companies Act 1985, s 612.
2 Companies Act 1948, s 229(2); Companies Act 1985, s 524(2).
3 Ibid, s 280; ibid, s 574.
4 *Re Fine Industrial Commodities Ltd* [1956] Ch 256, [1955] 3 All ER 707.
5 *In re Humber Ironworks and Shipbuilding Co* (1869) 4 Ch App 643.
6 However where a foreign currency liability has been converted into sterling as at the date of the commencement of the winding up (as it should be: *Re Lines Bros Ltd* [1983] Ch 1, [1982] 2 All ER 183, CA) the debt on which post-liquidation interest is to be calculated at the contractual rate is the sterling debt, not the reconverted foreign money liability: *Re Lines Bros Ltd (in liquidation) (No 2)* [1984] Ch 438, [1984] 2 WLR 905.
7 *Re Rolls Royce Ltd* [1974] 3 All ER 646, [1974] 1 WLR 1584.
8 See para 4.06, above.

THE INSOLVENCY ACT 1985

9.15   The Report of the Review Committee on Insolvency Law and Practice in 1982[1] made a number of recommendations regarding the recovery of interest on debts proved in an insolvency, whether individual or corporate. Supporting the criticisms of this branch of the law made earlier by the Law Commission in their Report No 88 on Interest,[2] they concluded[3] that:

(a) section 66 of the Act of 1914 should be repealed;

(b) the Court should have power in companies winding up to reopen extortionate credit agreements similar to the power under the Consumer Credit Act 1974 applicable to personal insolvencies;

(c) during the insolvency, in the event of there being a surplus after payment of all admitted debts and liabilities (including interest prior to the commencement of the insolvency, where applicable) interest should run on all such debts and liabilities until a final dividend is declared, the rate being that currently applicable to judgment debts at the commencement of the insolvency;

(d) the rate of rebate required where a creditor proves for a debt payable at a future date should be that currently applicable to judgment debts at the commencement of the insolvency; and

(e) these rules should be applicable in all forms of insolvency proceedings.

1 Cmnd 8558, chaired by Sir Kenneth Cork GBE.
2 (1978) Cmnd 7229.
3 Chapter 31, Interest on Debts: the recommendations are at para 1395 on p 316.

9.16 The changes recommended by the Review Committee on Insolvency Law are, for the most part, contained in the Insolvency Bill which is before Parliament at the time of going to press. It is assumed that it will in due course become the Insolvency Act 1985; but it may not be brought into operation for some time after that. Subject to changes which will no doubt be made during its passage through Parliament, the Bill will repeal section 66 of the Bankruptcy Act 1914[1] and thus free the creditor from the 5% limit: he will be able to prove in the bankruptcy or the winding up for whatever interest is owing to him at the commencement of the bankruptcy[2] or winding up[3] subject only to the court's power to reopen any extortionate transactions entered into within the preceding three years.[4] Provision for the discounting of interest on future debts is likely to be made in the Insolvency Rules.[5]

1 s 202, Sch 9. References in these notes to sections and Schedules are taken from the Bill, as introduced.
2 s 143 and the Individual Insolvency Rules made under s 184 and para 16 of Sch 6. See the definition of 'bankruptcy debt' in s 187 and the provisions of s 106(1) regarding the commencement of a bankruptcy.
3 Section 87 and the Company Insolvency Rules made under that section and para 11 of Sch 3 (by which the individual insolvency provisions may be applied). As regards the commencement of winding up, see Companies Act 1948, s 229 and Companies Act 1985, s 524.

4 ss 84 (companies) and 153 (individuals).
5 Sch 6, para 16.

9.17   As for the payment of interest for the period of the
insolvency, the Insolvency Bill provides, in clause 74 (companies)
and clause 146(4) and (5) (individuals), that where there is a surplus
after paying the debts admitted to proof it shall be applied in paying
interest from the date when the company went into liquidation (or
the commencement of the bankruptcy) at the rate then payable on
High Court judgments or the rate then applicable to the debt,
whichever may be higher. It is to be noted, however, that any loans
by the spouse of the bankrupt and interest on them, rank after the
payment of the interest payable on the other debts for the period of
the bankruptcy.[1]

1 Clause 146(6) of the Insolvency Bill as introduced.

Chapter 10

Tender before action, money in court and offers to settle

Tender before action

STOPPING INTEREST RUNNING BY TENDERING THE SUM DUE

10.01   In order to establish a defence of tender before action, the debtor need not tender anything in respect of interest on the debt which is tendered, unless the creditor has an accrued right to interest, eg under the contract. But where there is such a right, the debtor must tender a sum to cover the interest then due as well as the principal. The effect is to stop interest running from that date.[1] In order to have such an effect the normal requirements of a valid tender must be satisfied.[2] It must be a tender of the entire sum due[3] and the debtor may not pray in aid a set-off without the creditor's prior agreement.[4] Also the tender ought technically to be made by a production of cash in the exact amount, but unless this technical point is taken as a ground for rejecting what would otherwise be a valid tender it does not matter that the tender is made in the form of a cheque or that there is no production of currency or 'jingling of money'.[5] A more important requirement is that the tender must not be conditional: it must not, for instance, be made on the terms that the creditor gives up a claim other than that which is admitted to be due, or treats that other claim as being satisfied. On the other hand a valid tender may be made 'under protest' and it is not invalidated by the inclusion of a condition with which the creditor must in any case comply. For example, the debtor may when tendering the money due on promissory notes require, as a condition, that the notes be delivered up.[6] Also it was held in *Graham v Seal*[7] that the tender of a mortgage debt conditionally upon the mortgage then and there

102

granting a previously approved reconveyance was a good legal tender for the purpose of stopping interest running.

1 *Dent v Dunn* (1812) 3 Camp 296.
2 See Halsbury's Laws (4th edn), vol 9, paras 520–529.
3 *Read's Trustee in Bankruptcy v Smith* [1951] Ch 439, [1951] 1 All ER 406.
4 *Searles v Sadgrave* (1855) 5 E & B 639.
5 *Farquharson v Pearl Assurance Co Ltd* [1937] 3 All ER 124.
6 *Dent v Dunn*: see n 1, above.
7 (1918) 88 LJ Ch 31, CA.

TENDER AND PAYMENT INTO COURT AS A DEFENCE
10.02   If the creditor rejects the tender and, at a later stage, brings legal proceedings, the tender may be pleaded as a defence. However the money tendered must, at the same time, be paid into court.[1] The creditor may accept the money so tendered but the money in court may not be paid out without the leave of the court.[2] The requirement of a court order is to enable the court to make provision for the defendant's costs to be recouped out of the money in court, his defence of tender having been successful. This is the main difference between paying into court with a plea of tender and paying into court in satisfaction. Another difference is that the former can only arise in the case of a claim for a debt, whereas a payment into court in satisfaction can be made in the case of a claim for unliquidated damages. A third is that with a payment into court in support of a plea of tender, interest need not be paid into court beyond whatever was included in the tender; but in order to satisfy a claim for debt and interest where there has been no tender, interest should be paid in, calculated down to the date of payment.[3]

1 RSC Ord 18, r 16, CCR Ord 9, r 12.
2 RSC Ord 22, r 4, CCR Ord 11, r 4(2)(b). See Appendix B.
3 See para 10.04

Payment into court in satisfaction

TACTICAL CONSIDERATIONS
10.03   The payment into court in satisfaction is a most potent tactical weapon. In the High Court the procedure is governed by RSC Order 22, rule 1 and in the county court by CCR Order 11, rule 1(1)(a). The effect of such a payment is to make an offer to the plaintiff to settle the claim for the amount paid in. The fact that the payment has been made is not revealed to the court until the case has been decided[1] and the defendant may, and usually does, adhere to his pleaded defence on the question of liability at the same time as

paying money into court in satisfaction. On being notified of the payment the plaintiff has to decide whether to accept the money which is offered and to recover his legal costs down to the date of the payment into court,[2] or to go on with the case in the hope of recovering more, but with the risk of obtaining less (or indeed nothing at all) and having to pay both sides' costs, from the date of the payment. The defendant's usual tactic is to pay in a sum which is, on his evaluation of the case, enough to protect his position on costs, with perhaps a little bit more to be on the safe side; so the plaintiff's choice, whether or not to accept, is often very difficult: he has to weigh his chances of success on each of the issues in the case which will probably include, even in a straightforward personal injury case, issues on liability, contributory negligence, medical prognosis and impairment of earning capacity. Theoretically where the plaintiff is successful on some issues but not others, the court may award him the costs on the former and the defendant the costs on the latter,[3] but in practice, where there is a payment into court in satisfaction, the costs which are incurred by both sides thereafter go, on an all or nothing basis,[4] to the plaintiff if he beats the payment into court and, if he fails, to the defendant.[5]

1 RSC Ord 22 r 7; CCR Ord 11, r 7 (text in Appendix B); and see RSC Ord 59, r 12A regarding appeals.
2 Unless there are exceptional circumstances justifying a different result: *Seacroft Hotel (Teignmouth) v Goble* [1984] 3 All ER 116, [1984] 1 WLR 939, CA.
3 RSC Ord 62, rr 3, 5–8; CCR Ord 38, r 1.
4 Except that the liability of a legally assisted person to pay his own solicitor's costs will be limited to the contribution required to be paid under s 9 of the Legal Aid Act 1974 and his liability to pay the other side's costs will be limited by s 8(1)(e) to what is reasonable in all the circumstances.
5 *Hultquist v Universal Pattern Ltd.* [1960] 2QB 467, [1960] 2 All ER 266, CA.

SATISFYING THE CLAIM FOR INTEREST

10.04 Until recently a distinction was drawn between interest to which the plaintiff was entitled and interest which might be awarded as a matter of discretion but for which he had no cause of action. Where the former was claimed the defendant had to take account of the interest accrued to the date of payment when making a payment into court in satisfaction.[1] But the latter was not required to be taken into account.[2] This distinction has now gone. In accordance with the recommendations of the Law Commission in their Report on Interest,[3] the Rules of the Supreme Court and of the county courts have been amended[4] to provide, in effect, that a defendant who is paying money into court in satisfaction of a claim must cover any pleaded claim in respect of interest (under section 35A of the Supreme Court Act 1981 or section 69 of the County Courts Act

1984 or otherwise) or take the consequences of having paid into court a sum that is inadequate. Now that the plaintiff has to plead his claim for interest, wherever he is seeking an award, the defendant is better placed than formerly to decide what if anything may be recovered: if a claim for interest is pleaded it must be taken into account, but if not, not. Any payment into court which is intended to cover interest as well as principal should be calculated down to the date of the payment into court, except when accompanying a defence of tender, in which case it should be calculated down to the date of tender. This means that the plaintiff who accepts such an offer must forgo any interest in respect of the period between the date of the lodgment in court and the date of acceptance. There is theoretically an injustice here but the principle is well established[5] and any procedure which attempted to get over it would necessarily be extremely complicated and expensive to operate.[6] The defendant who makes a payment into court in respect of principal and interest is not bound to specify in his notice of payment whether it includes interest, nor to apportion it between interest and principal. The rules[7] allow a plaintiff to seek a court order for the defendant to divide up his payment into court, but only where he has made a single payment into court in respect of two or more causes of action, whereas a claim for a debt (or, as the case may be, damages) plus interest is one cause of action, not two.

1 *Kidd v Walker* (1831) 2 B v Ad 705; *The Norseman* [1957] P 224.
2 *Jefford v Gee* [1970] 2 QB 130, at 149–150.
3 Law Com No 88 (1978) (Cmnd 7229), paras 185–197.
4 RSC Ord 22, r 1(8) and CCR Ord 11, r 1(8) are reproduced in the Appendix B in their amended form.
5 See the cases cited in n 1.
6 As it is, the defendant receives no interest on the money either: SCFR r 30(2), CCFR r 17A(2).
7 RSC Ord 22, r 1(5); CCR Ord 11, r 1(6); see Appendix B for the text.

APPROPRIATION OF MONEY ALREADY IN COURT

10.05   RSC Order 22, rule 8(2) provides that a defendant who has been given leave to defend, under RSC Order 14, on condition that he brings a specified sum into court, may, unless the court otherwise orders, by notice appropriate all or some of that money, including interest accrued on it while in court,[1] to the plaintiff's claim so as to support a pleaded defence of tender[2] or, more usually, to turn the money already in court into a satisfaction payment which is offered to the plaintiff for acceptance on the usual terms. By this device the defendant achieves the same protection as if he had made a payment into court in satisfaction but does so without having to venture any further money than that which he has had to pay to obtain leave to defend. The same facility exists in the county court[3] but is not limited to the case where the defendant has to bring money into court as a condition of being granted leave to defend under CCR Order 9, rule 14 (which is the county court equivalent of RSC Order 14); in addition it is available in the county court as regards money paid into court in pursuance of an order made under CCR Order 13 rule 1(8)(c) (payment into court required as a condition of granting *any* application) and CCR Order 37 rule 8(1) (payment into court as a term on which execution is stayed).

1 SCFR r 27(3).
2 See para 10.02, above.
3 CCR Ord 11 r 9(2); CCFR 10(3).

ACCEPTANCE

10.06   The procedure and timetable for giving notice of acceptance of money paid into court in satisfaction differ: in the High Court the plaintiff has 21 days from receipt of the notice of the payment[1] and in the county court he has 14.[2] It is important that the notice of acceptance when given in the High Court should be in the correct form,[3] ie Form 24 in Appendix A for the Supreme Court Rules, but there is no prescribed form for the county court. Generally a plaintiff who accepts within the time allowed is entitled, by the rules of the High Court and of the county court, to have the money paid out to him forthwith; but in certain circumstances an order of the court is required[4] and, in the case of a legally aided plaintiff, the money has to be paid to his solicitor.[5] In either jurisdiction the court may grant the plaintiff leave to accept the money after the period for acceptance has expired but this will usually be on terms that he pays costs reasonably incurred by the defendant after the date of payment in.[6]

1 RSC Ord 22, r 3; see Appendix B for the text. Only 2 days are allowed for accepting a payment after the hearing has begun.
2 CCR Ord 11, r 3; see Appendix B for the text.
3 For example, in *Metroinvest Ansalt v Commercial Union Assurance Co* (1985) 129 Sol Jo 86, CA, the plaintiff gave notice of acceptance in the wrong form and the court allowed the defendant to withdraw the money in court.
4 RSC Ord 22, r 4(1), CCR Ord 11, r 4(2); see Appendix B.
5 RSC Ord 22, r 10, CCR Ord 11, r 4(4); see Appendix B.
6 RSC Ord 22, r 5, CCR Ord 11, r 5: *Griggs v Petts* [1940] 1 KB 198, [1939] 4 All ER 39, CA; *Gaskins v British Aluminium Co Ltd* [1976] QB 524, [1976] 1 All ER 208.

WITHDRAWAL

10.07   A notice of payment may not be withdrawn without the leave of the court, which may be granted on such terms as may be just.[1] Where leave is granted, an order will be made enabling the defendant to have the money in court paid out to him including not only the money paid in but interest which has accrued on it. The defendant should be careful to apply specifically for the payment out of the interest in such a situation: otherwise the plaintiff may, in due course, obtain an order for it to be paid out to him if the case goes in his favour, or it may languish for ever as an unclaimed balance.[2] The fact that the plaintiff has not accepted the payment within the time allowed is not by itself sufficient to justify an order that the defendant should be permitted to withdraw it. He must, in addition, show a good and sufficient reason for a change of attitude, such as mistake as to some material matter or a change in legal outlook brought about by a new judicial decision,[3] or, it may be supposed, being required to make an interim payment under RSC Order 29. The fact that the defendant has become insolvent is not by itself sufficient justification for allowing the money to be returned to him for the benefit of the general body of creditors: the plaintiff is entitled to retain the security of having the money in court.[4]

1 RSC Ord 22 r 1(3), CCR Ord 11 r 1(4); see Appendix B.
2 SCFR r 56; CCFR rr 35–39B.
3 *Cumper v Pothecary* [1941] 2 KB 58, [1941] 2 All ER 516, CA.
4 *W. A. Sherratt Ltd v John Bromley (Church Stretton) Ltd* [1985] 1 All ER 216, CA.

Other payments into court

PAYMENTS PURSUANT TO COURT ORDER
10.08   There are many situations in which a party is required by court order to pay money into court as a necessary step in a piece of litigation, often as a condition of being allowed to proceed further. The most obvious example is probably that of the defendant who is granted leave, under RSC Order 14, to defend proceedings, provided that he pays a certain sum of money into court. Having complied with the condition he may then proceed with his defence of the claim and may indeed appropriate the money in court, or some of it, to the satisfaction of the plaintiff's claim.[1] An equally common situation of money being paid into court pursuant to a court order is where a defendant who has allowed a judgment to go against him by default obtains an order for the judgment to be set aside, conditionally on his paying some or all of the plaintiff's claim into court. In the county court a defendant who has paid money into court in such a context may then appropriate some or all of it to the satisfaction of the plaintiff's claim:[2] but for some reason there is no equivalent facility in the High Court. Money may be ordered to be brought into

court in other situations where appropriation is not possible in the High Court or in the county court, for example where money is paid in as security for costs[3] or to preserve the subject matter of the dispute[4] or as an interim payment.[5] Money so lodged may not be accepted in satisfaction by the other party, nor may it be paid out to either side except on an order of the court, usually once the case has been decided or settled.[6] Likewise the interest accruing on the money paid into court may not be paid out either, except by order of the court.[7] There is, however, one very common situation in which money is required to be paid in and out without a court order, namely where a county court judgment is required to be satisfied by money being paid into court under section 99(3) of the County Courts Act 1959:[8] this is the exception which proves the rule, since it requires suitors' money (not funds) to be channelled by the judgment debtor through the court to the judgment creditor. The money is paid out to the judgment creditor automatically; there is no question of it being invested.

1 See para 10.05, above.
2 CCR Ord 11 r 9(2).
3 RSC Ord 23, CCR Ord 13, r 8 and Ord 50, r 9.
4 RSC Ord 29, r 2, applied in the county court by CCR Ord 13, r 7.
5 RSC Ord 29, r 13(1), CCR Ord 13, r 12.
6 RSC Ord 22, r 8, CCR Ord 11, r 9.
7 RSC Ord 92, r 1; CCFR r 26(1) provides, by implication, that, except where money may be paid out without an order (eg under r 11A(2) an order of the court is needed.
8 s 99(3) and also ss 168 to 174 and 174A have been repealed by s 75 and Sch 9 of the Administration of Justice Act 1982 but the repeal is not effective until a Commencement Order is made in this regard under s 76(2)(j)(iv) of that Act.

PAYMENTS PURSUANT TO STATUTE

10.09   The last class of payment into court to be considered is where money is lodged pursuant to statute. There are, on the one hand, statutory provisions which enable a fund to be lodged although there is no litigation pending in the court. In this category are lodgments under section 63 of the Trustee Act 1925 or under sections 84 or 136 of the Law of Property Act 1925 and with them may be grouped payments into court of life assurance money, under the Life Assurance Companies (Payment into Court) Act 1896 if no sufficient discharge for the payment can be obtained otherwise. On the other hand there are statutory lodgments which are required as an earnest of good faith and solvency.[1] Money paid into court pursuant to statute may be invested in any of the ways available for money paid in pursuant to court order.

1 Assurance Companies Act 1909, s 2, Industrial Assurance Act 1923, s 7(1), Prevention of Fraud (Investments) Act 1958, s 4, Compulsory Purchase Act 1965, Road Traffic Act 1972, ss 143, 144 and 146 and Part III of the Insurance Companies Regulations (SI 1981/1654).

PAYMENT INTO COURT IN A LIMITATION ACTION

10.10   The Merchant Shipping Acts 1894–1981 provide for a shipowner to limit his liability for losses incurred 'without his actual fault or privity' to an amount calculated by reference to the tonnage of the ship at so many special drawing rights ('SDRs') a ton. The shipowner brings a limitation action for a decree that he may limit his liability on this basis and if successful he is directed to constitute a fund, comprising the appropriate amount for the tonnage, plus interest from the date of the collision, so that the fund may be divided up pro rata amongst those suffering loss in the collision. It is sometimes advantageous for the shipowner to pay the money into court in advance of the order, because the conversion from SDRs into sterling takes place at the date of the payment, provided that enough is paid in for the purpose. There was at one time some controversy as to whether, in order to make a sufficient fund by an early payment into court, the shipowner had to pay into court not only the sterling equivalent of the requisite sum in SDRs but also interest on that sum from the date of the collision. However, in *Polish SS Co v Atlantic Maritime Co (the Garden City)*[1] the Court of Appeal held, reversing Parker J (1) that it is not necessary for interest to be paid into court or to be paid at any time before the grant of the decree; and (2) that the money accruing from the investment of the money in court does not become part of the fund, whether or not a sum is paid in in respect of interest. This second point is in line with the general approach to money paid into court to satisfy the other side's entitlement, namely that any increase in the fund which derives from its investment does not swell the amount which is on offer but is something apart which it is for the court to dispose of by order when the case is over. Accordingly, in the *Garden City* case, the limitation fund was directed by the Court of Appeal to be constituted out of that part of the money paid into court which was the sterling equivalent at that time of the gold franc (now SDR) equivalent, together with simple interest (at 8.25% per annum) on that sum from the date of the collision to the date of decree; everything else that accumulated in court was ordered to be paid back to the plaintiff shipowner.

1 [1984] 3 All ER 59, CA [1984] 3 WLR 300.

Investment of money in court

10.11   Where money is paid into court with a plea of tender,[1] or in satisfaction,[2] or pursuant to a court order[3] or statute[4] it is available for investment within certain limits. The limits are of four kinds:

(1) by statute, primarily sections 4 to 7 of the Administration of Justice Act 1965 (for the High Court) and section 168 of the County Courts Act 1959 (for the county court, the repeal of which section is not yet in force);[5]

(2) by rules of court, primarily RSC Order 22 (payment into court) and Order 80 rule 12 (control of money recovered by person under disability) and the county court equivalents, CCR Order 11 and Order 10, rule 11;

(3) by the Supreme Court Funds Rules 1975 as amended (SCFR) and the County Court Funds Rules 1965 as amended (CCFR); and

(4) by the discretion of the court.

Subject to these limitations, the three main methods by which court funds may be invested in the High Court and in the county court are by placing money on deposit, by placing it to the Short Term Investment Account and by placing it to long term investment in Common Investment Funds.

1 See para 10.02, above.
2 See paras 10.03–10.04, above.
3 See para 10.08, above.
4 See para 10.09, above.
5 See n 7 to para 10.08, above.

DEPOSIT
10.12   The general rule, in the High Court and in the county court, is that money paid into court in satisfaction is automatically placed on deposit when the time for acceptance has passed[1] and that it then attracts the deposit rate of interest, currently 8% per annum,[2] until the money is reinvested or paid out.[3] With other kinds of payment into court the deposit is made on the day when the relevant Schedule or authority is received in the Court Funds Office, or the effective date of lodgment, whichever is the later;[4] in other respects it is treated in the same way as satisfaction money.

1 SCFR r 30, CCFR r 9(6)(i).
2 SCFR r 31(1), CCFR r 23(1).
3 SCFR r31(1) and (2), CCFR r 23(2) and (3).
4 SCFR r 28, CCFR r 9(6)(ii).

SHORT TERM INVESTMENT

10.13   The Short Term Investment Account has always paid a higher rate of interest than money on deposit and at present it pays 12% per annum.[1] It used to be available in the High Court for the investment of satisfaction money and other funds generally but since the Funds Rules were amended, with effect from 1 April 1983,[2] its availability has been much more restricted. In the High Court the Short Term Investment Account is now available only for the investment of money which is payable to a person under a disability,[3] typically an injured minor plaintiff, whose claim has been determined or settled with the court's approval. In the county court, however, the facility for investment on the Short Term Investment Account remains more or less as it was: money paid in satisfaction of a claim by a person under disability is to be placed to that account automatically[4] and any other kind of payment which would otherwise be placed on deposit and would remain there may, if the court so orders, be placed to the Short Term Investment Account instead.[5] Whether the court would so order is another matter: the registrar might take the view that the Short Term Investment Account ought not to be used in the county court for purposes for which it may not be used in the High Court.[6]

1 SCFR r 37A.
2 Supreme Court Funds (Amendment) Rules 1983 (SI 1983/290) and County Court Funds (Amendment) Rules 1983 (SI 1983/291).
3 SCFR r 37.
4 CCFR r 17A(2).
5 CCFR r 17A (3).
6 See *Practice Direction* of 11 March 1983, [1983] 1 All ER 928 (text in Appendix C) for a statement of the main purpose of the amendments.

COMMON INVESTMENT FUNDS

10.14   Another possibility is to seek a court order for money in court to be placed to a long-term investment account, that is to say invested by the purchase of units in one of the three Common Investment Funds, set up under the Common Investment Funds Scheme 1965:[1]

(1) the Capital Fund, the primary purpose of which is to increase capital value over a period of at least five years;
(2) the High Yield Fund which aims to produce high income rather than capital growth but the income from which is subject to the deduction of tax, and
(3) the Gross Income Fund which has the same aim as (2) except that dividends are paid without the deduction of tax.

Common Investment Funds are inherently more speculative than deposit or short term investment because where market conditions are unfavourable the capital value of the units goes down. Nevertheless they are likely to have advantages in the long term and ought in the ordinary way to produce a marginally better return than ordinary unit trusts because they can be administered more cheaply. Investment in Common Investment Funds may well be appropriate for a plaintiff who has several years to go before he reaches the age of eighteen.

1 SI 1965/1467.

OTHER INVESTMENTS

10.15 Apart from those already mentioned, the investment possibilities are much wider in the High Court than in the county court. This difference stems from the High Court's powers of investment which exist independently of the Supreme Court Funds Rules made under sections 4(1) and 7(1) of the Administration of Justice Act 1965. These extra powers have their formal expression in RSC Order 22, rule 13(1) which allows funds to be invested in any manner specified in Part I and in paragraphs 1 to 10 and 12 of Part II of Schedule 1 to the Trustee Investments Act 1961, as supplemented by Part IV of that Schedule.[1] The possibilities opened up by these provisions include investment in National Savings Certificates and by deposit in the National Savings Bank (Part I of the Schedule) and, as regards paragraphs 1 to 10 and 12 of Part II, investment in Government stock, debentures, public authority securities, deposits with building societies, local authority stock and securities issued in the United Kingdom by the government of a Commonwealth country or a public or local authority in such a country; the rate of interest for local authority stock or Commonwealth securities may be fixed or, within certain limits, variable. It is doubtful whether the county courts have ever had inherent powers of investment other than those accorded by County Court Funds Rules[2] but even if such potential powers exist no rules of court have been made to give them efficacy.

1 The relevant text is set out in Appendix A.
2 The existing rules were made under s 168 of the County Courts Act 1959 which is due to be repealed. See n 8 to para 10.08

10.16 Investments of the kind just described cannot normally be made without a court order[1] and will normally be considered only where money needs to be invested over a long period eg for the benefit of a very young plaintiff. Theoretically, however, they are available for all money paid into, or transferred to, the High Court, and occasions may arise in which it would be appropriate to seek an order for, say, satisfaction money to be taken off deposit and placed instead with the National Savings Bank. The purchase of Government stock etc is also a possibility but it should be borne in mind that the expenses of any such purchase must be borne by the fund.[2] Another point to bear in mind is that applications regarding the investment of money in court are not the sole prerogative of the party making the payment: if a defendant has had to pay money into court as a condition of having the judgment set aside the plaintiff as well as the defendant may apply for an order for its investment.

1 Lodgments under the Prevention of Fraud (Investments) Act 1958 or the Insurance Companies Regulations 1981 (SI 1981/1654) are exceptional.
2 SCFR r 47, CCFR r 20(3)(b).

FOREIGN CURRENCY

10.17   Before the decision in *Miliangos v George Frank (Textiles) Ltd*[1] it was an established rule that any judgment in an English court and any execution to enforce it should be expressed in terms of sterling.[2] Claims were accordingly framed as claims in sterling and payments into court were made in sterling too. But the Practice Direction which followed the *Miliagos* decision[3] authorises, and indeed encourages, a payment into court of foreign currency in support of a plea of tender (of foreign currency) or to satisfy a foreign money liability claim. The investment of foreign currency presents practical difficulties unless it is first converted into sterling; and the *Miliangos* principle is that, in cases to which it applies,[4] there should be no conversion of the foreign currency until as close as may be practical to the date of payment to the plaintiff. The Supreme Court Funds Rules now deal expressly with payments into court of foreign currency and prohibit such payments except under RSC Order 22, rule 1 (tender or satisfaction) or with the court's permission.[5] As for investment, there is no automatic investment as there is for sterling, and foreign currency may not be placed on deposit or in any of the other conventional forms of investment. However, if an application is made, the court may direct that the foreign currency should be deposited on an interest-bearing account in that currency or any other currency.[6] The position in the county court is less clear. There is no express prohibition on the lodgment of foreign currency and in principle the Practice Direction for the High Court should be followed in the county court as well if possible. On the other hand the County Court Funds Rules do not provide expressly for the investment of foreign currency. If foreign currency is lodged in the county court it should be remitted, unconverted, to the Accountant General, in the same way as if it were sterling. It will not be invested unless the court so directs but arguably the county court has the same power as the High Court to direct that the foreign currency should be deposited in an interest-bearing account, the County Court Funds Rules being silent on the point.[7]

1 [1976] AC 443.
2 *Manners v Pearson* [1898] 1 Ch 581, CA.
3 [1976] 1 All ER 669, [1976] 1 WLR 83. See Appendix C for the text, as subsequently amended.
4 See n 2 to para 7.02, above.
5 SCFR r 21.
6 SCFR r 37C.
7 See County Courts Act 1984, s 76.

CHANGING FROM ONE INVESTMENT TO ANOTHER AND TRANSFER OF FUNDS BETWEEN COURTS

10.18   In order for funds to be moved from one kind of investment to another or between the High Court and county court an order or direction of the court in which the money is lodged is ordinarily required.[1] Where an order or direction is required it will usually be made only on the application of a party to the procedings, but in the county court directions may be given by the court of its own motion, without an application.[2] In the High Court there are specific provisions regarding the making of certain kinds of applications for the investment of funds[3] but in other respects the general provisions regarding the making of applications are applicable in both the High Court[4] and the county court.[5] Accordingly applications may be made ex parte or on notice, depending on the nature of the order or direction sought. Presumably where satisfaction money has not been accepted and the defendant applies for an order for its investment otherwise than on deposit the court will not usually require notice of the application to be given to the plaintiff. On the other hand notice of an application by the *plaintiff* regarding the investment of satisfaction money paid in by the defendant ought in the normal way to be given to the defendant. Likewise, in the case of an application on behalf of a minor plaintiff regarding the investment of money to which he is entitled notice to the defendant will not normally be required.[6] As regards transfer of funds between the High Court and the county court the different powers of investment mean that a transfer of the funds is sometimes to the advantage of the litigants[7] and a transfer may be justified on this ground. The procedure for the transfer is set out in the Funds Rules[8] and the procedures for applying for the necessary order is the same as for the other applications in relation to funds.

1 Instances of reinvestment without order are SCFR r 34(2); CCFR r 17.
2 CCR Ord 13, r 2.
3 RSC Ord 92, r 5 applies to applications made in the Chancery Division. See, too, Admiralty *Practice Direction* [1982] 2 All ER 480, [1982] 1 WLR 660.
4 RSC Ord 32.
5 CCR Ord 13, rr 1 and 2.
6 Supreme Court Practice (1985), 32/1–6/4.
7 Particularly transfer of minor's funds: *Practice Direction (Minors' Funds in Court)* [1983] 1 All ER 800 [1983] 1 WLR 278; Appendix C.
8 SCFR r 50 for transfer down and CCFR r 13(3) for transfer up.

Investment of money on behalf of persons under disability

MINORS

10.19   The jurisdiction to direct the investment of money belonging to a litigant who is under a disability is not the same as the jurisdiction to control the investment of money lodged in court. There is, however, a considerable overlap of function: the court fund facilities for investment are often the most convenient method of protecting the disabled litigant's interests. Provision is made in RSC Order 80, rules 12 and 13 and in CCR Order 10, rule 11 for the court to give directions as how the disabled person's money is to be invested and applied. No distinction is drawn, procedurally, between the disability which arises from minority on the one hand, and mental disorder on the other, but there are important differences of principle and of practice. As regards minors, the court has a protective role as parens patriae and has to consider what is in the minor's best interests having regard to his age and needs and the size of the fund. Where the sum is under £1,000 it may be appropriate to pay the money to the minor's parents or solicitors on an undertaking that it will be invested in, say, the purchase of National Savings Certificates; and in any case it is usual to make a small payment out of the fund at the conclusion of the litigation in order to provide the minor with some tangible consolation. Otherwise the money ought usually to be placed to the short term or long term investment account or, in the High Court, used to buy National Savings stock or Government or Local Government stock.[1] If it is necessary to transfer to the High Court in order to get a wider spread of investments and yet desirable to have the fund managed locally the usual course is for the fund to be transferred to the appropriate District Registry.[2] A third possibility, suitable only where the fund exceeds £60,000, is to set up a trust under arrangements made with the Public Trustee, for him to administer under the Public Trustee Act 1906. A standard form of trust has been worked out for this kind of case and it is sometimes known as a Standard Order 80/12/8 Trust. One of the disadvantages of this course is that fees have to be paid to the Public Trustee for his management of the trust, whereas no direct charge is made for the management of funds in court. The fourth possibility, which is likely to be no less expensive, is for the court to direct the setting up of a private trust under a deed which it has approved. If a suitable trust is already in existence the transfer to the trustees of the money in court may well be the best course, but in other cases the cost of setting up and managing the trust may outweigh the other advantages. It could however be justified by the need to invest money on the minor's behalf in ventures which are outside the prescribed provisions of the Trustee Investments Act 1961,[3] such as the acquisition or construction of suitable accommodation, particularly where he has special needs arising from physical disablement.

1 See paras 10.11–10.16.
2 *Practice Direction (Minors' Funds in Court)* [1983] 1 All ER 800, [1983] 1 WLR 278; see Appendix C for the text.
3 See para 10.15 and Appendix A, where the relevant Parts of the Schedule are set out.

PATIENTS

10.20   Much of the law applicable to the investment of funds on behalf of minors applies equally to the investment of funds on behalf of the mentally disordered ie persons who would be accepted by the Court of Protection as 'patients'[1] whose affairs could properly be controlled by that court, usually by means of a receivership order. There is, however, one important point of difference. Whereas the High Court has a protective role in respect of minors it is the Court of Protection which exercises the equivalent function in regard to the mentally disordered, except as regards the approval of settlements under RSC Order 80, rule 10. Moreover the powers of management and investment which are exercisable by that court are much greater[2] than those exercisable by the High Court in relation to minors. On the face of it, therefore, the funds of any mentally disordered plaintiff would be managed with greater advantage by the Court of Protection and, unless an order of receivership has already been made, the High Court ought to direct that the plaintiff's next friend should apply for an order of receivership as a preliminary to the funds being transferred to the Court of Protection. But there is a drawback: the Court of Protection charges fees for the management of the patient's funds, whereas the High Court does not. Where the fund is under £5,000 and the plaintiff patient has no other assets, it is often sensible for the money to remain in the

High Court. Conversely a fund of over £50,000 ought to be managed by the Court of Protection, since its powers are wider than those of the High Court. Any award between these two figures where the patient has any other assets or is intestate and incapable of making a will for himself would normally be appropriate for management by the Court of Protection. The Court fees for future management are properly recoverable against the defendant in the litigation as a head of damage.[3]

1 Mental Health Act 1983 s 94(2), RSC Ord 80, r 1.
2 Ibid, ss 95–98.
3 *Futej v Lewandowski* (1980) 124 Sol Jo 777; *Rialas v Mitchell* (1984) Times, 17 July, CA.

Alternatives to paying money into court

OFFERS TO SETTLE

10.21 The payment into court in satisfaction is a most useful tactical weapon.[1] But there are some situations in which it is not a practical possibility and it has one important drawback from the defendant's point of view, namely that it deprives him of the use of his money. Admittedly the money may be invested while it is in court but this is of no immediate benefit to him. In any case he might well want to apply the money to some other purpose, eg as working capital for a business venture or to pay for improvements to his home, or to buy a car. So it is worth considering alternative methods of forcing a settlement which do not require any money to be paid to anyone until the settlement has been achieved. In 1968 the Winn Report on Personal Injuries Litigation[2] recommended replacing the system of paying satisfaction money into court with a system of formal offers to settle that could not be referred to in court until the issues in the case had been decided but could then be referred to on the question of costs. This proposal has never been adopted and was rejected by the Cantley Working Party on Personal Injury Litigation[3] but two advances have been made along this front, one in regard to offers to settle contribution questions[4] and the other in regard to offers to settle a case where the issue of liability is to be tried well in advance of the issue as to the amount of damages.[5] More recently a much greater advance has been made by judicial ingenuity in getting round the old common law rule that an offer to settle could not be referred to on the question of costs if the offer was made 'without prejudice'[6] (as it must always be if the defendant is to retain the tactical advantage of putting the plaintiff to proof of every contentious issue in his case). The technique is to write what has come to be known as a *Calderbank* letter[7] which offers, without prejudice, to settle the case on terms but gives notice of the intention to bring the offer to the attention of the court on the question of costs should the offer not be accepted.

1 See para 10.03, above.
2 Cmnd 3691. See in particular paras 507–540 and Appendix 24 in the Report.
3 (1979) Cmnd 7476, paras 76–101.
4 RSC Ord 16, r 10; CCR Ord 12, r 7.
5 RSC Ord 33, r 4A.
6 *Walker v Wilsher* (1889) 23 QBD 335.
7 Named after the decision in *Calderbank v Calderbank*, [1976] Fam 93, [1975] 3 All ER 333 that, in matrimonial proceedings over money, an offer to settle could serve the same purpose, as regards costs, as a payment into court.

10.22   The use of a *Calderbank* letter was considered and approved in *McDonnell v McDonnell*[1] and in *Computer Machinery Co Ltd v Drescher*[2] and the latter case ventured on to new ground by suggesting that such a letter's utility was not confined to matrimonial procedings but was just as useful in other proceedings for which payment into court was not available, such as proceedings for an injunction. These points have been considered further by the Court of Appeal in *Cutts v Head*[3] and this decision is now clear authority for two complementary propositions. First, a *Calderbank* offer which reserves the right to bring the letter to the notice of the judge on the issue of costs after judgment in the action if the offer is refused is admissible on that issue even though written 'without prejudice'; it may be used without the consent of both parties in any litigation in which what is in issue is something more than a simple money claim for which a payment into court would be the appropriate way of proceeding. The second proposition is that such an offer may *not* be used as a substitute for payment into court which such a payment would be appropriate and, if so used, should not be treated as carrying the same consequences as a payment in.

1 [1977] 1 All ER 766, [1977] 1 WLR 34, CA.
2 [1983] 3 All ER 153, [1983] 1 WLR 1379.
3 [1984] 1 All ER 597, [1984] 2 WLR 349, CA. See too *Corby District Council v Holst & Co Ltd* [1985] 1 All ER 321, [1985] 1 WLR 427, CA, particularly on the second of the two propositions.

10.23   The way seems now to be clear for yet more extensive use of the *Calderbank* letter. Plainly it may be used between the start of proceedings and the conclusion where the claim is for some kind of relief other than debt or damages eg ancillary relief in matrimonial proceedings, equitable relief such as an injunction or declaration, judicial review and the various special orders that may be sought under special statutes. But that is not the end of it. It may, it seems, be used also in proceedings for debt or damages provided that payment into court is not appropriate. Thus a *Calderbank* letter may be used in connection with a claim for debt or damages that has been decided and is being appealed, or to protect a party's position on costs in connection with an interlocutory proceeding in an action for debt or damages. Most important of all there seems no reason why the would-be defendant to a claim for damages should not make a *Calderbank* offer to dispose of a claim without legal proceedings. Then if the plaintiff rejects the offer and sues the defendant may pay the same amount into court. He will then have protected himself in costs not only as regards the costs incurred after his payment in but, arguably, right back to the date of the *Calderbank* offer, so as to achieve much the same protection as if he had made a valid legal tender, but with the tactical advantage of being able to defend the case on the general merits at the same time. However, so long as what is made before action is not a valid tender but an offer 'without prejudice', the subsequent payment into court ought, it is suggested, to include interest down to the date of payment in, not just down to the date of the offer.

GIVING SECURITY WITHOUT MAKING A PAYMENT INTO COURT
10.24   As has been noted earlier, there are many situations in which a party is required to pay money into court as a condition of being allowed to proceed further.[1] Paying money into court in these circumstances is of no tactical advantage to the defendant and has the disadvantages noted already in connection with payments into court generally.[2] A defendant who is faced with the possibility of such an order should therefore consider what if any alternative form of security can reasonably be offered. One possibility is a solicitor's undertaking to be responsible for the other side's costs, a form of security which is frequently acceptable in the case of a plaintiff who is required to give security because he is resident outside the jurisdiction. Another possibility is a banker's guarantee, such as was offered in *Rosengrens Ltd v Safe Deposit Centres Ltd*[3] and was commended by the Court of Appeal as a better security in the circumstances than the payment into court of part only of the sum in dispute. A third possibility which is only marginally more advantageous than paying money into court is depositing money not with the court but with an interest-bearing account in the joint names of both parties' solicitors. No doubt other methods may be devised, borrowing from the experiences of the Commercial Court[4] and the Court of Admiralty;[5] if an acceptable form of security can be

devised that protects the plaintiff and still leaves the defendant in control of his money, its advantages from the defendant's point of view are considerable. The *Rosengrens* decision suggests that the courts are moving in favour of such alternatives to requiring money to be paid into court.[6]

1 See para 10.08, above.
2 See para 10.21 above.
3 [1984] 3 All ER 198, CA.
4 See the comments of the Court of Appeal, in the *Rosengrens* case, on the practice of the Commercial Court.
5 Something might be devised on the lines of the Bail Bond: see RSC Ord 75, r 16, Form 11 in Appendix B to the Rules.
6 Although not to the extent of inventing new Rules of Court: *Corby District Council v Holst & Co Ltd* [1985] 1 All ER 321 [1985] 1 WLR 427, CA.

Chapter 11

Tax

Interest on tax

11.01   The law regarding interest on tax is rather simpler than that regarding tax on interest. It is set out in sections 86 to 92 of the Taxes Management Act 1970. The main provisions are in section 86 to the effect that any assessments to income tax under Schedule A or D, or charging income tax at a rate other than the basic rate, and any assessments to capital gains tax or corporation tax, other than advance corporation tax,[1] carry interest at a prescribed rate from the date when the tax is due to be paid until it is in fact paid, but must be remitted on any tax paid within two months.[2] In the case of tax recovered to make good loss due to the taxpayer's fault the interest is backdated to the date when the tax should have been paid in the first place.[3] Arrears of interest may be recovered by any means of recovery available in respect of the tax itself, including distraint upon the taxpayer's goods, chattels, lands, tenements and premises.[4]

1 Interest on overdue advance corporation tax and income tax on company payments are dealt with in Taxes Management Act 1970, s 87.
2 Taxes Management Act 1970, s 86.
3 Ibid, s 88.
4 Taxes Management Act 1970, ss 61 and 69.

Tax on interest

11.02   As a general rule income in the form of interest is paid gross and is taxable in the hands of the recipient[1] under Schedule D Case III of the Income and Corporation Taxes Act 1970 (ICTA).[2] There are, however, several exceptions[3] and some interest payments which are exempt from tax altogether. Further, as regards interest which are not exempt, there are certain circumstances in which tax is required to be deducted and remitted to Inland Revenue before the interest reaches the person to whom it is owed.

1 The charge is on the person receiving or entitled to the interest, ICTA s 114.
2 ICTA, s 109(2)(a).
3 See, in particular, paras 11.06–11.14, below.

EXCEPTION FOR INTEREST ON PERSONAL INJURY COMPENSATION

11.03 An important exception to the general rule, that interest is taxable, is made for interest on personal injury compensation: section 375A[1] of ICTA provides, in its amended form,[2] as follows:

(1) The following interest shall not be regarded as income for any income tax purpose—
  (a) Any interest on damages in respect of personal injuries to a plaintiff or any other person, or in respect of a person's death, which is included in any sum for which judgment is given by virtue of a provision to which this paragraph applies; and
  (b) any interest on damages or solatium in respect of personal injuries sustained by a pursuer or by any other person, decree for payment of which is included in any interlocutor by virtue of section 1 of the Interest on Damages (Scotland) Act 1958.

(1A) A payment in satisfaction of a cause of action, including a payment into court, shall not be regarded as income for any income tax purpose to the extent to which it is in respect of interest which would fall within subsection (1) above if included in a sum for which a judgment is given or if decree for payment of it were included in an interlocutor.

(1B) The provisions to which subsection (1)(a) of this section applies are—
  (a) section 3 of the Law Reform (Miscellaneous Provisions) Act 1934;
  (b) section 17 of the Law Reform (Miscellaneous Provisions) Act (Northern Ireland) 1937;
  (c) section 35A of the Supreme Court Act 1981;
  (d) section 69 of the County Courts 1984;
  (e) section 33A of the Judicature (Northern Ireland) Act 1978; and
  (f) Article 45A of the County Courts (Northern Ireland) Order 1980.

(2) In this section 'personal injuries' includes any disease and any impairment of a person's physical or mental condition.

1 Added by Finance Act 1971, s 19.
2 Amended by Finance Act 1981, s 39, Administration of Justice Act 1982, s 74 and County Courts Act 1984, Sch 2.

11.04 The broad effect of the section is to exempt from tax the interest element in compensation for injuries whether the claim is litigated or not. However, tax is not exempt as regards interest on any compensation for damage to property, or on debts or on damages where the claim is not related to wrongful injury to the person, or death. Where a court decides a case and awards interest it will be obvious how much, if any, of the award is in the excepted category. But most litigation is disposed of without a formal decision; either there is a settlement out of court or the plaintiff accepts money paid into court in satisfaction. So the interest element in the compensation may be left unidentified. But the prudent course is to come to terms about interest when reaching a settlement, whether or not it involves accepting money in court, and to provide in the agreement that interest on all or part of the claim should be waived or that the money should be apportioned, so much to damages of a certain kind, so much to interest and so on. In arriving at an agreement the parties may properly have regard to the fiscal implications of identifying part of the money as being paid in respect of interest.[1]

1 *Jefford v Gee* [1970] 2 QB 130, at 150, [1970] 1 All ER 1202, at 1212.

Deduction of tax

11.05 Interest which is not exempt counts as taxable income for the purposes of Case III under Schedule D. On the face of it, this is more important to the recipient taxpayer than to the paying party. But there are various situations in which the person by, or through whom, the interest is paid may be required to deduct a sum equivalent to tax at the basic rate and to remit it to Inland Revenue. If he fails to deduct when he should have done he is accountable to the Revenue for the difference. If, on the other hand, he makes a wrongful deduction he may be liable to the person entitled to payment.[1]

1 See for instance *Corinthian Securities Ltd v Cato* [1970] 1 QB 377, [1969] 3 All ER 1168, CA.

SECTION 54

11.06 The main provision for deducting tax from payments of interest is section 54(1) of the Income and Corporation Taxes Act 1970, which provides as follows:

(1) Subject to subsections (2) and (3) below, where any yearly interest of money chargeable to tax under Case III of Schedule D is paid —
  (a) otherwise than in a fiduciary or representative capacity, by a company or local authority, or
  (b) by or on behalf of a partnership of which a company is a member, or

(c) by any person to another person whose usual place of abode is outside the United Kingdom, the person by or through whom the payment is made shall, on making the payment, deduct out of it a sum representing the amount of income tax thereon for the year in which payment is made.

11.07   Subsection (2) excludes from subsection (1) interest paid to a United Kingdom bank on an advance, or by such a bank in the ordinary course of business. Subsection (3) attracts the provisions of section 53(2) to (4) whereby the party who ought to make the deduction has to deliver to the inspector an account of the payment and is chargeable to tax on it at the basic rate. By section 55, if the payee so requests, the paying party who has made a deduction under section 54(1) must supply a certificate of deduction, which the payee needs for the adjustment of his own tax position.

'YEARLY INTEREST OF MONEY'
11.08   'Yearly interest of money' does not mean merely interest calculated at an annual rate. But it is not at all easy to see, from the authorities, what it does mean. The broad distinction seems to be between 'investment interest' on the one hand and 'default interest' on the other: the former is normally yearly interest money and the latter is normally not. But a short term investment eg a bank deposit which may be withdrawn at any time, does not produce 'yearly' interest[1] and, with contractual interest, the distinction between yearly interest and short largely depends on the intention of the parties.[2] With statutory interest it is more difficult.

1 See the Inland Revenue Statement in the Appendix; also *Garston Overseers v Carlisle* [1915] 3 KB 381.
2 *Cairns v MacDiarmid (Inspector of Taxes)* [1983] STC 178, CA.

INVESTMENT INTEREST
11.09   Interest payable under the terms of a mortgage is almost inevitably yearly interest of money, because of the element of investment; this is so notwithstanding the usual provisions for the mortgage debt to be repaid within six months.[1] Likewise interest for which provision is made on the face of a bill of exchange or other security will probably be classed as yearly interest.[2] On the other hand the interest recoverable as liquidated damages on the dishonour of the bill is probably not yearly interest of money.[3] Interest payable for a period of delay in completion of a purchase of land has been held to be yearly interest of money[4] on an analogy with a land mortgage, although it must be said that, nowadays at least, it would be most unusual for completion to be delayed for more than a year. It has also been held that the interest which a person in a fiduciary

position is ordered by the court to pay as part of an order for the restitution of profits made by a misuse of his position of trust, is yearly interest of money.[5]

1 *Corinthian Securities Ltd v Cato* [1970] 1 QB 377, [1969] 3 All ER 1168, CA.
2 *Ward v Anglo-American Oil Co Ltd* (1934) 19 TC 94.
3 *Goslings and Sharpe v Blake* (1889) 23 QBD 324.
4 *Bebb v Bunny* (1854) 1 K & J 216. And see the Inland Revenue Statement in Appendix G.
5 *Regal (Hastings) Ltd v Gulliver* (1944) 24 ATC 297.

DEFAULT INTEREST

11.10   It was said, obiter, in *Re Cooper*[1] that interest payable on a High Court judgment is not yearly interest of money. The authority of this case is much strengthened by the later case of *Gateshead Corpn v Lumsden*,[2] in which it was held that the interest which a highway authority was entitled to recover from a frontager in respect of the contribution that he owed towards the cost of their making up the road was not yearly interest of money, even though several years' interest were allowed to accrue. It was pointed out in that case that the right to interest had not been provided for by the agreement of the parties and that the debt on which the interest accrued was recoverable on demand at any time.[3] These observations give some support to the view, advanced earlier, that default interest (and particularly default interest arising by statute) ought not normally to be classed as yearly interest, even though the period of default may last longer than a year before payment is recovered. Dicta in *Jefford v Gee*[4] go the other way, suggesting that where interest is awarded pursuant to statute for a period of years it must count as yearly interest of money, on the authority of *Riches v Westminster Bank Ltd*;[5] but that case merely decided that the money was taxable as interest, not that it was *yearly* interest. Accordingly the question whether default interest and, particularly, interest recovered under section 33A of the Supreme Court Act 1981 and section 69 of the County Court Act 1984, is 'yearly interest of money' cannot be regarded as finally settled.

1 [1911] 2 KB 550.
2 [1914] 2 KB 883, CA.
3 Ibid at 890. On the latter point see too *Garston Overseers v Carlisle* [1915] 3 KB 381 at 386.
4 [1970] 2 QB, 130 at 149, [1970] 1 All ER 1202, 1210.
5 [1947] AC 390, [1947] 1 All ER 469.

THE CASES TO WHICH SECTION 54 APPLIES

11.11   The cases to which section 54 applies seldom affect interest payments by individuals. The main categories are payments by a company or local authority or a partnership of which a company is a member. But there is one situation in which an individual may be required to deduct tax from a payment of yearly interest and that is where the person entitled to it is someone whose usual place of abode is outside the United Kingdom.[1] The paying party and his solicitor may not know whether the payee's usual place of abode is outside the United Kingdom, but if a paying solicitor mistakenly pays interest gross on the faith of an assurance by the recipient's solicitor that to the best of his knowledge the recipient's usual place of abode is in the UK the Revenue will not seek to make the paying solicitor accountable for the tax that ought to have been deducted.[2]

1 s 54(1)(c); at para 11.06, above.
2 See the Inland Revenue Statement in Appendix G.

THE PERSON BY OR THROUGH WHOM PAYMENT IS MADE

11.12　　The person by whom payment of yearly interest is made is bound to deduct tax in the situations to which section 54(1) applies. But he may not do so and it is of importance to the recipient to know whether he has done so and, if so, to be given the appropriate certificate so as to make the necessary adjustments to his own tax position. The recipient may assume that tax has not been deducted unless the payer makes it clear that it has;[1] likewise where money is paid into court to satisfy a claim which includes a claim for interest the plaintiff may assume that there has been no deduction of tax unless notified to the contrary.[2]

1 *Hemsworth v Hemsworth* [1946] KB 431, [1946] 2 All ER 117.
2 *The Norseman* [1957] P 224, [1957] 2 All ER 660.

11.13　　A person *through* whom payment is made includes the paying party's authorised agents, who may be a firm of solicitors, as in *Rye and Eyre v IRC*.[1] Where the agents are bound to deduct tax, the obligation under section 53 to render an account to the inspector applies and they are assessable in respect of the tax they ought to have deducted.[2]

1 [1935] AC 274.
2 ICTA 1970, ss 53(2) to (4) and s 54(3).

DEDUCTION OF TAX BY DEPOSIT-TAKING INSTITUTIONS

11.14　　Building societies are enabled, by section 343 of the Income and Corporation Taxes Act 1970, to enter into arrangements for accounting for their tax at a special rate, as a result of which interest paid to its depositors is treated as income paid net after the deduction of tax at the basic rate. Accordingly the depositor may have to pay extra tax if he is being taxed on a higher rate. However he does not get anything back in respect of the tax notionally deducted if his income is not sufficient to bring him into tax at the basic rate. More recently, banks, including the Post Office and trustee savings banks, but not the National Savings Bank, have been brought within a similar regime under sections 26 and 27 of the Finance Act 1984 and Schedule 8 of that Act. The effect is that deposit interest which is payable to an individual is treated as income paid net after the deduction of tax at the basic rate, as in the case of building societies, but where he has declared in writing to the deposit-taker that he is not ordinarily resident in the United Kingdom, interest standing to his name in a designated account is paid gross,[1] subject to what is said later about being taxable in the hands of his agent.[3]

1 Finance Act 1984, Sch 8 para 3(3)(h). For the effect in relation to bank deposit interest on solicitors' client accounts see the Law Society's statement (1985) 82 Law Society's Gazette pp 738 740, the material parts of which are set out in Appendix G.
2 Ibid, s 27(2).
3 See paras 11.17.

EUROBONDS
11.15   Section 35 of the Finance Act 1984 permits interest on quoted Eurobonds issued by UK companies to be paid without deduction of tax in certain circumstances including the case where the beneficial owner who is entitled to the interest is not resident in the United Kingdom. In other cases, where the payment is made by or through a person who is in the United Kingdom, tax must be deducted except where the quoted Eurobond is held in a recognised clearing system.[1]

1 In exercise of its powers under s 35(7) and (8), the Board of Inland Revenue has designated the Cedel and Euro-clear clearing systems, as recognised clearing systems for the purpose of s 35.

UNTAXED INTEREST PAID TO NON-RESIDENTS
11.16   Accordingly, whereas interest which is paid to persons not resident in the United Kingdom will have to be paid under deduction of tax in the case of 'yearly interest of money', it ought normally to be possible for bank interest and Eurobond interest to be paid gross. The recipient will then receive the benefit, as well, of Extra-Statutory Concession B13 which is as follows:[1]

Where for any year of assessment, for the whole of which he is regarded as being not resident in the UK, a person receives interest (eg bank interest) without deduction of tax and is neither chargeable in the name of an agent under s 78, Taxes Management Act 1970, nor has a branch in this country which has the management or control of the interest, no action is taken to pursue his liability to income tax except so far as it can be recovered by set-off in a claim to relief (eg under s 27 of the Income and Corporation Taxes Act 1970) in respect of taxed income from UK sources. This concession does not apply to the corporation tax chargeable on the income of the UK branch or agency of a non-resident company.

1 Quoted from the Inland Revenue booklet, IRI—Extra-Statutory Concessions.

DEDUCTION OF TAX BY THE NON-RESIDENT'S UK AGENT

11.17   Extra-Statutory Concession B13 applies where the interest is paid direct to the non-resident in question. If it is paid to his agent in the United Kingdom it will be chargeable to tax in the agent's hands on his principal's behalf under section 78 of the Taxes Management Act 1970.[1] Furthermore, under section 114 of the Income and Corporations Taxes Act 1970 the agent is himself liable to tax as the recipient of the interest, although not beneficially entitled.[2] So, one way or another, the United Kingdom agent is required to deduct tax at the basic rate. This applies in particular to a solicitor whose client is resident outside the United Kingdom and with whom the client has deposited money on which interest is due to be paid gross. The solicitor in such a case should retain tax at the basic rate for the year in which the interest is paid or credited when transmitting or accounting to the client for the interest. He should also, for each year of assessment in which he receives designated deposit account interest for one or more non-resident clients, notify the inspector of taxes of the fact and after the end of the year the inspector will issue the appropriate form requiring details. However, where he accounts to the client by paying the client a sum out of his own money equivalent to the interest earned[3] he should pay the sum gross and will accordingly be assessed to income tax only on the net interest retained on undesignated clients' accounts in the year.[4]

1 ie chargeable at the basic rate unless the sum is itself sufficient to make the non-resident person liable to higher rates of tax.
2 Again the liability is at the basic rate: *Aplin v White* [1973] STC 322.
3 Solicitors' Account (Deposit Interest) Rules 1975, r 2 (1)(b).
4 See Inland Revenue Statement, and The Law Society's statement, in Appendix G.

Value added tax

11.18   Liability for value added tax[1] impinges very little upon the law and practice relating to the recovery of interest. This particular tax is charged on the supply of goods or services, where it is a taxable supply made by a taxable person in the course or furtherance of any business carried on by him.[2] But financial services are exempt if they fall within Group 5 of Schedule 6, which contains the following items:

1 The issue, transfer or receipt of, or any dealing with, money, any security for money or any note or order for the payment of money.[3]

2 The making of any advance or the granting of any credit.

3 The provision of the facility of instalment credit finance in a hire-purchase, conditional sale or credit sale agreement for which facility a separate charge is made and disclosed to the recipient of the supply of goods.

4 The provision of administrative arrangements and documentation and the transfer of title to the goods in connection with the supply described in item 3 if the total consideration therefore is specified in the agreement and does not exceed £10.

5 The making of arrangements for any transaction comprised in item 1, 2, 3 or 4.

6 The issue, transfer or receipt of, or any dealing with, any security or secondary security within the definition in section 42 of the Exchange Control Act 1947.

7 The operation of any current, deposit or savings account.

1 Value Added Tax Act 1983 consolidates earlier legislation on their topic.
2 Value Added Tax Act 1983, s 2.
3 Item 1 does not include anything included in item 6.

11.19 The granting of credit is accordingly exempt as a service and the interest charge made for such a service is not subject to value added tax. That still leaves for consideration the interest which may be charged or claimed in respect of chargeable goods or services where the customer has defaulted in payment. The answer appears to be that value added tax is calculated in relation to the cash value of the goods or services,[1] without regard to any extra liability that may arise because of the customer's failure to pay on time.[2] Thus the supplier who recovers interest from his defaulting customer, which is calculated on the full price, inclusive of value added tax, is not liable to account to Customs and Excise for that part of the interest which relates to the element of value added tax: he may keep it all (subject, of course, to income or cooperation tax) as compensation for being kept out of the money that was due to him.

11.20 *Tax*

1 Value Added Tax Act 1983, ss 10–12.
2 Indeed, if a discount is allowed for prompt payment, the value is to be treated as reduced by the discount, even if the payment is not made on time: Sch 4, paras 4 and 5.

11.20   A final point to note about value added tax is that arrears used not to carry interest; but if clause 17 of the 1985 Finance Bill becomes law arrears of value added tax will carry interest in much the same circumstances as arrears of income tax and corporation tax.[1]

1 See para 11.01, above.

Appendix A
Statutes

Contents

Judgments Act 1838 (c 110)

Judgment debts to carry interest
17. Every judgment debt shall carry interest at the rate of fifteen[1] pounds per centum per annum from the time of entering up the judgment until the same shall be satisfied, and such interest may be levied under a writ of execution on such judgment.

Decrees and orders of courts of equity, &c to have effect of judgments
18. All decrees and orders of courts of equity, and all rules of courts of common law whereby any sum of money, or any costs, charges, or expences, shall be payable to any person, shall have the effect of judgments in the superior courts of common law, and the persons to whom any such monies, or costs, charges, or expences, shall be payable, shall be deemed judgment creditors within the meaning of this Act; and all powers hereby given to the judges of the superior courts of common law with respect to matters depending in the same courts shall and may be exercised by courts of equity with respect to matters therein depending and all remedies hereby given to judgment creditors are in like manner given to persons to whom any monies, or costs, charges, or expences, are by such orders or rules respectively directed to be paid.

1 For rates see Appendix E.

Bills of Exchange Act 1882 (c 61)

PART I — PRELIMINARY

Interpretation of terms
2. In this Act, unless the context otherwise requires, —
"Acceptance" means an acceptance completed by delivery or notification.
"Action" includes counter claim and set off.
"Banker" includes a body of persons whether incorporated or not who carry on the business of banking.
"Bankrupt" includes any person whose estate is vested in a trustee or assignee under the law for the time being in force relating to bankruptcy.
"Bearer" means the person in possession of a bill or note which is payable to bearer.
"Bill" means bill of exchange, and "note" means promissory note.
"Delivery" means transfer of possession, actual or constructive, from one person to another.
"Holder" means the payee or indorsee of a bill or note who is in possession of it, or the bearer thereof.
"Indorsement" means an indorsement completed by delivery.

"Issue" means the first delivery of a bill or note, complete in form to a person who takes it as a holder.

"Person" includes a body of persons whether incorporated or not.

"Value" means valuable consideration.

"Written" includes printed, and "writing" includes print.

PART II—FORM AND INTERPRETATION

Bill of exchange defined

3. (1) A bill of exchange is an unconditional order in writing, addressed by one person to another, signed by the person giving it, requiring the person to whom it is addressed to pay on demand or at a fixed or determinable future time a sum certain in money to or to the order of a specified person, or to bearer.

(2) An instrument which does not comply with these conditions, or which orders any act to be done in addition to the payment of money, is not a bill of exchange.

(3) An order to pay out a particular fund is not unconditional within the meaning of this section; but an unqualified order to pay, coupled with (a) an indication of a particular fund out of which the drawee is to re-imburse himself or a particular account to be debited with the amount, or (b) a statement of the transaction which gives rise to the bill, is unconditional.

(4) A bill is not valid by reason—

(a) That it is not dated;

(b) That it does not specify the value given, or that any value has been given therefor;

(c) That it does not specify the place where it is drawn or the place where it is payable.

.   .   .

Measure of damages against parties to dishonoured bill

57. Where a bill is dishonoured, the measure of damages, which shall be deemed to be liquidated damages, shall be as follows:

(1) The holder may recover from any party liable on the bill, and the drawer who has been compelled to pay the bill may recover from the acceptor, and an indorser who has been compelled to pay the bill may recover from the acceptor or from the drawer, or from a prior indorser—

(a) The amount of the bill:

(b) Interest thereon from the time of presentment for payment if the bill is payable on demand, and from the maturity of the bill in any other case:

(c) The expenses of noting, or, when protest is necessary, and the protest has been extended, the expenses of protest.

(2) [Repealed]

(3) Where by this Act interest may be recovered as damages, such interest may, if justice require it, be withheld wholly or in part, and where a bill is

expressed to be payable with interest at a given rate, interest as damages may or may not be given at the same rate as interest proper.

Law Reform (Miscellaneous Provisions) Act 1934 s 3, including the provisions introduced by the Administration of Justice Act 1969, s 22.

Power of courts of record to award interest on debts and damages
3.(1) In any proceedings tried in any court of record for the recovery of any debt or damages, the court may, if it thinks fit, order that there shall be included in the sum for which judgment is given interest at such rate as it thinks fit on the whole or any part of the debt or damages for the whole or any part of the period between the date when the cause of action arose and the date of the judgment:

Provided that nothing in this section –
(a) shall authorise the giving of interest upon interest; or
(b) shall apply in relation to any debt upon which interest is payable as of right whether by virtue of any agreement or otherwise; or
(c) shall affect the damages recoverable for the dishonour of a bill of exchange.

(1A) Where in any such proceedings as are mentioned in subsection (1) of this section judgment is given for a sum which (apart from interest on damages) exceeds £200 and represents or includes damages in respect of personal injuries to the plaintiff or any other person, or in respect of a person's death, then (without prejudice to the exercise of the power conferred by that subsection in relation to any part of that sum which does not represent such damages) the court shall exercise that power so as to include in that sum interest on those damages or on such part of them as the court considers appropriate, unless the court is satisfied that there are special reasons why no interest should be given in respect of those damages.

(1B) Any order under this section may provide for interest to be calculated at different rates in respect of different parts of the period for which interest is given, whether that period is the whole or part of the period mentioned in subsection (1) of this section.

(1C) For the avoidance of doubt it is hereby declared that in determining, for the purposes of any enactment contained in the County Courts Act 1959, whether an amount exceeds, or is less than, a sum specified in that enactment, no account shall be taken of any power exercisable by virtue of this section of any order made in the exercise of such a power.

(1D) In this section "personal injuries" includes any disease and any impairment of a person's physical or mental condition, and any reference to the County Courts Act 1959 is a reference to that Act as (whether by virtue of the Administration of Justice Act 1969 or otherwise) that Act has effect for the time being.

Arbitration Act 1950 (c 27)

PART I

.   .   .

Power of arbitrator to award interest

19A. (1) Unless a contrary intention is expressed therein, every arbitration agreement shall, where such a provision is applicable to the reference, be deemed to contain a provision that the arbitrator or umpire may, if he thinks fit, award simple interest at such rate as he thinks fit—

    (a) on any sum which is the subject of the reference but which is paid before the award, for such period ending not later than the date of the payment as he thinks fit; and

    (b) on any sum which he awards, for such period ending not later than the date of the award as he thinks fit.

(2) The power to award interest conferred on an arbitrator or umpire by subsection (1) above is without prejudice to any other power of an arbitrator or umpire to award interest.

Interest on awards

20. A sum directed to be paid by an award shall, unless the award otherwise directs, carry interest as from the date of the award and at the same rate as a judgment debt.

.   .   .

Enforcement of award

26. (1) An award on an arbitration agreement may, by leave of the High Court or judge thereof, be enforced in the same manner as a judgment or order to the same effect, and where leave is so given, judgment may be entered in terms of the award.

    (2) If—

        (a) the amount sought to be recovered does not exceed the county court limit, and

        (b) a county court so orders,

it shall be recoverable (by execution issued from the county court or otherwise) as if payable under an order of that court and shall not be enforceable under subsection (1) above.

(3) An application to the High Court under this section shall preclude an application to a county court and an application to a county court under this section shall preclude an application to the High Court.

(4) In subsection 2(a) above 'the county court limit' means the county court limit which for the time being is the county court limit for the purposes of section 16 of the County Courts Act 1984 (money recoverable by statute).

.   .   .

Crown to be bound

30. This Part of this Act shall apply to any arbitration to which His Majesty, either in right of the Crown or of the Duchy of Lancaster or otherwise, or the Duke of Cornwall, is a party.

Application of Part I to statutory arbitrations
31. (1) Subject to the provisions of section thirty-three of this Act, this Part of this Act, except the provisions thereof specified in subsection (2) of this section, shall apply to every arbitration under any other Act (whether passed before or after the commencement of this Act) as if the arbitration were pursuant to an arbitration agreement and as if that other Act were an arbitration agreement, except in so far as this Act is inconsistent with that other Act or with any rules or procedures authorised or recognised thereby.

(2) The provisions referred to in subsection (1) of this section are subsection (1) of section two, section three, section five, subsection (3) of section eighteen and sections twenty-four, twenty-five, twenty-seven and twenty-nine.

Meaning of 'arbitration agreement'
32. In this Part of this Act, unless the context otherwise requires, the expression "arbitration agreement" means a written agreement to submit present or future differences to arbitration, whether an arbitrator is named therein or not.

.   .   .

PART II—ENFORCEMENT OF CERTAIN FOREIGN AWARDS

Application of Part II
35. (1) This Part of this Act applies to any award made after the twenty-eighth day of July, nineteen hundred and twenty-four—
  - (a) in pursuance of an agreement for arbitration to which the protocol set out in the First Schedule to this Act applies; and
  - (b) between persons of whom one is subject to the jurisdiction of some one of such Powers as His Majesty, being satisfied that reciprocal provisions have been made, may by Order in Council declare to be parties to the convention set out in the Second Schedule to this Act, and of whom the other is subject to the jurisdiction of some other of the Powers aforesaid; and
  - (c) in one of such territories as His Majesty, being satisfied that reciprocal provisions have been made, may by Order in Council declare to be territories to which the said convention applies,

and an award to which this Part of this Act applies is in this Part of this Act referred to as "a foreign award".

(2) His Majesty may by a subsequent Order in Council vary or revoke any Order previously made under this section.

(3) Any Order in Council under section one of the Arbitration (Foreign Awards) Act, 1930, which is in force at the commencement of this Act shall have effect as if it had been made under this section.

Effect of foreign awards
36. (1) A foreign award shall, subject to the provisions of this Part of this

Act, be enforceable in England either by action or in the same manner as the award of an arbitrator is enforceable by virtue of section twenty-six of this Act.

(2) Any foreign award which would be enforceable under this Part of this Act shall be treated as binding for all purposes on the persons as between whom it was made, and may accordingly be relied on by any of those persons by way of defence, set off or otherwise in any legal proceedings in England, and any references in this Part of this Act to enforcing a foreign award shall be construed as including references to relying on an award.

Conditions for enforcement of foreign awards

37. (1) In order that a foreign award may be enforceable under this Part of this Act it must have—

(a) been made in pursuance of an agreement for arbitration which was valid under the law by which it was governed;

(b) been made by the tribunal provided for in the agreement or constituted in manner agreed upon by the parties;

(c) been made in conformity with the law governing the arbitration procedure;

(d) become final in the country in which it was made;

(e) been in respect of a matter which may lawfully be referred to arbitration under the law of England;

and the enforcement thereof must not be contrary to the public policy or the law of England.

(2) Subject to the provisions of this subsection, a foreign award shall not be enforceable under this Part of this Act if the Court dealing with the case is satisfied that—

(a) the award has been annulled in the country in which it was made; or

(b) the party against whom it is sought to enforce the award was not given notice of the arbitration proceedings in sufficient time to enable him to present his case, or was under some legal incapacity and was not properly represented; or

(c) the award does not deal with all the questions referred or contains decisions on matters beyond the scope of the agreement for arbitration:

Provided that, if the award does not deal with all the questions referred, the Court may, if it thinks fit, either postpone the enforcement of the award or order its enforcement subject to the giving of such security by the person seeking to enforce it as the Court may think fit.

(3) If a party seeking to resist the enforcement of a foreign award proves that there is any ground other than the non-existence of the conditions specified in paragraphs (a) (b) and (c) of subsection (1) of this section, or the existence of the conditions specified in paragraphs (b) and (c) of subsection (2) of this section, entitling him to contest the validity of the award, the Court may, if it thinks fit, either refuse to enforce the award or adjourn the hearing until after the expiration of such period as appears the Court to be

reasonably sufficient to enable that party to take the necessary steps to have the award annulled by the competent tribunal.

Evidence
38. (1) The party seeking to enforce a foreign award must produce—
  (a) the original award or a copy thereof duly authenticated in manner required by the law of the country in which it was made; and
  (b) evidence proving that the award has become final; and
  (c) such evidence as may be necessary to prove that the award is a foreign award and that the conditions mentioned in paragraphs (a) (b) and (c) of subsection (1) of the last foregoing section are satisfied.

(2) In any case where any document required to be produced under subsection (1) of this section is in a foreign language, it shall be the duty of the party seeking to enforce the award to produce a translation certified as correct by a diplomatic or consular agent of the country to which that party belongs, or certified as correct in such other manner as may be sufficient according to the law of England.

(3) Subject to the provisions of this section, rules of Court may be made under section 84 of the Supreme Court Act 1981, with respect to the evidence which must be furnished by a party seeking to enforce an award under this Part of this Act.

Meaning of "final award"
39. For the purposes of this Part of this Act, an award shall not be deemed final if any proceedings for the purpose of contesting the validity of the award are pending in the country in which it was made.

Saving for other rights, etc.
40. Nothing in this Part of this Act shall—
  (a) prejudice any rights which any person would have had of enforcing in England any award or of availing himself in England of any award if neither this Part of this Act nor Part I of the Arbitration (Foreign Awards) Act 1930, had been enacted; or
  (b) apply to any award made on an arbitration agreement governed by the law of England.

.   .   .

Trustee Investments Act 1961 (c 62)

FIRST SCHEDULE

MANNER OF INVESTMENT

PART I—NARROWER-RANGE INVESTMENTS NOT REQUIRING ADVICE

1. In Defence Bonds, National Savings Certificates and Ulster Savings

Certificates, Ulster Development Bonds, National Development Bonds, British Savings Bonds, National Savings Income Bonds, National Savings Deposit Bonds.

2. In deposits in the National Savings Bank and deposits in a bank or department thereof certified under subsection (3) of section nine of the Finance Act, 1956.

PART II — NARROWER-RANGE INVESTMENTS REQUIRING ADVICE

1. In securities issued by Her Majesty's Government in the United Kingdom, the Government of Northern Ireland or the Government of the Isle of Man, not being securities falling within Part I of this Schedule and being fixed-interest securities registered in the United Kingdom or the Isle of Man, Treasury Bills or Tax Reserve Certificates, or any variable interest securities issued by Her Majesty's Government in the United Kingdom and registered in the United Kingdom.

2. In any securities the payment of interest on which is guaranteed by her Majesty's Government in the United Kingdom or the Government of Northern Ireland.

3. In fixed-interest securities issued in the United Kingdom by any public authority or nationalised industry or undertaking in the United Kingdom.

4. In fixed-interest securities issued in the United Kingdom by the government of any overseas territory within the Commonwealth or by any public or local authority within such a territory, being securities registered in the United Kingdom.

References in this paragraph to an overseas territory or to the government of such a territory shall be construed as if they occurred in the Overseas Service Act, 1958.

4A. In securities issued in the United Kingdom by the government of an overseas territory within the Commonwealth or by any public or local authority within such a territory, being securities registered in the United Kingdom and in respect of which the rate of interest is variable by reference to one or more of the following:–
   (a) the Bank of England's minimum lending rate;
   (b) the average rate of discount on allotment on 91-day Treasury bills;
   (c) a yield on 91-day Treasury bills;
   (d) a London sterling inter-bank offered rate;
   (e) a London sterling certificate of deposit rate.
References in this paragraph to an overseas territory or to the government of such a territory shall be construed as if they occurred in the Overseas Service Act 1958.

5. In fixed-interest securities issued in the United Kingdom by the African Development Bank, the Asian Development Bank, the Caribbean Development Bank, the International Finance Corporation, the International

Monetary Fund or by the International Bank for Reconstruction and Development, being securities registered in the United Kingdom.

In fixed-interest securities issued in the United Kingdom by the Inter-American Development Bank.

In fixed interest securities issued in the United Kingdom by the European Atomic Energy Community, the European Economic Community, the European Investment Bank or by the European Coal and Steel Community, being securities registered in the United Kingdom.

5A. In securities issued in the United Kingdom by
  (i) the International Bank for Reconstruction and Development or by the European Investment Bank or by the European Coal and Steel Community, being securities registered in the United Kingdom or
  (ii) the Inter-American Development Bank
being securities in respect of which the rate of interest is variable by reference to one or more of the following:
  (a) the Bank of England's minimum lending rate;
  (b) the average rate of discount on allotment on 91-day Treasury bills;
  (c) a yield on 91-day Treasury bills;
  (d) a London sterling inter-bank offered rate;
  (e) a London sterling certificate of deposit rate.

5B. In securities issued in the United Kingdom by the African Development Bank, the Asian Development Bank, the Caribbean Development Bank, the European Atomic Energy Community, the European Economic Community, the International Finance Corporation or by the International Monetary Fund, being securities registered in the United Kingdom and in respect of which the rate of interest is variable by reference to one or more of the following:–
  (a) The average rate of discount on allotment on 91-day Treasury Bills;
  (b) a yield 91-day Treasury Bills;
  (c) a London sterling inter-bank offered rate;
  (d) a London sterling certificate of deposit rate.

6. In debentures issued in the United Kingdom by a company incorporated in the United Kingdom, being debentures registered in the United Kingdom.

7. In stock of the Bank of Ireland.
  In Bank of Ireland 7 per cent Loan Stock 1986/91.

8. In debentures issued by the Agricultural Mortgage Corporation Limited or the Scottish Agricultural Corporation Limited.

9. In loans to any authority to which this paragraph applies charged on all or any of the revenues of the authority or on a fund into which all or any of those revenues are payable, in any fixed-interest securities issued in the United Kingdom by any such authority for the purpose of borrowing money so charged, and in deposits with any such authority by way of temporary loan made on the giving of a receipt for the loan by the treasurer or other similar officer of the authority and on the giving of an undertaking by the authority that, if requested to charge the loan as aforesaid, it will either comply with the request or repay the loan.

This paragraph applies to the following authorities, that is to say—

(a) any local authority in the United Kingdom;

(b) any authority all the members of which are appointed or elected by one or more local authorities in the United Kingdom;

(c) any authority the majority of the members of which are appointed or elected by one or more local authorities in the United Kingdom, being an authority which by virtue of any enactment has power to issue a precept to a local authority in England and Wales, or a requisition to a local authority in Scotland, or to the expenses of which, by virtue of any enactment, a local authority in the United Kingdom is or can be required to contribute;

(d) the Receiver for the Metropolitan Police District or a combined police authority (within the meaning of the Police Act, 1946);

(e) the Belfast City and District Water Commissioners;

(f) the Great Ouse Water Authority;

(g) any district council in Northern Ireland.

9A. In any securities issued in the United Kingdom by any authority to which paragraph 9 applies for the purpose of borrowing money charged on all or any of the revenues of the authority or on a fund into which all or any of these revenues are payable and being securities in respect of which the rate of interest is variable by reference to one or more of the following:

(a) the Bank of England's minimum lending rate;

(b) the average rate of discount on allotment on 91-day Treasury bills;

(c) a yield on 91-day Treasury bills;

(d) a London sterling inter-bank offered rate;

(e) a London sterling certificate of deposit rate.

10. In debentures or in the guaranteed or preference stock of any incorporated company, being statutory water undertakers within the meaning of the Water Act, 1945, or any corresponding enactment in force in Northern Ireland, and having during each of the ten years immediately preceding the calendar year in which the investment was made paid a dividend of not less than $3\frac{1}{2}$ per cent on its ordinary shares.

.   .   .

12. In loans to and deposits in a building society designated under section 1 of the House Purchase and Housing Act, 1949.

.   .   .

PART IV — SUPPLEMENTAL

1. The securities mentioned in Part I to III of this Schedule do not include any securities where the holder can be required to accept repayment of the principal, or the payment of any interest, otherwise than in sterling.

2. The securities mentioned in paragraphs 1 to 8 of Part II, other than Treasury Bills or Tax Reserve Certificates, securities issued before the passing of this act by the government of the Isle of Man, securities falling within paragraph 4 of the said Part II issued before the passing of this Act or securities falling within paragraph 9 of that Part, and the securities mentioned in paragraph 1 of Part III of this Schedule, do not include —
- (a) securities the price of which is not quoted on a recognised stock exchange within the meaning of the Prevention of Fraud (Investments) Act, 1958, or the Belfast stock exchange;
- (b) shares or debenture stock not fully paid up (except shares or debenture stock which by the terms of issue are required to be fully paid up within nine months of the date of issue).

3. The securities mentioned in paragraph 6 of Part II and paragraph 1 of Part III of this Schedule do not include —
- (a) shares of debentures of an incorporated company of which the total issued and paid up share capital is less than one million pounds;
- (b) shares or debentures of an incorporated company which has not in each of the five years immediately preceding the calendar year in which the investment is made paid a dividend on all the shares issued by the company, excluding any shares issued after the dividend was declared and any shares which by their terms of issue did not rank for the dividend for that year.

For the purposes of sub-paragraph (b) of this paragraph a company formed —
- (i) to take over the business of another company or other companies, or
- (ii) to acquire the securities of, or control of, another company or other companies,

or for either of those purposes and for other purposes shall be deemed to have paid a dividend as mentioned in that sub-paragraph in any year in which such a dividend has been paid by the other company or all the other companies, as the case may be.

4. In this Schedule, unless the context otherwise requires, the following expressions have the meanings hereby respectively assigned to them, that is to say —

"debenture" includes debenture stock and bonds, whether constituting a charge on assets or not, and loan stock or notes;

"enactment" includes an enactment of the Parliament of Northern Ireland;

"fixed-interest securities" means securities which under their terms of issue bear a fixed rate of interest;

"local authority" in relation to the United Kingdom, means any of the following authorities—
- (a) in England and Wales, the council of a county, a . . . borough, an urban or rural district or a parish, the Common Council of the City of London the Greater London council and the Council of the Isles of Scilly;
- (b) in Scotland, a local authority within the meaning of the Local Government (Scotland) Act, 1947;

"securities" includes shares, debentures, Treasury Bills and Tax Reserve Certificates;

"share" includes stock;

"Treasury Bills" includes . . . bills issued by Her Majesty's Government in the United Kingdom and Northern Ireland Treasury Bills.

5. It is hereby declared that in this Schedule "mortgage" in relation to freehold or leasehold property in Northern Ireland, includes a registered charge which, by virtue of subsection (4) of section forty of the Local Registration of Title (Ireland) Act, 1891, or any other enactment, operates as a mortgage by deed.

6. References in this Schedule to an incorporated company are references to a company incorporated by or under any enactment and include references to a body of persons established for the purpose of trading for profit and incorporated by Royal Charter.

7. The references in paragraph 12 of Part II and paragraph 2 of Part III of this Schedule to a building society designated under section one of the House Purchase and Housing Act, 1959, include references to a permanent society incorporated under the Building Societies Acts (Northern Ireland) 1874 to 1940 for the time being designated by the Registrar for Northern Ireland under subsection (2) of that section (which enables such a society to be so designated for the purpose of trustees' powers of investment specified in paragraph (a) of subsection (1) of that section).

Consumer Credit Act 1974 (c 39)

PART I—DIRECTOR GENERAL OF FAIR TRADING

General functions of Director
1. (1) It is the duty of the Director General of Fair Trading ("the Director")—
- (a) to administer the licensing system set up by this Act,
- (b) to exercise the adjudicating functions conferred on him by this Act in relation to the issue, renewal, variation, suspension and revocation of licences, and other matters,
- (c) generally to superintend the working and enforcement of this Act, and regulations made under it, and

(d) where necessary or expedient, himself to take steps to enforce this Act, and regulations so made.

(2) It is the duty of the Director, so far as appears to him to be practicable and having regard both to the national interest and the interests of persons carrying on business to which this Act applies and their customers, to keep under review and from time to time advise the Secretary of State about—

    (a) social and commercial developments in the United Kingdom and elsewhere relating to the provision of credit or bailment or (in Scotland) hiring of goods to individuals, and related activities: and

    (b) the working and enforcement of this Act and orders and regulations made under it.

[31 July 1974]

.   .   .

PART II—CREDIT AGREEMENTS, HIRE AGREEMENTS AND LINKED
TRANSACTIONS [31 July1974]

Consumer credit agreements

8. (1) A personal credit agreement is an agreement between and individual ("the debtor") and any other person ("the creditor") by which the creditor provides the debtor with credit of any amount.

(2) A consumer credit agreement is a personal credit agreement by which the creditor provides the debtor with credit not exceeding £15,000.

(3) A consumer credit agreement is a regulated agreement within the meaning of this Act if it is not an agreement (an "exempt agreement") specified in or under section 16. [see Sch 3, para 1, below.]

Meaning of credit

9. (1) In this Act "credit" includes a cash loan, and any other form of financial accommodation.

(2) Where credit is provided otherwise than in sterling it shall be treated for the purposes of this Act as provided in sterling of an equivalent amount.

(3) Without prejudice to the generality of subsection (1), the person by whom goods are bailed or (in Scotland) hired to an individual under a hire-purchase agreement shall be taken to provide him with fixed-sum credit to finance the transaction of an amount equal to the total price of the goods less the aggregate of the deposit (if any) and the total charge for credit.

(4) For the purposes of this Act, an item entering into the total charge for credit shall not be treated as credit even though time is allowed for its payment.

Running-account credit and fixed-sum credit

10. (1) For the purposes of this Act—

    (a) running-account credit is a facility under a personal credit agreement whereby the debtor is enabled to receive from time to time (whether in his own person, or by another person) from the creditor or a third party cash, goods and services (or any of them) to an amount or value such that taking into account payments made by or to the credit oi the debtor, the credit limit (if any) is not at any time exceeded; and

(b) fixed-sum credit is any other facility under a personal credit agreement whereby the debtor is enabled to receive credit (whether in one amount or by instalments).

(2) In relation to running-account credit "credit limit" means, as respects any period, the maximum debit balance which, under the credit agreement, is allowed to stand on the account during that period, disregarding any term of the agreement allowing that maximum to be exceeded merely temporarily.

(3) For the purposes of section 8 (2), running-account credit shall be taken not to exceed the amount specified in that subsection ("the specified amount") if—

(a) the credit limit does not exceed the specified amount; or

(b) whether or not there is a credit limit, and if there is, notwithstanding that it exceeds the specified amount,—

(i) the debtor is not enabled to draw at any one time an amount which, so far as (having regard to section 9 (4)) it represents credit, exceeds the specified amount, or

(ii) the agreement provides that, if the debit balance rises above a given amount (not exceeding the specified amount), the rate of the total charge for credit increases or any other condition favouring the creditor or his associate comes into operation, or

(iii) at the time the agreement is made it is probable, having regard to the terms of the agreement and any other relevant considerations, that the debit balance will not at any time rise above the specified amount.

Restricted-use credit and unrestricted-use credit

11. (1) A restricted-use credit agreement is a regulated consumer credit agreement—

(a) to finance a transaction between the debtor and the creditor, whether forming part of that agreement or not, or

(b) to finance a transaction between the debtor and a person (the "supplier") other than the creditor, or

(c) to refinance any existing indebtedness of the debtor's, whether to the creditor or another person.

and "restricted-use credit" shall be construed accordingly.

(2) An unrestricted-use credit agreement is a regulated consumer credit agreement not falling within subsection (1), and "unrestricted-use credit" shall be construed accordingly.

(3) An agreement does not fall within subsection (1) if the credit is in fact provided in such a way as to leave the debtor free to use it as he chooses, even though certain uses would contravene that or any other agreement.

Debtor-creditor-supplier agreements

12. A debtor-creditor-supplier agreement is a regulated consumer agreement being—

(a) a restricted-use credit agreement which falls within section 11(1) (a), or
(b) a restricted-use credit agreement which falls within section 11 (1) (b) and is made by the creditor under pre-existing arrangements, or in contemplation of future arrangements, between himself and the supplier, or
(c) an unrestricted-use credit agreement which is made by the creditor under pre-existing arrangements between himself and a person (the "supplier") other than the debtor in the knowledge that the credit is to be used to finance a transaction between the debtor and the supplier.

Debtor-creditor agreements
13. A debtor-creditor agreement is a regulated consumer credit agreement being—
(a) a restricted-use credit agreement which falls within section 11 (1) (b) but is not made by the creditor under pre-existing arrangements, or in contemplation of future arrangements, between himself and the supplier, or
(b) a restricted-use credit agreement which falls within section 11 (1) (c), or
(c) an unrestricted-use credit agreement which is not made by the creditor under pre-existing arrangements between himself and a person (the "supplier") other than the debtor in the knowledge that the credit is to be used to finance a transaction between the debtor and the supplier.

Credit-token agreements
14. (1) A credit-token is a card, check, voucher, coupon, stamp, form, booklet or other document or thing given to an individual by a person carrying on a consumer credit business, who undertakes—
(a) that on the production of it (whether or not some other action is also required) he will supply cash, goods and services (or any of them) on credit, or
(b) that where, on the production of it to a third party (whether or not any other action is also required), the third party supplies cash, goods and services (or any of them), he will pay the third party for them (whether or not deducting any discount or commission), in return for payment to him by the individual.

(2) A credit-token agreement is a regulated agreement for the provision of credit in connection with the use of a credit-token.

(3) Without prejudice to the generality of section 9 (1), the person who gives to an individual an undertaking falling within subsection (1) (b) shall be taken to provide him with credit drawn on whenever a third party supplies him with cash, goods or services.

(4) For the purposes of subsection (1), use of an object to operate a machine provided by the person giving the object or a third party shall be treated as the production of the object to him.

Consumer hire agreements

15. (1) A consumer hire agreement is an agreement made by a person with an individual (the "hirer") for the bailment or (in Scotland) the hiring of goods to the hirer, being an agreement which—

(a) is not a hire-purchase agreement, and

(b) is capable of subsisting for more than three months, and

(c) does not require the hirer to make payments exceeding £15,000.

(2) A consumer hire agreement is a regulated agreement if it is not an exempt agreement.

Exempt agreements

16. (1) This Act does not regulate a consumer credit agreement where the creditor is a local authority or building society, or a body specified, or of a description specified, in an order made by the Secretary of State, being—

(a) an insurance company,

(b) a friendly society,

(c) an organisation of employers or organisation of workers,

(d) a charity

(e) a land improvement company, or

(f) a body corporate named or specifically referred to in any public general Act.

(2) Subsection (1) applies only where the agreement is—

(a) a debtor-creditor-supplier agreement financing—

  (i) the purchase of land, or

  (ii) the provision of dwellings on any land,

  and secured by a land mortgage on that land; or

(b) a debtor-creditor agreement secured by any land mortgage; or

(c) a debtor-creditor-supplier agreement financing a transaction which is a linked transaction in relation to—

    (i) an agreement falling within paragraph (a), or

    (ii) an agreement falling within paragraph (b) financing—

      (aa) the purchase of any land, or

      (bb) the provision of dwellings on any land,

and secured by a land mortgage on the land referred to in paragraph (a) or, as the case may be, the land referred to in sub-paragraph (ii).

(3) The Secretary of State shall not make, vary or revoke an order—

(a) under subsection (1) (a) without consulting the Minister of the Crown responsible for insurance companies,

(b) under subsection (1) (b) without consulting the Chief Registrar of Friendly Societies,

(c) under subsection (1) (d) without consulting the Charity Commissioners, or

(d) under subsection (1) (e) or (f) without consulting any Minister of the Crown with responsibilities concerning the body in question.

(4) An order under subsection (1) relating to body may be limited so as to apply only to agreements to that body of a description specified in the order.

(5) The Secretary of State may by order provide that this Act shall not regulate other consumer credit agreements where—

(a) the number of payments to be made by the debtor does not exceed the number specified for that purpose in the order, or

(b) the rate of the total charge does not exceed the rate so specified, or

(c) an agreement has a connection with a country outside the United Kingdom.

(6) The Secretary of State may by order provide that this Act shall not regulate consumer hire agreements of a description specified in the order where—

(a) the owner is a body corporate authorised by or under any enactment to supply electricity, gas or water, and

(b) the subject of the agreement is a meter or metering equipment, or where the owner is a public telecommunications operator specified in the order.

(7) Nothing in this section affects the application of sections 137 to 140 (extortionate credit bargains).

.   .   .

Small agreements

17. (1) A small agreement is—

(a) a regulated consumer credit agreement for credit not exceeding £50, other than a hire-purchase or conditional sale agreement; or

(b) a regulated consumer hire agreement which does not require the hirer to make payments exceeding £50,

being an agreement which is either unsecured or secured by a guarantee or indemnity only (whether or not the guarantee or indemnity is itself secured).

(2) Section 10 (3) (a) applies for the purposes of subsection (1) as it applies for the purposes of section 8 (2).

(3) Where—

(a) two or more small agreements are made at or about the same time between the same parties, and

(b) it appears probable that they would instead have been made as a single agreement but for the desire to avoid the operation of provisions of this Act which would have applied to that single agreement but, apart from this subsection, are not applicable to the small agreements,

this Act applies to the small agreements as if they were regulated agreements other than small agreements.

(4) If, apart from this subsection (3) does not apply to any agreements but would apply if, for any party or parties to any of the agreements, there were substituted an associate of that party, or associates of each of those parties, as the case may be, then subsection (3) shall apply to the agreements.

Multiple agreements

18. (1) This section applies to an agreement (a "multiple agreement") if its terms are such as—

    (a) to place a part of it within one category of agreement mentioned in this Act, and another part of it within a different category of agreement so mentioned, or within a category of agreement not so mentioned, or

    (b) to place it, or a part of it, within two or more categories of agreement so mentioned.

(2) Where a part of an agreement falls within subsection (1), that part shall be treated for the purposes of this Act as a separate agreement.

(3) Where an agreement falls within subsection (1) (b), it shall be treated as an agreement in each of the categories in question, and this Act shall apply to it accordingly.

(4) Where under subsection (2) a part of a multiple agreement is to be treated as a separate agreement, the multiple agreement shall (with any necessary modifications) be construed accordingly; and any sum payable under the multiple agreement, if not apportioned by the parties, shall for the purposes of proceedings in any court relating to the multiple agreement be apportioned by the Court as may be requisite.

(5) In the case of an agreement for running-account credit, a term of the agreement allowing the credit limit to be exceeded merely temporarily shall not be treated as a separate agreement or as providing fixed-sum credit in respect of the excess.

(6) This Act does not apply to a multiple agreement so far as the agreement relates to goods if under the agreement payments are to be made in respect of the goods in the form of rent (other than a rentcharge) issuing out of land.

Linked transactions [see Sch 3, para 2, below.]

19. (1) A transaction entered into by the debtor or hirer, or a relative of his, with any other person ("the other party"), except one for the provision of security, is a linked transaction in relation to an actual or prospective regulated agreement (the "principal agreement") of which it does not form part if—

    (a) the transaction is entered into in compliance with a term of the principal agreement; or

    (b) the principal agreement is a debtor-creditor-supplier agreement and the transaction is financed, or to be financed, by the principal agreement; or

    (c) the other party is a person mentioned in subsection (2), and a person so mentioned initiated the transaction by suggesting it to the debtor or hirer, or his relative, who enters into it—

        (i) to induce the creditor or owner to enter into the principal agreement, or

        (ii) for another purpose related to the principal agreement, or

        (iii) where the principal agreement is a restricted-use credit agreement, for a purpose related to a transaction financed, or to be financed, by the principal agreement.

(2) The persons referred to in subsection (1) (c) are—

(a) the creditor or owner, or his associate;

(b) a person who, in the negotiation of the transaction, is represented by a credit-broker who is also a negotiator in antecedent negotiations for the principal agreement;

(c) a person who, at the time the transaction is initiated, knows that the principal agreement has been made or contemplates that it might be made.

(3) A linked transaction entered into before the making of the principal agreement has no effect until such time (if any) as that agreement is made. [see Sch 3, para 3, below.]

(4) Regulations may exclude linked transactions of the prescribed description from the operation of subsection (3).

Total charge for credit [see Sch 3, para 4, below.]

20. (1) The Secretary of State shall make regulations containing such provisions as appear to him appropriate for determining the true cost to the debtor of the credit provided or to be provided under an actual or prospective consumer credit agreement (the "total charge for credit"), and regulations so made shall prescribe—

(a) what items are to be treated as entering into the total charge for credit, and how their amount is to be ascertained;

(b) the method of calculating the rate of the total charge for credit.

(2) Regulations under subsection (1) may provide for the whole or part of the amount payable by the debtor or his relative under any linked transaction to be included in the total charge for credit, whether or not the creditor is a party to the transaction or derives benefit from it.

PART III—LICENSING OF CREDIT AND HIRE BUSINESSES [31 July 1974]

Licensing principles

Businesses needing a licence [see Sch 3, para 5, below.]

21. Subject to this section, a licence is required to carry on a consumer credit business or consumer hire business.

(2) A local authority does not need a licence to carry on a business.

(3) A body corporate empowered by a public general Act naming it to carry on a business does not need a licence to do so.

.   .   .

Enforcement of agreements made by unlicensed trader [see Sch 3, para 7, below.]

40. (1) A regulated agreement, other than a non-commercial agreement, if made when the creditor or owner was unlicensed, is enforceable against the debtor or hirer only where the Director has made an order under this section which applies to the agreement.

(2) Where during any period an unlicensed person (the "trader") was carrying on a consumer credit business or consumer hire business, he or his

151

successor in title may apply to the Director for an order that regulated agreements made by the trader during that period are to be treated as if he had been licensed.

(3) Unless the Director determines to make an order under subsection (2) in accordance with the application, he shall, before determining the application, by notice—
  (a) inform the applicant, giving his reasons, that, as the case may be, he is minded to refuse the application, or to grant it in terms different from those applied for, describing them, and
  (b) invite the applicant to submit to the Director representations in support of his application in accordance with section 34.

(4) In determining whether or not to make an order under subsection (2) in respect of any period the Director shall consider, in addition to any other relevant factors—
  (a) how far, if at all, debtors or hirers under regulated agreements made by the trader during that period were prejudiced by the trader's conduct,
  (b) whether or not the Director would have been likely to grant a licence covering that period on an application by the trader, and
  (c) the degree of culpability for the failure to obtain a licence.

(5) If the Director thinks fit, he may in an order under subsection (2)—
  (a) limit the order to specified agreements, or agreements of a specified description or made at a specified time;
  (b) make the order conditional on the doing of specified acts by the applicant.

.   .   .

Preliminary matters

Disclosure of information
55. (1) Regulations may require specified information to be disclosed in the prescribed manner to the debtor or hirer before a regulated agreement is made.

(2) A regulated agreement is not properly executed unless regulations under subsection (1) were complied with before the making of the agreement.

Antecedent negotiations [see Sch 3, para 12, below.]
56. (1) In this Act "antecedent negotiations" means any negotiations with the debtor or hirer—
  (a) conducted by the creditor or owner in relation to the making of any regulated agreement, or
  (b) conducted by a credit-broker in relation to goods sold or proposed to be sold by the credit-broker to the creditor before forming the

subject-matter of a debtor-creditor-supplier agreement within section 12 (a), or

(c) conducted by the supplier in relation to a transaction financed or proposed to be financed by a debtor-credit-supplier agreement within section 12 (b) or (c),

and "negotiator" means the person by whom negotiations are so conducted with the debtor or hirer.

(2) Negotiations with the debtor in a case falling within subsection (1) (b) or (c) shall be deemed to be conducted by the negotiator in the capacity of agent of the creditor as well as in his actual capacity.

(3) An agreement is void if, and to the extent that, it purports in relation to an actual or prospective regulated agreement—

(a) to provide that a person acting as, or on behalf of, a negotiator is to be treated as the agent of the debtor or hirer, or

(b) to relieve a person from liability for acts or omissions of any person acting as, or on behalf of, a negotiator.

(4) For the purposes of this Act, antecedent negotiations shall be taken to begin when the negotiator and the debtor or hirer first enter into communication (including communication by advertisement), and to include any representations made by the negotiator to the debtor or hirer and any other dealings between them.

Withdrawal from prospective agreement [19 May 1985]
57. (1) The withdrawal of a party from a prospective regulated agreement shall operate to apply this Part to the agreement, any linked transaction and any other thing done in anticipation of the making of the agreement as it would apply if the agreement were made and then cancelled under section 69.

(2) The giving to a party of a written or oral notice which, however expressed, indicates the intention of the other party to withdraw from a prospective regulated agreement operates as a withdrawal from it.

(3) Each of the following shall be deemed to be the agent of the creditor or owner for the purpose of receiving a notice under subsection (2)—

(a) a credit-broker or supplier who is the negotiator in antecedent negotiations, and

(b) any person who, in the course of a business carried on by him, acts on behalf of the debtor or hirer in any negotiations for the agreement.

(4) Where the agreement, if made, would not be a cancellable agreement, subsection (1) shall nevertheless apply as if the contrary were the case.

Opportunity for withdrawal from prospective land mortgage [19 May 1985]
58. (1) Before sending to the debtor or hirer, for his signature, an unexecuted agreement in a case where the prospective regulated agreement is to be secured on land (the "mortgaged land"), the creditor or owner shall give the debtor or hirer a copy of the unexecuted agreement which contains a notice in the prescribed form indicating the right of the debtor or hirer to withdraw from the prospective agreement, and how and when the right is exercisable,

together with a copy of any other document referred to in the unexecuted agreement.

(2) Subsection (1) does not apply to—
(a) a restricted-use credit agreement to finance the purchase of the mortgaged land, or
(b) an agreement for a bridging loan in connection with the purchase of the mortgaged land or other land.

Agreement to enter future agreement void [19 May 1985]

59. (1) An agreement is void, if, and to the extent that, it purports to bind a person to enter as debtor or hirer into a prospective regulated agreement.

(2) Regulations may exclude from the operation of subsection (1) agreements such as are described in the regulations.

Making the agreement

Form and content of agreements [31July 1974]

60. (1) The Secretary of State shall make regulations as to the form and content of documents embodying regulated agreements, and the regulations shall contain such provisions as appear to him appropriate with a view to ensuring that the debtor or hirer is made aware of—
(a) the rights and duties conferred or imposed on him by the agreement,
(b) the amount and rate of the total charge for credit (in the case of a consumer credit agreement),
(c) the protection and remedies available to him under this Act, and
(d) any other matters which, in the opinion of the Secretary of State, it is desirable for him to know about in connection with agreement.

(2) Regulations under subsection (1) may in particular—
(a) require specified information to be handled in the prescribed manner in documents, and other specified material to be excluded;
(b) contain requirements to ensure that specified information is clearly brought to the attention of the debtor or hirer, and that one part of a document is not given insufficient or excessive prominence compared with another.

(3) If, on an application made to the Director by a person carrying on a consumer credit business or a consumer hire business, it appears to the Director impracticable for the applicant to comply with any requirement of regulations under subsection (1) in a particular case, he may, by notice to the applicant direct that the requirements be waived or varied in relation to such agreements, and subject to such conditions (if any), as he may specify, and this Act and the regulations shall have effect accordingly.

(4) The Director shall give notice under subsection (3) only if he is satisfied that to do so would not prejudice the interests of debtors or hirers.

Signing of agreement [19 May 1985]

61. (1) A regulated agreement is not properly executed unless—
(a) a document in the prescribed form itself containing all the prescribed

Consumer Credit Act 1974 (c 39)

terms and conforming to regulations under section (6) (1) is signed in the prescribed manner both by the debtor or hirer and by or on behalf of the creditor or owner, and

(b) the document embodies all the terms of the agreement, other than implied terms, and

(c) the document is, when presented or sent to the debtor or hirer for signature, in such a state that all its terms are readily legible.

(2) In addition, where the agreement is one to which section 58 (1) applies, it is not properly executed unless—

(a) the requirements of section 58 (1) were complied with, and

(b) the unexecuted agreement was sent, for his signature, to the debtor or hirer by post not less than seven days after a copy of it was given to him under section 58 (1), and

(c) during the consideration period, the creditor or owner refrained from approaching the debtor or hirer (whether in person, by telephone or letter, or in any other way) except in response to a specific request made by the debtor or hirer after the beginning of the consideration period, and

(d) no notice of withdrawal by the debtor or hirer was received by the creditor or owner before the sending of the unexecuted agreement.

(3) In subsection (2) (c), "the consideration period" means the period beginning with the giving of the copy under section 58(1) and ending—

(a) at the expiry of seven days after the day on which the unexecuted agreement is sent, for his signature, to the debtor or hirer, or

(b) on its return by the debtor or hirer after signature by him, whichever first occurs.

(4) Where the debtor or hirer is a partnership or an unincorporated body of persons, subsection (1) (a) shall apply with the substitution for "by the debtor or hirer" or "by or on behalf of the debtor or hirer".

Duty to supply copy of unexecuted agreement [19 May 1985]
62. (1) If the unexecuted agreement is presented personally to the debtor or hirer for his signature, but on the occasion when he signs it the document does not become an executed agreement, a copy of it, and of any other document referred to in it, must be there and then delivered to him.

(2) If the unexecuted agreement is sent to the debtor or hirer for his signature, a copy of it, and of any other document referred to in it, must be sent to him at the same time.

(3) A regulated agreement is not properly executed if the requirements of this section are not observed.

Duty to supply copy of executed agreement [19 May 1985]
63. (1) If the unexecuted agreement is presented personally to the debtor or hirer for his signature, and on the occasion when he signs it the document becomes an executed agreement, a copy of the executed agreement, and of any other document referred to in it must be there and then delivered to him.

(2) A copy of the executed agreement, and of any other document referred

155

to in it, must be given to the debtor or hirer within the seven days following the making of the agreement unless—

(a) subsection (1) applies, or

(b) the unexecuted agreement was sent to the debtor or hirer for his signature and, on the occasion of his signing it, the documents became an executed agreement.

(3) In the case of a cancellable agreement, a copy under subsection (2) must be sent by post.

(4) In the case of a credit-token agreement, a copy under subsection (2) need not be given within the seven days following the making of the agreement if it is given before at the time when the credit-token is given to the debtor.

(5) A regulated agreement is not properly executed if the requirements of this section are not observed.

Duty to give notice of cancellation rights [19 May 1985]

64. (1) In the case of a cancellable agreement, a notice in the prescribed form indicating the right of the debtor or hirer to cancel the agreement, how and when that right is exercisable, and the name and address of a person to whom notice of cancellation may be given, —

(a) must be included in every copy given to the debtor or hirer under section 62 or 63, and

(b) except where section 63 (2) applied, must also be sent by post to the debtor or hirer within the seven days following the making of the agreement.

(2) In the case of a credit-token agreement, a notice under subsection (1) (b) need not be sent by post within the seven days following the making of the agreement if either—

(a) it is sent by post to the debtor or hirer before the credit-token is given to him, or

(b) it is sent by post to him together with the credit-token.

(3) Regulations may provide that except where section 63 (2) applied a notice sent under subsection (1) (b) shall be accompanied by a further copy of the executed agreement, and of any other document referred to in it.

(4) Regulations may provide that subsection (1) (b) is not to apply in the case of agreements such as are described in the regulations, being agreements made by a particular person, if—

(a) on an application by that person to the Director, the Director has determined that having regard to—

(i) the manner in which antecedent negotiations for agreements with the applicant of that description are conducted, and

(ii) the information provided to debtors or hirers before such agreements are made,

the requirement imposed by subsection (1) (b) can be dispensed with without prejudicing the interests of debtors or hirers; and

(b) any conditions imposed by the Director in making the determination are complied with.

(5) A cancellable agreement is not properly executed if the requirements of this section are not observable.

Consequences of improper execution [19 May 1985]
65. (1) An improperly-executed regulated agreement is enforceable against the debtor or hirer on an order of the court only.

(2) A retaking of goods or land to which a regulated agreement relates is an enforcement of the agreement.

Acceptance of credit-tokens [19 May 1985]
66. (1) The debtor shall not be liable under a credit-token agreement for use made of the credit-token by any person unless the debtor had previously accepted the credit-token, or the use constituted an acceptance of it by him.

(2) The debtor accepts a credit-token when—
(a) it is signed, or
(b) a receipt for it is signed, or
(c) it is first used,
either by the debtor himself or by a person who, pursuant to the agreement, is authorised by him to use it,

Cancellation of certain agreements within cooling-off period

Cancellable agreements [19 May 1985]
67. A regulated agreement may be cancelled by the debtor or hirer in accordance with this Part if the antecedent negotiations included oral representations made when in the presence of the debtor or hirer by an individual acting as, or on behalf of, the negotiator, unless—
(a) the agreement is secured on land, or is a restricted-use credit agreement to finance the purchase of land or is an agreement for a bridging loan in connection with the purchase of land, or
(b) the unexecuted agreement is signed by the debtor or hirer at premises at which any of the following is carrying on any business (whether on a permanent or temporary basis)—
(i) the creditor or owner;
(ii) any party to a linked transaction (other than the debtor or hirer or a relative of his);
(iii) the negotiator in any antecedent negotiations.

Cooling-off period [19 May 1985]
68. The debtor or hirer may serve notice of cancellation of a cancellable agreement between his signing of the unexecuted agreement and—
(a) the end of the fifth day following the day on which he received a copy under section 63 (2) or a notice under section 64 (1) (b), or
(b) if (by virtue of regulations made under section 64 (4)) section 64 (1) (b) does not apply, the end of the fourteenth day following the day on which he signed the unexecuted agreement.

Notice of cancellation [19 May 1985]

69. (1) If within the period specified in section 68 the debtor or hirer under a cancellable agreement serves on—

    (a) the creditor or owner, or

    (b) the person specified in the notice under section 64 (1), or

    (c) A person who (whether by virtue of subsection (6) or otherwise) is the agent of the creditor or owner,

a notice (a "notice of cancellation") which, however expressed and whether or not conforming to the notice given under section 64 (1), indicates the intention of the debtor or hirer to withdraw from the agreement, the notice shall operate—

    (i) to cancel the agreement, and any linked transaction, and

    (ii) to withdraw any offer by the debtor or hirer, or his relative, to enter into a linked transaction.

(2) In the case of a debtor-creditor-supplier agreement for restricted-use credit financing—

    (a) the doing of work or supply of goods to meet an emergency, or

    (b) the supply of goods which, before service of the notice of cancellation, had by the act of the debtor or his relative become incorporated in any land or thing not comprised in the agreement or any linked transaction,

subsection (1) shall apply with the substitution of the following for paragraph (i)—

    "(i) to cancel only such provisions of the agreement and any linked transaction as—

        (aa) relate to the provision of credit, or

        (bb) require the debtor to pay an item in the total charge for credit, or

        (cc) subject the debtor to any obligation other than to pay for the doing of the said work, or the supply of the said goods".

(3) Except so far as is otherwise provided, references in this Act to the cancellation of an agreement or transaction do not include a case within subsection (2).

(4) Except as otherwise provided by or under this Act, an agreement or transaction cancelled under subsection (1) shall be treated as if it had never been entered into.

(5) Regulations may exclude linked transactions of the prescribed description from subsection (1) (i) or (ii).

(6) Each of the following shall be deemed to be the agent of the creditor or owner for the purpose of receiving a notice of cancellation—

    (a) a credit-broker or supplier who is the negotiator in antecedent negotiations, and

    (b) any person who, in the course of a business carried on by him, acts on behalf of the debtor or hirer in any negotiation for the agreement.

(7) Whether or not it is actually received by him, a notice of cancellation sent by post to a person shall be deemed to be served on him at the time of posting.

Cancellation: recovery of money paid by debtor or hirer [19 May 1985]

70. (1) On the cancellation of a regulated agreement, and of any linked transaction,—

- (a) any sum paid by the debtor or hirer, or his relative, under or in contemplation of the agreement or transaction, including any item in the total charge for credit, shall become repayable, and
- (b) any sum, including any item in the total charge for credit, which but for the cancellation is, or would or might become, payable by the debtor or hirer, or his relative, under the agreement or transaction shall cease to be, or shall not become, so payable, and
- (c) in the case of a debtor-creditor-supplier agreement falling within section 12 (b), any sum paid on the debtor's behalf by the creditor to the supplier shall become repayable to the creditor.

(2) If, under the terms of a cancelled agreement or transaction, the debtor or hirer, or his relative, is in possession of any goods, he shall have a lien on them for any sum repayable to him under subsection (1) in respect of that agreement or transaction, or any other linked transaction.

(3) A sum repayable under subsection (1) is repayable by the person to whom it was originally paid, but in the case of a debtor-creditor-agreement falling within section 12 (b) the creditor and the supplier shall be under a joint and several liability to repay sums paid by the debtor, or his relative under the agreement or under a linked transaction falling within section 19 (1) (b) and accordingly, in such a case, the creditor shall be entitled, in accordance with rules of court, to have the supplier made a party to any proceedings brought against the creditor to recover any such sums.

(4) Subject to any agreement between them, the creditor shall be entitled to be indemnified by the supplier for loss suffered by the creditor in satisfying his liability under subsection (3), including costs reasonably incurred by him in defending proceedings instituted by the debtor.

(5) Subsection (1) does not apply to any sum which, if not paid by a debtor, would be payable by virtue of section 71, and applies to a sum paid or payable by a debtor for the issue of a credit-token only where the credit-token has been returned to the creditor or surrendered to a supplier.

(6) If the total charge for credit includes an item in respect of a fee or commission charged by a credit-broker, the amount repayable under subsection (1) in respect of that item shall be the excess over £3 of the fee or commission.

(7) If the total charge for credit includes any sum payable or paid by the debtor to a credit-broker otherwise than in respect of a fee or commission charged by him, that sum shall for the purposes of subsection (6) be treated as if it were such a fee or commission.

(8) So far only as is necessary to give effect to section 69 (2), this section applies to an agreement or transaction within that subsection as it applies to a cancelled agreement or transaction.

Cancellation: repayment of credit [19 May 1985]

71. (1) Notwithstanding the cancellation of a regulated consumer credit agreement, other than a debtor-creditor-supplier agreement for restricted-use credit, the agreement shall continue in force so far as it relates to repayment of credit and payment of interest.

(2) If, following the cancellation of a regulated consumer credit agreement, the debtor repays the whole or a portion of the credit—
  (a) before the expiry of one month following service of the notice of cancellation, or
  (b) in the case of a credit repayable by instalments, before the date on which the first instalment is due,
no interest shall be payable on the amount repaid.

(3) If the whole of a credit repayable by instalments is not repaid on or before the date specified in subsection (2) (b), the debtor shall not be liable to repay any of the credit except on receipt of a request in writing in the prescribed form, signed by or on behalf of the creditor, stating the amounts of the remaining instalments (recalculated by the creditor as nearly as may be in accordance with the agreement and without extending the repayment period), but excluding any sum other than principal and interest.

(4) Repayment of a credit, or payment of interest, under a cancelled agreement shall be treated as duly made if it is made to any person on whom, under section 69, a notice of cancellation could have been served, other than a person referred to in section 69 (6) (b).

Cancellation: return of goods [19 May 1985]
72. (1) This section applies where any agreement or transaction relating to goods, being—
  (a) a restricted-use-creditor-supplier agreement, a consumer hire agreement, or a linked transaction to which the debtor or hirer under any regulated agreement is a party, or
  (b) a linked transaction to which a relative of the debtor or hirer under any regulated agreement is a party,
is cancelled after the debtor or hirer (in a case within paragraph (a)) or the relative (in a case within paragraph (b)) has acquired possession of the goods by virtue of the agreement or transaction.

(2) In this section—
(a) "the possessor" means the person who has acquired possession of the goods as mentioned in subsection (1),
  (b) "the other party" means the person from whom the possessor acquired possession, and
  (c) "the pre-cancellation period" means the period beginning when the possessor acquired possession and ending with the cancellation.

(3) The possessor shall be treated as having been under a duty throughout the precancellation period—
  (a) to retain possession of the goods, and
  (b) to take reasonable care of them.

(4) On the cancellation, the possessor shall be under a duty, subject to any lien, to restore the goods to the other party in accordance with this section,

and meanwhile to retain possession of the goods and take reasonable care of them.

(5) The possessor shall not be under any duty to deliver the goods except at his own premises and in pursuance of a request in writing signed by or on behalf of the other party and served on the possessor either before, or at the time when, the goods are collected from those premises.

(6) If the possessor—

(a) delivers the goods (whether at his own premises or elsewhere) to any person on whom, under section 69, a notice of cancellation could have been served (other than a person referred to in section 69 (6) (b)), or

(b) send the goods at his own expense to such a person,

he shall be discharged from any duty to retain the goods or deliver them to any person.

(7) Where the possessor delivers the goods as mentioned in subsection (6) (a), his obligation to take care of the goods shall cease; and if he sends the goods as mentioned in subsection (6) (b), he shall be under a duty to take reasonable care to see that they are received by the other party and not damaged in transit, but in other respects his duty to take care of the goods shall cease.

(8) Where, at any time during the period of 21 days following the cancellation, the possessor receives such a request as is mentioned in subsection (5), and unreasonably refuses or unreasonably fails to comply with it, his duty to take reasonable care of the goods shall continue until he delivers or sends the goods as mentioned in subsection (6), but if within that period he does not receive such a request his duty to take reasonable care of the goods shall cease at the end of that period.

(9) The preceding provisions of this section do not apply to—

(a) perishable goods, or

(b) goods which by their nature are consumed by use and which, before the cancellation, where so consumed, or

(c) goods supplied to meet an emergency, or

(d) goods which, before the cancellation, had become incorporated in any land or thing not comprised in the cancelled agreement or a linked transaction.

(10) Where the address of the possessor is specified in the executed agreement, references in this section to his own premises are to that address and no other.

(11) Breach of a duty imposed by this section is actionable as a breach of statutory duty.

Cancellation: goods given in part-exchange [19 May 1985]

73. (1) This section applies on the cancellation of a regulated agreement where, in antecedent negotiations, the negotiator agreed to take goods in part-exchange (the "part-exchange goods") and those goods have been delivered to him.

(2) Unless, before the end of the period of ten days beginning with the

date of cancellation, the part-exchange goods are returned to the debtor or hirer in a condition substantially as good as when they were delivered to the negotiator, the debtor or hirer shall be entitled to recover from the negotiator a sum equal to the part-exchange allowance (as defined in subsection (7) (b)).

(3) In the case of a debtor-creditor-supplier agreement within section 12 (b), the negotiator and the creditor shall be under a joint and several liability to pay to the debtor a sum recoverable under subsection (2).

(4) Subject to any agreement between them, the creditor shall be entitled to be indemnified by the negotiator for loss suffered by the creditor in satisfying his liability under subsection (3), including costs reasonably incurred by him in defending proceedings instituted by the debtor.

(5) During the period of ten days beginning with the date of cancellation, the debtor or hirer, if he is in possession of goods to which the cancelled agreement relates, shall have a lien on them for—

    (a) delivery of the part-exchange goods, in a condition substantially as good as when they were delivered to the negotiator, or

    (b) a sum equal to the part-exchange allowance;

and if the lien continues to the end of that period it shall thereafter subsist only as a lien for a sum equal to the part-exchange allowance.

(6) Where the debtor or hirer recovers from the negotiator or creditor, or both of them jointly, a sum equal to the part-exchange allowance, then, if the title of the debtor or hirer to the part-exchange goods has not vested in the negotiator, it shall so vest on the recovery of that sum.

(7) For the purposes of this section—

    (a) the negotiator shall be treated as having agreed to take goods in part-exchange if, in pursuance of the antecedent negotiations, he either purchased or agreed to purchase those goods or accepted or agreed to accept them as part of the consideration for the cancelled agreement, and

    (b) the part-exchange allowance shall be the sum agreed as such in the antecedent negotiations or, if no such agreement was arrived at, such sum as it would have been reasonable to allow in respect of the part-exchange goods if no notice of cancellation had been served.

(8) In an action brought against the creditor for a sum recoverable under subsection (2), he shall be entitled, in accordance with rules of court, to have the negotiator made a party to the proceedings.

Exclusion of certain agreements from Part V

Exclusion of certain agreements from Part V [31 July 1974]

74. (1) This Part (except section 56) does not apply to—

    (a) a non-commercial agreement, or

    (b) a debtor-creditor agreement enabling the debtor to overdraw on a current account, or

    (c) a debtor agreement to finance the making of such payments arising on, or connected with, the death of a person as may be prescribed.

(2) This Part (except sections 55 and 56) does not apply to a small debtor-creditor-supplier agreement for restricted-use credit.

(3) Subsection (1) (b) or (c) applies only where the Director so determines, and such a determination–

(a) may be made subject to such conditions as the Director thinks fit, and

(b) shall be made only if the Director is of opinion that it is not against the interest of debtors.

(3A) Notwithstanding anything in subsection (3) (b) above, in relation to a debtor-creditor agreement under which the creditor is the Bank of England or a bank within the meaning of the Bankers' Books Evidence Act 1879, the Director shall make a determination that subsection (1) (b) above applies unless he considers that it would be against the public interest to do so.

(4) If any term of an agreement falling within subsection (1) (c) or (2) is expressed in writing, regulations under section 60 (1) shall apply to that term (subject to section 60 (3)) as if the agreement were a regulated agreement not falling within subsection (1) (c) or (2).

PART VI—MATTERS ARISING DURING CURRENCY OF CREDIT OR HIRE AGREEMENTS

Liability of creditor for breaches by supplier [see Sch 3, para 15, below.]

75. (1) If the debtor under a debtor-creditor-supplier agreement falling within section 12 (b) or (c) has, in relation to a transaction financed by the agreement, any claim against the supplier in respect of a misrepresentation or breach of contract, he shall have a like claim against the creditor, who, with the supplier, shall accordingly be jointly and severally liable to the debtor.

(2) Subject to any agreement between them, the creditor shall be entitled to be indemnified by the supplier for loss suffered by the creditor in satisfying his liability under subsection (1), including costs reasonably incurred by him in defending proceedings instituted by the debtor.

(3) Subsection (1) does not apply to a claim—

(a) under a non-commercial agreement, or

(b) so far as the claim relates to any single item to which the supplier has attached a cash price not exceeding £100 or more than £30,000.

(4) This section applies notwithwithstanding that the debtor, in entering into the transaction, exceeded the credit limit or otherwise contravened any term of the agreement.

(5) In an action brought against the creditor under subsection (1) he shall be entitled, in accordance with rules of court, to have the supplier made a party to the proceedings.

Duty to give notice before taking certain action [19May 1985: see Sch 3, para 16, below.]

76. (1) The creditor or owner is not entitled to enforce a term of a regulated agreement by—

(a) demanding earlier payment of any sum, or

(b) recovering possession of any goods or land, or

(c) treating any right conferred on the debtor or hirer by the agreement as terminated, restricted or deferred,

except by or after giving the debtor or hirer not less than seven days' notice of his intention to do so.

(2) Subsection (1) applies only where—

(a) a period for the duration of the agreement is specified in the agreement and

(b) that period has not ended when the creditor or owner does an act mentioned in subsection (1).

but so applies notwithstanding that, under the agreement, any party is entitled to terminate before the end of the period so specified.

(3) A notice under subsection (1) is ineffective if not in the prescribed form.

(4) Subsection (1) does not prevent a creditor from treating the right to draw on any credit as restricted or deferred and taking such steps as may be necessary to make the restriction or deferment effective.

(5) Regulations may provide that subsection (1) is not to apply to agreements described by the regulations.

(6) Subsection (1) does not apply to a right of enforcement arising by reason of any breach by the debtor or hirer of the regulated agreement.

Duty to give information to debtor under fixed-sum credit agreement [19 May 1985; see Sch 3, para 17, below.]

77. (1) The creditor under a regulated agreement for fixed-sum credit, within the prescribed period after receiving a request in writing to that effect from the debtor and payment of a fee of 50 new pence, shall give the debtor a copy of the executed agreement (if any) and of any other document referred to in it, together with a statement signed by or on behalf of the creditor showing, according to the information to which it is practicable for him to refer,—

(a) the total sum paid under the agreement by the debtor;

(b) the total sum which has become payable under the agreement by the debtor but remains unpaid, and the various amounts comprised in that total sum, with the date when each became due; and

(c) the total sum which is to become payable under the agreement by the debtor, and the various amounts comprised in that total sum, with the date, or mode of determining the date, when each becomes due.

(2) If the creditor possesses insufficient information to enable him to ascertain the amounts and dates mentioned in subsection (1) (c), he shall be taken to comply with that paragraph if his statement under subsection (1) gives the basis on which, under the regulated agreement, they would fall to be ascertained.

(3) Subsection (1) does not apply to—

(a) an agreement under which no sum is, or will or may become, payable by the debtor, or

(b) a request made less than one month after a previous request under that subsection relating to the same agreement was complied with.

(4) If the creditor under an agreement fails to comply with subsection (1)—

(a) he is not entitled, while the default continues, to enforce the agreement; and

(b) if the default continues for one month he commits and offence.

(5) This section does not apply to a non-commercial agreement.

Duty to give information to debtor under running-account credit agreement
[19 May 1985; see Sch 3, para 17, below.]

78. (1) The creditor under a regulated agreement for running-account credit, within the prescribed period after receiving a request in writing to that effect from the debtor and payment of a fee of 50 new pence, shall give the debtor a copy of the executed agreement (if any) and of any other documents referred to in it, together with a statement signed by or on behalf of the creditor showing, according to the information to which it is practicable for him to refer,—

(a) the state of the account, and

(b) the amount, if any, currently payable under the agreement by the debtor to the creditor, and

(c) the amounts and due dates of any payments which, if the debtor does not draw further on the account, will later become payable under the agreement by the debtor to the creditor.

(2) If the creditor possesses insufficient information to enable him to ascertain the amounts and dates mentioned in subsection (1) (c), he shall be taken to comply with that paragraph if his statement under subsection (1) gives the basis on which, under the regulated agreement, they would fall to be ascertained.

(3) Subsection (1) does not apply to—

(a) an agreement under which no sum is, or will or may become, payable by the debtor, or

(b) a request made less than one month after a previous request under that subsection relating to the same agreement was complied with.

(4) Where running-account credit is provided under a regulated agreement, the creditor shall give the debtor statements in the prescribed form, and with the prescribed contents—

(c) showing according to the information to which it is practicable for him to refer, the state of the account at regular intervals of not more than twelve months, and

(b) where the agreement provides, in relation to specified periods, for the making of payments by the debtor, or the charging against him of interest or any other sum, showing according to the information to which it is practicable for him to refer the state of the account at the end of each of those periods during which there is any movement in the account.

(5) A statement under subsection (4) shall be given within the prescribed period after the end of the period to which the statement relates.

(6) If the creditor under an agreement fails to comply with subsection (1)—

    (a) he is not entitled, while the default continues, to enforce the agreement; and

    (b) if the default continues for one month he commits an offence.

(7) This section does not apply to a non-commercial agreement, and subsections (4) and (5) do not apply to a small agreement.

Duty to give hirer information [19 May 1985; see Sch 3, para 17, below.]

79. (1) The owner under a regulated consumer hire agreement, within the prescribed period after receiving a request in writing to that effect from the hirer and payment of a fee of 50 new pence shall give to the hirer a copy of the executed agreement and of any other document referred to in it, together with a statement signed by or on behalf of the owner showing, according to the information to which it is practicable for him to refer, the total sum which has become payable under the agreement by the hirer but remains unpaid and the various amounts comprised in that total sum, with the date when each became due.

(2) Subsection (1) does not apply to—

    (a) an agreement under which no sum is, or will or may become payable by the hirer, or

    (b) a request made less than one month after a previous request under that subsection relating to the same agreement was complied with.

(3) If the owner under an agreement fails to comply with subsection (1)—

    (a) he is not entitled, while the default continues, to enforce the agreement; and

    (b) if the default continues for one month he commits an offence.

(4) This section does not apply to a non-commercial agreement.

Debtor or hirer to give information about goods [19 May 1985]

80. (1) Where a regulated agreement, other than a non-commercial agreement, requires the debtor or hirer to keep goods to which the agreement relates in his possession or control, he shall, within seven working days after he has received a request in writing to that effect from the creditor or owner, tell the creditor or owner where the goods are.

(2) If the debtor or hirer fails to comply with subsection (1), and the default continues for 14 days, he commits an offence.

Appropriation of payments [19 May 1985]

81. (1) Where a debtor or hirer is liable to make to the same person payments in respect of two or more regulated agreements, he shall be entitled, on making any payment in respect of the agreements which is not sufficient to discharge the total amount then due under all the agreements to appropriate the sum so paid by him—

(a) in towards the satisfaction of the sum due under any one of the agreements or

(b) in or towards the satisfaction of the sums due under any two or more of the agreements in such proportions as he thinks fit.

(2) If the debtor or hirer fails to make any such appropriation where one or more of the agreements is—

(a) a hire-purchase agreement or conditional sale agreement, or

(b) a consumer hire agreement, or

(c) an agreement in relation to which any security is provided,

the payment shall be appropriated towards the satisfaction of the sums due under the several agreements respectively in the proportions which those sums bear to one another.

Variation of agreements [1 April 1977]

82. (1) Where, under a power contained in a regulated agreement, the creditor or owner varies the agreement, the variation shall not take effect before notice of it is given to the debtor or hirer in the prescribed manner.

(2) Where an agreement (a "modifying agreement") varies or supplements an earlier agreement, the modifying agreements shall for the purposes of this Act be treated as—

(a) revoking the earlier agreement, and

(b) containing provisions reproducing the combined effect of the two agreements,

and obligations outstanding in relation to the earlier agreement shall accordingly be treated as outstanding instead in relation to the modifying agreement.

(3) If the earlier agreement is a regulated agreement but (apart from this subsection) the modifying agreement is not then, unless the modifying agreement is for running-account credit, it shall be treated as a regulated agreement.

(4) If the earlier agreement is a regulated agreement for running-account credit, and by the modifying agreement the creditor allows the credit limit to be exceeded but intends the excess to be merely temporary, Part V (except section 56) shall not apply to the modifying agreement.

(5) If—

(a) the earlier agreement is a cancellable agreement, and

(b) the modifying agreement is made within the period applicable under section 68 to the earlier agreement,

then, whether or not the modifying agreement would, apart from this subsection, be a cancellable agreement, it shall be treated as a cancellable agreement in respect of which a notice may be served under section 68 not later than the end of the period applicable under that section to the earlier agreement.

(6) Except under subsection (5), a modifying agreement shall not be treated as a cancellable agreement.

(7) This section does not apply to a non-commercial agreement.

Appendix A

Liability for misuse of credit facilities [19 May 1985; see Sch 3, para 20, below.]

83. (1) The debtor under a regulated consumer credit agreement shall not be liable to the creditor for any loss arising from use of the credit facility by another person not acting, or to be treated as acting, as the debtor's agent.

(2) This section does not apply to a non-commercial agreement, or to any loss in so far as it arises from misuse of an instrument to which section 4 of the Cheques Act 1957 applies.

Misuse of credit-tokens [19 May 1985; see Sch 3, para 20, below.]

84. (1) Section 83 does not prevent the debtor under a credit-token agreement from being made liable to the extent of £50 (or the credit limit if lower) for loss to the creditor arising from use of the credit-token by other persons during a period beginning when the credit-token ceases to be in the possession of any authorised person and ending when the credit-token is once more in the possession of an authorised person.

(2) Section 83 does not prevent the debtor under a credit-token agreement from being made liable to any extent for loss to the creditor from use of the credit-token by a person who acquired possession of it with the debtor's consent.

(3) Subsections (1) and (2) shall not apply to any use of the credit-token after the creditor has been given oral or written notice that it is lost or stolen, or is for any other reason liable to misuse.

(4) Subsections (1) and (2) shall not apply unless there are contained in the credit-token agreement in the prescribed manner particulars of the name, address and telephone number of a person stated to be the person to whom notice is to be given under subsection (3).

(5) Notice under subsection (3) takes effect when received, but where it is given orally, and the agreement so requires, it shall be treated as not taking effect if not confirmed in writing within seven days.

(6) Any sum paid by the debtor for the issue of the credit-token, to the extent (if any) that it has not been previously offset by use made of the credit-token, shall be treated as paid towards satisfaction of any liability under subsection (1) or (2).

(7) The debtor, the creditor, and any person authorised by the debtor to use the credit-token, shall be authorised persons for the purposes of subsection (1).

(8) Where two or more credit-tokens are given under on credit-token agreement, the preceding provisions of this section apply to each credit-token separately.

Duty on issue of new credit-tokens [19 May 1985; see Sch 3, para 21, below.]

85. (1) Whenever, in connection with a credit-token agreement, a credit-token (other than the first) is given by the creditor to the debtor, the creditor shall give the debtor a copy of the executed agreement (if any) and of any other document referred to in it.

(2) If the creditor fails to comply with this section —

(a) he is not entitled, while the default continues, to enforce the agreement; and

(b) if the default continues for one month he commits an offence.

(3) The section does not apply to a small agreement.

Death of debtor or hirer [19 May 1985; see Sch 3, para 22, below.]

86. (1) The creditor or owner under a regulated agreement is not entitled, by reason of the death of the debtor or hirer, to do an act specified in paragraphs (a) to (e) of section 87 (1) if at the death the agreement is fully secured.

(2) If at the death of the debtor or hirer a regulated agreement is only partly secured or is unsecured, the creditor or owner is entitled, by reason of the death of the debtor or hirer, to do an act specified in paragraphs (a) to (e) of section 87 (1) on an order of the court only.

(3) This section applies in relation to the termination of an agreement only where—

(a) a period for its duration is specified in the agreement, and

(b) that period has not ended when the creditor or owner purports to terminate the agreement.

but so applies notwithstanding that, under the agreement, any party is entitled to terminate it before the end of the period so specified.

(4) This section does not prevent the creditor from treating the right to draw on any credit as restricted or deferred, and taking such steps as may be necessary to make the restriction or deferment effective.

(5) This section does not affect the operation of any agreement providing for payment of sums—

(a) due under the regulated agreement, or

(b) becoming due under it on the death of the debtor or hirer,

out of the proceeds of a policy of assurance on his life.

(6) For the purposes of this section an act is done by reason of the death of the debtor or hirer if it is done under a power conferred by the agreement which is—

(a) exercisable on his death, or

(b) exercisable at will and exercised at any time after his death.

PART VII—DEFAULT AND TERMINATION

Default notices

Need for default notice [19 May 1985; see Sch 3, para 35, below.]

87. (1) Service of a notice on the debtor or hirer in accordance with section 88 (a "default notice") is necessary before the creditor or owner can become entitled, by reason of any breach by the debtor or hirer of a regulated agreement,—

(a) to terminate the agreement, or

(b) to demand earlier payment of any sum, or

(c) to recover possession of any goods or land, or

(d) to treat any right conferred on the debtor or hirer by the agreement as terminated, restricted or deferred, or

(e) to enforce any security.

(2) Subsection (1) does not prevent the creditor from treating the right to draw upon any credit as restricted or deferred, and taking such steps as may be necessary to make the restriction or deferment effective.

(3) The doing of an act by which a floating charge becomes fixed is not enforcement of a security.

(4) Regulations may provide that subsection (1) is not to apply to agreements described by the regulations.

Contents and effect of default notice [19 May 1985; see Sch 3, para 35, below.]

88. (1) The default notice must be in the prescribed form and specify—

(a) the nature of the alleged breach;

(b) if the breach is capable of remedy, what action is required to remedy it and date before which that action is to be taken;

(c) if the breach is not capable of remedy, the sum (if any) required to be paid as compensation for the breach and the date before which it is to be paid.

(2) A date specified under subsection (1) must not be less than seven days after the date of service of the default notice, and the creditor or owner shall not take action such as is mentioned in section 87 (1) before the date so specified or (if no requirement is made under subsection (1)) before those seven days have elapsed.

(3) The default notice must not treat as a breach of failure to comply with a provision of the agreement which becomes operative only on breach of some other provision, but if the breach of that other provision is not duly remedied or compensation demanded under subsection (1) is not duly paid, or (where no requirement is made under subsection (1)) if the seven days mentioned in subsection (2) have elapsed, the creditor or owner may treat the failure as a breach and section 87 (1) shall not apply to it.

(4) The default notice must contain information in the prescribed terms about the consequences of failure to comply with it.

(5) A default notice making a requirement under subsection (1) may include a provision for the taking of action such as is mentioned in section 87 (1) at any time after the restriction imposed by subsection (2) will cease, together with a statement that the provision will be ineffective if the breach is duly remedied or the compensation duly paid.

Compliance with default notice [19 May 1985; see Sch 3, para 35, below.]

89. If before the date specified for that purpose in the default notice the debtor or hirer takes the action specified under section 88 (1) (b) or (c) the breach shall be treated as not having occurred.

Further restriction of remedies for default

Retaking of protected hire-purchase etc. goods [19 May 1985]
90. (1) At any time when—
(a) the debtor in breach of a regulated hire-purchase or a regulated conditional sale agreement relating to goods, and
(b) the debtor has paid to the creditor one-third or more of the total price of the goods, and
(c) the property in the goods remains in the creditor,
the creditor is not entitled to recover possession of the goods from the debtor except on an order of the court.

(2) Where under a hire-purchase or conditional sale agreement the creditor is required to carry out any installation and the agreement specifies, as part of the total price, the amount to be paid in respect of the installation (the "installation charge") the reference in subsection (1) (b) to one-third of the total price shall be construed as a reference to the aggregate of the installation charge and one-third of the remainder of the total price.

(3) In a case where—
(a) subsection (1) is satisfied, but not subsection (1) (b), and
(b) subsection (1) (b) was satisfied on a previous occasion in relation to an earlier agreement, being a regulated hire-purchase or regulated conditional sale agreement, between the same parties, and relating to any of the goods comprised in the later agreement (whether or not other goods were also included),
subsection (1) shall apply to the later agreement with the omission of paragraph (b).

(4) If the later agreement is a modifying agreement, subsection (3) shall apply with the substitution, for the second reference to the later agreement, of a reference to the modifying agreement.

(5) Subsection (1) shall not apply, or shall cease to apply, to an agreement if the debtor has terminated, or terminates, the agreement.

(6) Where subsection (1) applies to an agreement at the death of the debtor, it shall continue to apply (in relation to the possessor of the goods) until the grant of probate or administration, or (in Scotland) confirmation (on which the personal representative would fall to be treated as the debtor).

(7) Goods falling within this section are in this Act referred to as "protected goods".

Consequences of breach of s 90 [19 May 1985]
91. If goods are recovered by the creditor in contravention of section 90—
(a) the regulated agreement, if not previously terminated, shall terminate, and
(b) the debtor shall be released from all liability under the agreement, and shall be entitled to recover from the creditor all sums paid by the debtor under the agreement.

171

Recovery of possession of goods or land [19 May 1985, see Sch 3, para 35, below.]

92. (1) Except under an order of the court, the creditor or owner shall not be entitled to enter any premises to take possession of goods subject to a regulated hire-purchase agreement, regulated conditional sale agreement or regulated consumer hire agreement.

(2) At any time when the debtor is in breach of a regulated conditional sale agreement relating to land, the creditor is entitled to recover possession of the land from the debtor or any person claiming under him, on an order of the court only.

(3) An entry in contravention of subsection (1) or (2) is actionable as a breach of statutory duty.

Interest not to be increased on default [19 May 1985]

93. The debtor under a regulated consumer credit agreement shall not be obliged to pay interest on sums which, in breach of the agreement are unpaid by him at a rate —

    (a) where the total charge for credit includes an item in respect of interest, exceeding the rate of that interest, or

    (b) in any other case, exceeding what would be the rate of the total charge for credit if any items included in the total charge for credit by virtue of section 20 (2) were disregarded.

Early payment by debtor

Right to complete payments ahead of time [19 May 1985; see Sch 3, para 35, below.]

94. (1) The debtor under a regulated consumer credit agreement is entitled at any time, by notice to the creditor and the payment to the creditor of all amounts payable by the debtor to him under the agreement (less any rebate allowable under section 95), to discharge the debtor's indebtedness under the agreement.

(2) A notice under subsection (1) may embody the exercise by the debtor of any option to purchase goods conferred on him by the agreement, and deal with any other matter arising on, or in relation to, the termination of the agreement.

Rebate on early settlement [19 May 1985; see Sch 3, para 35, below.]

95. (1) Regulations may provide for the allowance of a rebate of charges for credit to the debtor under a regulated consumer credit agreement where, under section 94, on refinancing, on breach of the agreement, or for any other reason, his indebtedness is discharged or becomes payable before the time fixed by the agreement, or any sum becomes payable by him before the time so fixed.

(2) Regulations under subsection (1) may provide for calculation of the rebate by reference to any sums paid or payable by the debtor or his relative under or in connection with the agreement (whether to the creditor or some

other person), including sums under linked transactions and other items in the total charge for credit.

Effect on linked transactions [May 1985; see Sch 3, para 35, below.]
96. (1) Where for any reason the indebtedness of the debtor under a regulated consumer credit agreement is discharged before the time fixed by the agreement, he, and any relative of his, shall at the same time be discharged from any liability under a linked transaction, other than a debt which has already become payable.

(2) Subsection (1) does not apply to a linked transaction which is itself an agreement providing the debtor or his relative with credit.

(3) Regulations may exclude linked transactions of the prescribed description from the operation of subsection (1).

Duty to give information [19 May 1985; see Sch 3, para 35, below.]
97. (1) The creditor under a regulated consumer credit agreement, within the prescribed period after he has received a request in writing to that effect from the debtor, shall give the debtor a statement in the prescribed form indicating, according to the information to which it is practicable for him to refer, the amount of the payment required to discharge the debtor's indebtedness under the agreement, together with the prescribed particulars showing how the amount is arrived at.

(2) Subsection (1) does not apply to a request made less than one month after a previous request under that subsection relating to the same agreement was complied with.

(3) If the creditor fails to comply with subsection (1)—
(a) he is not entitled, while the default continues, to enforce the agreement; and
(b) if the default continues for one month he commits an offence.

Termination of agreements

Duty to give notice of termination (non-default cases) [19 May 1985; see Sch 3, para 35, below.]
98. (1) The creditor or owner is not entitled to terminate a regulated agreement except by or after giving the debtor or hirer not less than seven days' notice of the termination.

(2) Subsection (1) applies only where—
(a) a period for the duration of the agreement is specified in the agreement, and
(b) that period has not ended when the creditor or owner does an act mentioned in subsection (1),
but so applies notwithstanding that, under the agreement, any party is entitled to terminate it before the end of the period so specified.

(3) A notice under subsection (1) is ineffective if not in the prescribed form.

(4) Subsection (1) does not prevent a creditor from treating the right to

draw on any credit as restricted or deferred and taking such steps as may be necessary to make the restriction or deferment effective.

(5) Regulations may provide that subsection (1) is not to apply to agreements described by the regulations.

(6) Subsection (1) does not apply to the termination of a regulated agreement by reason of any breach by the debtor or hirer of the agreement.

Right to terminate hire-purchase etc agreements [19 May 1985]

99. (1) At any time before the final payment by the debtor under a regulated hire-purchase or regulated conditional sale agreement falls due, the debtor shall be entitled to terminate the agreement by giving notice to any person entitled or authorised to receive the sums payable under the agreement.

(2) Termination of an agreement under subsection (1) does not affect any liability under the agreement which has accrued before the termination.

(3) Subsection (1) does not apply to a conditional sale agreement relating to land after the title to the land has passed to the debtor.

(4) In the case of a conditional sale agreement relating to goods, where the property in the goods, have become vested in the debtor, is transferred to a person who does not become the debtor under the agreement, the debtor shall not thereafter be entitled to terminate the agreement under subsection (1).

(5) Subject to subsection (4), where a debtor under a conditional sale agreement relating to goods terminates the agreement under this section after the property in the goods has become vested in him, the property in the goods shall thereupon vest in the person (the "previous owner") in whom it was vested immediately before it became vested in the debtor:

Provided that if the previous owner has died, or any other event has occurred whereby that property, if vested in him immediately before that event, would thereupon have vested in some other person, the property shall be treated as having devolved as if it had been vested in the previous owner immediately before his death or immediately before that event, as the case may be.

Liability of a debtor on termination of hire-purchase etc agreement [19 May 1985]

100. (1) Where a regulated hire-purchase or regulated conditional sale agreement is terminated under section 99 the debtor shall be liable, unless the agreement provides for a smaller payment, or does not provide for any payment, to pay the creditor the amount (if any) by which one-half of the total price exceeds the aggregate of the sums paid and the sums due in respect of the total price immediately before the termination.

(2) Where under a hire-purchase or conditional sale agreement the creditor is required to carry out any installation and the agreement specifies, as part of the total price, the amount to be paid in respect of the installation (the "installation charge") the reference in subsection (1) to one-half of the total price shall be construed as a reference to the aggregate of the installation charge and one-half of the remainder of the total price.

(3) If in any action the court is satisfied that a sum less than the amount specified in subsection (1) would be equal to the loss sustained by the creditor in consequence of the termination of the agreement by the debtor, the court may make an order for the payment of that sum in lieu of the amount specified in subsection (1).

(4) If the debtor has contravened an obligation to take reasonable care of the goods or land, the amount arrived at under subsection (1) shall be increased by the sum required to recompensate the creditor for that contravention, and subsection (2) shall have effect accordingly.

(5) Where the debtor on the termination of the agreement, wrongfully retains possession of goods to which the agreement relates, then, in any action brought by the creditor to recover possession of the goods from the debtor, the court, unless it is satisfied that having regard to the circumstances it would not be just to do so, shall order the goods to be delivered to the creditor without giving the debtor an option to pay the value of the goods.

Right to terminate hire agreement [19 May 1985]
101. (1) The hirer under a regulated consumer hire agreement is entitled to terminate the agreement by giving notice to any person entitled or authorised to receive the sums payable under the agreement.

(2) Termination of an agreement under subsection (1) does not affect any liability under the agreement which has accrued before the termination.

(3) A notice under subsection (1) shall not expire earlier than eighteen months after the making of the agreement, but apart from that the minimum period of notice to be given under subsection (1), unless the agreement provides for a shorter period, is as follows.

(4) If the agreement provides for the making of payments by the hirer to the owner at equal intervals, the minimum period of notice is the length of one interval or three months, whichever is less.

(5) If the agreement provides for the making of such payments at differing intervals, the minimum period of notice is the length of the shortest interval or three months, whichever is less.

(6) In any other case, the minimum period of notice is three months.

(7) This section does not apply to —
(a) any agreement which provides for the making by the hirer of payments which in total (and without breach of the agreement) exceed £900 in any year, or
(b) any agreement where —
   (i) goods are bailed or (in Scotland) hired to the hirer for the purposes of a business carried on by him, or the hirer holds himself out as requiring the goods for those purposes, and
   (ii) the goods are selected by the hirer, and acquired by the owner for the purposes of the agreement at the request of the hirer from any person other than the owner's associate, or
(c) any agreement where the hirer requires, or holds himself out as

requiring, the goods for the purpose of bailing or hiring them to other persons in the course of a business carried on by him.

(8) If, on an application made to the Director by a person carrying on a consumer hire business, it appears to the Director that it would be in the interest of hirers to do so, he may by notice to the applicant, and subject to such conditions (if any) as the Director may specify, this Act shall have effect accordingly.

(9) In the case of a modifying agreement, subsection (3) shall apply with the substitution, for "the making of the agreement" of "the making of the original agreement".

Agency for receiving notice of rescission [19 May 1985]

102. (1) Where the debtor or hirer under a regulated agreement claims to have a right to rescind the agreement, each of the following shall be deemed to be the agent of the creditor or owner for the purpose of receiving any notice rescinding the agreement which is served by the debtor or hirer—

(a) a credit-broker or supplier who was the negotiator in antecedent negotiations, and

(b) any person who, in the course of a business carried on by him, acted on behalf of the debtor or hirer in any negotiations for the agreement.

(2) In subsection (1) "rescind" does not include—

(a) service of a notice of cancellation, or

(b) termination of an agreement under section 99 or 101 or by the exercise of a right or power in that behalf expressly conferred by the agreement.

Termination statements [19 May 1985; see Sch 3, para 35, below.]

103. (1) If an individual (the "customer") serves on any person (the "trader") a notice—

(a) stating that—

(i) the customer was the debtor or hirer under a regulated agreement described in the notice, and the trader was the creditor or owner under the agreement, and

(ii) the cusomter has discharged his indebtedness to the trader under the agreement, and

(iii) the agreement has ceased to have any operation; and

(b) requiring the trader to give the customer a notice, signed by or on behalf of the trader, confirming that those statements are correct,

the trader shall, within the prescribed period after receiving the notice, either comply with it or serve on the customer a counter-notice stating that, as the case may be, he disputes the correctness of the notice or asserts that the customer is not indebted to him under the agreement.

(2) Where the trader disputes the correctness of the notice he shall give particulars of the way in which he alleges it to be wrong.

(3) Subsection (1) does not apply in relation to any agreement if the trader has previously complied with that subsection on the service of a notice under it with respect to that agreement.

(4) Subsection (1) does not apply to a non-commercial agreement.

(5) If the trader fails to comply with subsection (1), and the default continues for one month, he commits an offence.

.   .   .

General

Form and content of securities [19 May 1985]

105. (1) Any security provided in relation to a regulated agreement shall be expressed in writing.

(2) Regulations may prescribe the form and content of documents ("security instruments") to be made in compliance with subsection (1).

3 Regulations under subsection (2) may in particular—

(a) require specified information to be included in the prescribed manner in documents, and other specified material to be excluded;

(b) contain requirements to ensure that specified information is clearly brought to the attention of the surety, and that one part of a document is not given insufficient or excessive prominence compared with another.

(4) A security instrument is not properly executed unless—

(a) a document in the prescribed form, itself containing all the prescribed terms and conforming to regulations under subsection (2), is signed in the prescribed manner by or on behalf of the surety, and

(b) the document embodies all the terms of the security, other than implied terms, and

(c) the document, when presented or sent for the purpose of being signed or on behalf of the surety, is in such state that its terms are readily legible, and

(d) when the document is presented or sent for the purpose of being signed by or on behalf of the surety there is also presented or sent a copy of the document.

(5) A security instrument is not properly executed unless—

(a) where the security is provided after, or at the time when, the regulated agreement is made, a copy of the executed agreement, together with a copy of any other document referred to in it, is given to the surety at the time the security is provided, or

(b) where the security is provided before the regulated agreement is made, a copy of the executed agreement, together with a copy of any other document referred to in it, is given to the surety within seven days after the regulated agreement is made.

(6) Subsection (1) does not apply to a security provided by the debtor or hirer.

(7) If—

(a) in contravention of subsection (1) a security is not expressed in writing, or

177

(b) a security instrument is improperly executed,

the security, so far as provided in relation to a regulated agreement, is enforceable against the surety on an order of the court only.

(8) If an application for an order under subsection (7) is dismissed (except on technical grounds only) section 106 (ineffective securities) shall apply to the security.

(9) Regulations under section 60 (1) shall include provision requiring documents embodying regulated agreements also to embody any security provided in relation to a regulated agreement by the debtor or hirer.

Ineffective securities [31 July 1974]

106. Where under any provision of this Act, this section is applied to any security provided in relation to a regulated agreement, then, subject to section 177 (saving for registered charges),—

- (a) the security, so far as it is so provided, shall be treated as never having effect;
- (b) any property lodged with the creditor or owner solely for the purposes of the security as so provided shall be returned by him forthwith;
- (c) the creditor or owner shall take any necessary action to remove or cancel an entry in any register, so far as the entry relates to the security as so provided; and
- (d) any amount received by the creditor or owner on realisation of the security shall, so far as it is referable to the agreement, be repaid to the surety.

Duty to give information to surety under fixed-sum credit agreements [19 May 1985; see Sch 3, para 37, below.]

107. (1) The creditor under a regulated agreement for fixed-sum credit in relation to which security is provided, within the prescribed period after receiving a request in writing to that effect from the surety and payment of a fee of 50 new pence, shall give to the surety (if a different person from the debtor)—

- (a) a copy of the executed agreement (if any) and of any other document referred to in it;
- (b) a copy of the security instrument (if any); and
- (c) a statement signed by or on behalf of the creditor showing, according to the information to which it is practicable for him to refer,—
  - (i) the total sum paid under the agreement by the debtor,
  - (ii) the total sum which has become payable under the agreement by the debtor but remains unpaid, and the various amounts comprised in that total sum, with the date when each became due, and
  - (iii) the total sum which is to become payable under the agreement by the debtor, and the various amounts comprised in that total sum, with the date, or mode of determining the date, when each becomes due.

(2) If the creditor possesses insufficient information to enable him to

ascertain the amounts and dates mentioned in subsection (1) (c) (iii), he shall be taken to comply with that sub-paragraph if his statement under subsection (1) (c) gives the basis on which, under the regulated agreement, they would fall to be ascertained.

(3) Subsection (1) does not apply to—
(a) an agreement under which no sum is, or will or may become, payable by the debtor, or
(b) a request made less than one month after a previous request under that subsection relating to the same agreement was complied with.

(4) If the creditor under an agreement fails to comply with subsection (1)—
(a) he is not entitled, while the default continues, to enforce the security, so far as provided in relation to the agreement; and
(b) if the default continues for one month he commits an offence.

(5) This section does not apply to a non-commercial agreement.

Duty to give information to surety under running-account credit agreement
[19 May 1985; see Sch 3, para 37, below.]
108. (1) The creditor under a regulated agreement for running-account credit in relation to which security is provided, within the prescribed period after receiving a request in writing to that effect from the surety and payment of a fee of 50 new pence, shall give to the surety (if a different person from the debtor)—
(a) a copy of the executed agreement (if any) and of any other document referred to in it;
(b) a copy of the security instrument (if any); and
(c) a statement signed by or on behalf of the creditor showing, according to the information to which it is practicable for him to refer,—
(i) the state of the account, and
(ii) the amount, if any, currently payable under the agreement by the debtor to the creditor, and
(iii) the amounts and due dates of any payments which, if the debtor does not draw further on the account, will later become payable under the agreement by the debtor to the creditor.

(2) If the creditor possesses insufficient information to enable him to ascertain the amounts and dates mentioned in subsection (1) (c) (iii), he shall be taken to comply with that sub-paragraph if his statement under subsection (1) (c) gives the basis on which, under the regulated agreement, they would fall to be ascertained.

(3) Subsection (1) does not apply to—
(a) an agreement under which no sum is, or will or may become; payable by the debtor, or
(b) a request made less than one month after a previous request under that subsection relating to the same agreement was complied with.

(4) If the creditor under an agreement fails to comply with subsection (1)—

(a) he is not entitled, while the default continues, to enforce the security, so far as provided in relation to the agreement; and

(b) if the default continues for one month he commits an offence

(5) This section does not apply to a non-commercial agreement.

Duty to give information to surety under consumer hire agreement [19 May 1985; see Sch 3, para 37, below.]

109. (1) The owner under a regulated consumer hire agreement in relation to which security is provided, within the prescribed period after receiving a request in writing to that effect from the surety and payment of a fee of 50 new pence, shall give to the surety (if a different person from the hirer)—

(a) a copy of the executed agreement and of any other document referred to in it;

(b) a copy of the security instrument (if any); and

(c) a statement signed by or on behalf of the owner showing, according to the information to which it is practicable for him to refer, the total sum which has become payable under the agreement by the hirer but remains unpaid and the various amounts comprised in that total sum, with the date when each became due.

(2) Subsection (1) does not apply to—

(a) an agreement under which no sum is, or will or may become, payable by the hirer, or

(b) a request made less than one month after a previous request under that subsection relating to the same agreement was complied with.

(3) If the owner under an agreement fails to comply with subsection (1)—

(a) he is not entitled, while the default continues, to enforce the security, so far as provided in relation to the agreement; and

(b) if the default continues for one month he commits an offence.

(4) This section does not apply to a non-commercial agreement.

Duty to give information to debtor or hirer [19 May 1985; see Sch 3, para 37, below.]

110. (1) The creditor or owner under a regulated agreement, within the prescribed period after receiving a request in writing to that effect from the debtor or hirer and payment of a fee of new pence, shall give the debtor or hirer a copy of any security instrument executed in relation to the agreement after the making of the agreement.

(2) Subsection (1) does not apply to—

(a) a non-commercial agreement, or

(b) an agreement under which no sum is, or will or may become, payable by the debtor or hirer, or

(c) a request made less than one month after a previous request under subsection (1) relating to the same agreement was complied with.   (3) If the creditor or owner under an agreement fails to comply with subsection (1)—

(a) he is not entitled, while the default continues, to enforce the security (so far as provided in relation to the agreement); and

(b) if the default continues for one month he commits an offence.

Duty to give surety copy of default etc notice [19 May 1985; see Sch 3 para 38, below].

111. (1) When a default notice or a notice under section 76 (1) or 98 (1) is served on a debtor or hirer, a copy of the notice shall be served by the creditor or owner on any surety (if a different person from the debtor or hirer).

(2) If the creditor or owner fails to comply with subsection (1) in the case of any surety, the security is enforceable against the surety (in respect of the breach or other matter to which the notice relates) on an order of the court only.

Realisation of securities [31 July 1974]

112. Subject to section 121, regulations may provide for any matters relating to the sale or other realisation, by the creditor or owner, of property over which any right has been provided by way of security in relation to an actual or prospective regulated agreement, other than a non-commercial agreement

Act not to be evaded by use of security [31 July 1974]

113. (1) Where a security is provided in relation to an actual or prospective regulated agreement, the security shall not be enforced so as to benefit the creditor or owner, directly or indirectly, to an extent greater (whether as respects the amount of any payment or the time or manner of its being made) than would be the case if the security were not provided and any obligations of the debtor or hirer, or his relative, under or in relation to the agreement were carried out to the extent (if any) to which they would be enforced under this Act.

(2) In accordance with subsection (1), where a regulated agreement is enforceable on an order of the court or the Director only, any security provided in relation to the agreement is enforceable (so far as provided in relation to the agreement) where such an order has been made in relation to the agreement, but not otherwise.

(3) Where—

(a) a regulated agreement is cancelled under section 69 (1) or becomes subject to section 69 (2), or

(b) a regulated agreement is terminated under section 91, or

(c) in relation to any agreement an application for an order under section 40 (2), 65 (1), 124 (1) or 149 (2) is dismissed (except on technical grounds only), or

(d) a declaration is made by the court under section 142 (1) (refusal of enforcement order) as respects any regulated agreement,

section 106 shall apply to any security provided in relation to the agreement.

(4) Where subsection (3) (d) applies and the declaration relates to a part only of the regulated agreement, section 106 shall apply to the security only so far as it concerns that part.

(5) In the case of a cancelled agreement, the duty imposed on the debtor or hirer by section 71 or 72 shall not be enforceable before the creditor or

owner has discharged any duty imposed on him by section 106 (as applied by subsection (3) (a)).

(6) If the security is provided in relation to a prospective agreement or transaction, the security shall be enforceable in relation to the agreement or transaction only after the time (if any) when the agreement is made; and until that time the person providing the security shall be entitled, by notice to the creditor or owner, to require that section 106 shall thereupon apply to the security.

(7) Where an indemnity is given in a case where the debtor or hirer is a minor, or is otherwise not of full capacity, the reference in subsection (1) to the extent to which his obligations would be enforced shall be read in relation to the indemnity as a reference to the extent to which they would be enforced if he were of full capacity.

(8) Subsections (1) to (3) also apply where a security is provided in relation to an actual or prospective linked transaction, and in that case —

(a) references to the agreement shall be read as references to the linked transaction, and

(b) references to the creditor or owner shall be read as references to any person (other than the debtor or hirer, or his relative) who is a party, or prospective party, to the linked transaction.

.   .   .

Negotiable instruments

Restrictions on taking and negotiating instruments [19 May 1985]

123. (1) A creditor or owner shall not take a negotiable instrument, other than a bank note or cheque, in discharge of any sum payable —

(a) by the debtor or hirer under a regulated agreement, or

(b) by any person as surety in relation to the agreement.

(2) The creditor or owner shall not negotiate a cheque taken by him in discharge of a sum payable as mentioned in subsection (1) except to a banker (within the meaning of the Bills of Exchange Act 1882).

(3) The creditor or owner shall not take a negotiable instrument as security for the discharge of any sum payable as mentioned in subsection (1).

(4) A person takes a negotiable instrument as security for the discharge of a sum if the sum is intended to be paid in some other way, and the negotiable instrument is to be presented for payment only if the sum is not paid in that way.

(5) This section does not apply where the regulated agreement is a non-commercial agreement.

(6) The Secretary of State may by order provide that this section shall not apply where the regulated agreement has a connection with a country outside the United Kingdom.

Consequences of breach of s 123 [19 May 1985]

124. (1) After any contravention of section 123 has occurred in relation to a sum payable as mentioned in section 123(1)(*a*), the agreement under which the sum is payable is enforceable against the debtor or hirer on an order of the court only.

(2) After any contravention of section 123 has occurred in relation to a sum payable by any surety, the security is enforceable on an order of the court only.

(3) Where an application for an order under subsection (2) is dismissed (except on technical grounds only) section 106 shall apply to the security.

Holders in due course [19 May 1985]

125. (1) A person who takes a negotiable instrument in contravention of section 123(1) or (3) is not a holder in due course, and is not entitled to enforce the instrument.

(2) Where a person negotiates a cheque in contravention of section 123(2), his doing so constitutes a defect in his title within the meaning of the Bills of Exchange Act 1882.

(3) If a person mentioned in section 123(1)*(a)* or *(b)* ("the protected person") becomes liable to a holder in due course of an instrument taken from the protected person in contravention of section 123(1) or (3), or taken from the protected person and negotiated in contravention of section 123(2), the creditor or owner shall indemnify the protected person in respect of that liability.

(4) Nothing in this Act affects the rights of the holder in due course of any negotiable instrument.

Land mortgages

Enforcement of land mortgages [9 May 1985]

126. A land mortgage securing a regulated agreement is enforceable (so far as provided in relation to the agreement) on an order of the court only.

PART IX—JUDICIAL CONTROL

Enforcement of certain regulated agreements and securities

Enforcement orders in cases of infringement [31 July 1974]

127. (1) In the case of an application for an enforcement order under—

  (a) section 65 (1) (improperly executed agreements), or
  (b) section 105 (7) or (b) (improperly executed security instruments), or
  (c) section 111 (2) (failure to serve copy of notice on surety), or
  (d) section 124 (1) or (2) (taking of negotiable instrument in contravention of section 123),

the court shall dismiss the application if, but (subject to subsections (3) and (4)) only if, it considers it just to do so having regard to—

   (i) prejudice caused to any person by the contravention in question, and the degree of culpability for it; and
   (ii) the powers conferred on the court by subsection (2) and sections 135 and 136.

(2) If it appears to the court just to do so, it may in an enforcement order

reduce or discharge any sum payable by the debtor or hirer, or any surety, so as to compensate him for prejudice suffered as a result of the contravention in question.

(3) The court shall not make an enforcement order under section 65 (1) if section 61 (1) (a) (signing of agreements) was not complied with unless a document (whether or not in the prescribed form and complying with regulations under section 60 (1)) itself containing all the prescribed terms of the agreement was signed by the debtor or hirer (whether or not in the prescribed manner).

(4) The court shall not make an enforcement order under section 65 (1) in the case of a cancellable agreement if—

(a) a provision of section 62 or 63 was not complied with, and the creditor or owner did not give a copy of the executed agreement, and of any other document referred to in it, to the debtor or hirer before the commencement of the proceedings in which the order is sought, or

(b) section 64 (1) was not complied with.

(5) Where an enforcement order is made in a case to which subsection (3) applies, the order may direct that the regulated agreement is to have effect as if it did not include a term omitted from the document signed by the debtor or hirer.

Enforcement orders on death of debtor or hirer [31 July 1974]

128. The court shall make an order under section 86 (2) if, but only if, the creditor or owner proves that he has been unable to satisfy himself that the present and future obligations of the debtor or hirer under the agreement are likely to be discharged.

Extension of time

Time orders [31 July 1974]

129. (1) If it appears to the court just to do so—

(a) on an application for an enforcement order; or

(b) on an application made by a debtor or hirer under this paragraph after service on him of—

(i) a default notice, or

(ii) a notice under section 76 (1) or 98 (1); or

(c) in an action brought by a creditor or owner to enforce a regulated agreement or any security, or recover possession of any goods or land to which a regulated agreement relates,

the court may make an order under this section (a "time order").

(2) A time order shall provide for one or both of the following, as the court considers just—

(a) the payment by the debtor or hirer or any surety of any sum owed under a regulated agreement or a security by such instalments, payable at such times, as the court, having regard to the means of the debtor or hirer and any surety, considers reasonable;

(b) the remedying by the debtor or hirer of any breach of a regulated agreement (other than non-payment of money) within such period as the court may specify.

Supplemental provisions about time orders [31 July 1974]

130. (1) Where in accordance with rules of court an offer to pay any sum by instalments is made by the debtor or hirer and accepted by the creditor or owner, the court may in accordance with rules of court make a time order under section 129 (2) (a) giving effect to the offer without hearing evidence of means.

(2) In the case of a hire-purchase or conditional sale agreement only, a time order under section 129 (2) (a) may deal with sums which, although not payable by the debtor at the time the order is made, would if the agreement continued in force become payable under it subsequently.

(3) A time order under section 129 (2) (a) shall not be made where the regulated agreement is secured by a pledge if, by virtue of regulations made under section 76 (5), 87 (4) or 98 (5), service of a notice is not necessary for enforcement of the pledge.

(4) Where, following the making of a time order in relation to a regulated hire-purchase or conditional sale agreement or a regulated consumer hire agreement, the debtor or hirer is in possession of the goods, he shall be treated (except in the case of a debtor to whom the creditor's title has passed) as a bailiee or (in Scotland) a custodier of the goods under the terms of the agreement, notwithstanding that the agreement has been terminated.

(5) Without prejudice to anything done by the creditor or owner before the commencement of the period specified in a time order made under section 129 (2) (b) ("the relevant period")—

(a) he shall not while the relevant period subsists take in relation to the agreement any action such as is mentioned in section 87 (1);

(b) where—

(i) a provision of the agreement ("the secondary provision") becomes operative only on breach of another provision of the agreement ("the primary provision"), and

(ii) the time order provides for the remedying of such a breach of the primary provision within the relevant period.

he shall not treat the secondary provision as operative before the end of that period;

(c) if while the relevant period subsists the breach to which the order relates is remedied it shall be treated as not having occurred.

(6) On the application of any person affected by a time order, the court may vary or revoke the order.

Protection of property pending proceedings

Protection orders [31 July 1974]

131. The court, on the application of the creditor or owner under a regulated agreement, may make such orders as it thinks just for protecting any property of the creditor or owner, or property subject to any security, from damage or depreciation pending the determination of any proceedings under this Act, including orders restricting or prohibiting use of the property or giving directions as to its custody.

Hire and hire-purchase etc agreements

Financial relief for hirer [31 July 1974]

132. (1) Where the owner under a regulated consumer hire agreement recovers possession of goods to which the agreement relates otherwise than by action, the hirer may apply to the court for an order that—

(a) the whole or part of any sum paid by the hirer to the owner in respect of the goods shall be repaid, and

(b) the obligation to pay the whole or part of any sum owed by the hirer to the owner in respect of the goods shall cease.

and if it appears to the court just to do so, having regard to the extent of the enjoyment of the goods by the hirer, the court shall grant the application in full or in part.

(2) Where in proceedings relating to a regulated consumer hire agreement the court makes an order for the delivery to the owner of goods to which the agreement relates the court may include in the order the like provision as may be made in an order under subsection (1).

Hire-purchase etc agreements: special powers of court [31 July 1974]

133. (1) If, in relation to a regulated hire-purchase or conditional sale agreement, it appears to the court just to do so—

(a) on an application for an enforcement order or time order; or

(b) in an action brought by the creditor to recover possession of goods to which the agreement relates.

the court may—

(i) make an order (a "return order") for the return to the creditor of goods to which the agreement relates;

(ii) make an order (a "transfer order") for the transfer to the debtor of the creditor's title to certain goods to which the agreement relates ("the transferred goods"), and the return to the creditor of the remainder of the goods.

(2) In determining for the purposes of this section how much of the total price has been paid ("the paid-up sum"), the court may—

(a) treat any sum paid by the debtor, or owed by the creditor, in relation to the goods as part of the paid-up-sum;

(b) deduct any sum owed by the debtor in relation to the goods (otherwise than as part of the total price) from the paid-up sum,

and make corresponding reductions in amounts so owed.

(3) Where a transfer is made, the transferred goods shall be such of the goods to which the agreement relates as the court thinks just; but a transfer order shall be made only where the paid-up sum exceeds the part of the total price referable to the transferred goods by an amount equal to at least one-third of the unpaid balance of the total price.

(4) Notwithstanding the making of a return order or transfer order, the debtor may at any time before the goods enter the possession of the creditor, on payment of the balance of the total price and the fulfilment of any other necessary conditions, claim the goods ordered to be returned to the creditor.

(5) When, in pursuance of a time order or under this section, the total price of goods under a regulated hire-purchase agreement or regulated conditional sale agreement is paid and any other necessary conditions are fulfilled, the creditor's title to the goods vests in the debtor.

(6) If, in contravention of a return order or transfer order, any goods to which the order relates are not returned to the creditor, on the application of the creditor, may—

(a) revoke so much of the order as relates to those goods, and
(b) order the debtor to pay the creditor the unpaid portion of so much of the total price as is referable to those goods.

(7) For the purposes of this section, the part of the total price referable to any goods is the part assigned to those goods by the agreement or (if no such assignment is made) the part determined by the court to be reasonable.

Evidence of adverse detention in hire-purchase etc cases [31 July 1974]
134. (1) Where goods are comprised in a regulated hire-purchase agreement, regulated conditional sale agreement or regulated consumer hire agreement, and the creditor or owner—

(a) brings an action or makes an application to enforce a right to recover possession of the goods from the debtor or hirer, and
(b) proves that a demand for the delivery of the goods was included in the default notice under section 88 (5), or that, after the right to recover possession of the goods accrued but before the action was begun or the application was made, he made a request in writing to the debtor or hirer to surrender the goods.

then, for the purposes of the claim, of the creditor or owner to recover possession of the goods, the possession of them by the debtor or hirer shall be deemed to be adverse to the creditor or owner.

(2) In subsection (1) "the debtor or hirer" includes a person in possession of the goods at any time between the debtor's or hirer's death and the grant of probate or administration, or (in Scotland) confirmation.

(3) Nothing in this section affects a claim for damages for conversion or (in Scotland) for delict.

Supplemental provisions as to orders

Power to impose conditions or suspend operation of order [31 July 1974]
135. If it considers it just to do so, the court may in an order made by it in relation to a regulated agreement include provisions—

(a) making the operation of any term of the order conditional on the doing of specified acts by any party to the proceedings;
(b) suspending the operation of any term of the order either—
  (i) until such time as the court subsequently directs, or

(ii) until the occurrence of a specified act or omission.

(2) The court shall not suspend the operation of a term requiring the delivery up of goods by any person unless satisfied that the goods are in his possession or control.

(3) In the case of a consumer hire agreement, the court shall not so use its powers under subsection (1) (b) as to extend the period for which, under the terms of the agreement, the hirer is entitled to possession of the goods to which the agreement relates.

(4) On the application of any person affected by a provision included under subsection (1), the court may vary the provision.

Power to vary agreements and securities [31 July 1974]
136. The court may in an order made by it under this Act include such provision as it considers just for amending any agreement or security in consequence of a term of the order.

Extortionate credit bargains

Extortionate credit bargains [see Sch 3, paras 42 and 43 below.]
137. (1) If the court finds a credit bargain extortionate it may reopen the credit agreement so as to do justice between the parties.

(2) In this section and sections 138 to 140—
  (a) "credit agreement" means any agreement between an individual (the "debtor") and any other person (the "creditor") by which the creditor provides the debtor with credit of any amount, and
  (b) "credit bargain"—
    (i) where no transaction other than the credit agreement is to be taken into account in computing the total charge for credit, means the credit agreement, or
    (ii) where one or more other transactions are to be so taken into account, means the credit agreement and those other transactions, taken together.

When bargains are extortionate [see Sch 3, paras 42 and 43 below.]
138. (1) A credit bargain is extortionate if it—
  (a) requires the debtor or a relative of his to make payments (whether unconditionally, or on certain contingencies) which are grossly exorbitant, or
  (b) otherwise grossly contravenes ordinary principles of fair dealing.

(2) In determining whether a credit bargain is extortionate, regard shall be had to such evidence as is adduced concerning—
  (a) interest rates prevailing at the time it was made,
  (b) the factors mentioned in subsection (3) to (5), and
  (c) any other relevant considerations.

(3) Factors applicable under subsection (2) in relation to the debtor include—
  (a) his age, experience, business capacity and state of health; and

    (b) the degree to which, at the time of making the credit bargain, he was under financial pressure, and the nature of that pressure.

(4) Factors applicable under subsection (2) in relation to the creditor include—

    (a) the degree of risk accepted by him, having regard to the value of any security provided;

    (b) his relationship to the debtor; and

    (c) whether or not a colourable cash price was quoted for any goods or services included in the credit bargain.

(5) Factors applicable under subsection (2) in relation to a linked transaction include the question how far the transaction was reasonably required for the protection of debtor or creditor, or was in the interest of the debtor.

Reopening of extortionate agreements [see Sch 3, paras 42 and 43, below.]
139.—(1) A credit agreement may, if the court thinks just, be reopened on the ground that the credit bargain is extortionate—

    (a) on an application for the purpose made by the debtor or any surety to the High Court, county court or sheriff court; or

    (b) at the instance of the debtor or a surety in any proceedings to which the debtor and creditor are parties, being proceedings to enforce the credit agreement, any security relating to it, or any linked transaction; or

    (c) at the instance of the debtor or a surety in other proceedings in any court where the amount paid or payable under the credit agreement is relevant.

(2) In reopening the agreement, the court may, for the purpose of relieving the debtor or a surety from payment of any sum in excess of that fairly due and reasonable, by order—

    (a) direct accounts to be taken, or (in Scotland) an accounting to be made, between any persons,

    (b) set aside the whole or part of any obligation imposed on the debtor or a surety by the credit bargain or any related agreement,

    (c) require the creditor to repay the whole or part of any sum paid under the credit bargain or any related agreement by the debtor or a surety, whether paid to the creditor or any other person,

    (d) direct the return to the surety of any property provided for the purposes of the security, or

    (e) alter the terms of the credit agreement or any security instrument.

(3) An order may be made under subsection (2) notwithstanding that its effect is to place a burden on the creditor in respect of an advantage unfairly enjoyed by another person who is a party to a linked transaction.

(4) An order under subsection (2) shall not alter the effect of any judgment.

(5) In England and Wales an application under subsection (1) (a) shall be brought only in the county court in the case of—

    (a) a regulated agreement, or

(b) an agreement (not being a regulated agreement) under which the creditor provides the debtor with fixed-sum credit not exceeding the county court limit or running-account credit on which the credit limit does not exceed the county court limit.

(5A) In the preceding subsection "the county court limit" means the county court limit for the time being specified by an Order in Council under section 145 of the County Courts Act 1984 as the county court limit for the purposes of that subsection

. . .

Interpretation of sections 137 to 139 [see Sch 3, paras 42 and 43 below.]
140. Where the credit agreement is not a regulated agreement, expressions used in sections 137 to 139 which, apart from this section, apply only to regulated agreements, shall be construed as nearly as may be as if the credit agreement were a regulated agreement.

Miscellaneous

Jurisdiction and parties [31 July 1974]
141. (1) In England and Wales the county court shall have jurisdiction to hear and determine—
(a) any action by the creditor or owner to enforce a regulated agreement or any security relating to it;
(b) any action to enforce any linked transaction against the debtor or hirer or his relative,
and such an action shall not be brought in any other court.

(2) Where an action or application is brought in the High Court which, by virtue of this Act, ought to have been brought in the county court it shall not be treated as improperly brought, but shall be transferred to the county court.

. . .

(5) Except as may be provided by rules of court, all the parties to a regulated agreement, and any surety, shall be made parties to any proceedings relating to the agreement.

Power to declare rights of parties [31 July 1974]
142. (1) Where under any provision of this Act a thing can be done by a creditor or owner on an enforcement order only, and either—
(a) the court dismisses (except on technical grounds only) an application for the enforcement order, or
(b) where no such application has been made or such an application has been dismissed on technical grounds only, an interested party applies to the court for a declaration under this subsection,
the court may if it thinks just make a declaration that the creditor or owner

is not entitled to do that thing, and thereafter no application for an enforcement order in respect of it shall be entertained.

(2) Where—

(a) a regulated agreement or linked transaction is cancelled under section 69 (1), or becomes subject to section 69 (2), or

(b) a regulated agreement is terminated under section 91,

and an interested party applies to the court for a declaration under this subsection, the court may make a declaration to that effect.

.   .   .

PART X—ANCILLARY CREDIT BUSINESS

Definitions

Types of ancillary credit business [31 July 1974]

145. (1) An ancillary credit business is any business so far as it comprises or relates to—

(a) credit-brokerage,

(b) debt-adjusting,

(c) debt-counselling,

(d) debt-collecting, or

(e) the operation of a credit reference agency.

(2) Subject to section 146 (5), credit brokerage is the effecting of introductions—

(a) of individuals desiring to obtain credit—

(i) to persons carrying on businesses to which this sub-paragraph applies, or

(ii) in the case of an individual desiring to obtain credit to finance the acquisition or provision of a dwelling occupied or to be occupied by himself or his relative, to any person carrying on a business in the course of which he provides credit secured on land, or

(b) of individuals desiring to obtain goods on hire to persons carrying on businesses to which this paragraph applies, or

(c) of individuals desiring to obtain credit, or to obtain goods on hire, to other credit-brokers.

(3) Subsection (2) (a) (i) applies to—

(a) a consumer credit business;

(b) a business which comprises or relates to consumer credit agreements being, otherwise than by virtue of section 16 (5) (a), exempt agreements;

(c) a business which comprises or relates to unregulated agreements where—

(i) the proper law of the agreement is the law of a country outside the United Kingdom, and

(ii) if the proper law of the agreement were the law of a part of the United Kingdom it would be a regulated consumer credit agreement.

(4) Subsection (2) (b) applies to—

(a) a consumer hire business;

(b) a business which comprises or relates to unregulated agreements where—

(i) the proper law of the agreement is the law of a country outside the United Kingdom, and

(ii) if the proper law of the agreement were the law of a part of the United Kingdom it would be a regulated consumer hire agreement.

(5) Subject to section 146 (6), debt-adjusting is, in relation to debts due under consumer credit agreements or consumer hire agreements,—

(a) negotiating with the creditor or owner, on behalf of the debtor or hirer, terms for the discharge of a debt, or

(b) taking over, in return for payments by the debtor or hirer, his obligation to discharge a debt, or

(c) any similar activity concerned with the liquidation of a debt.

(6) Subject to section 146 (6), debt-counselling is the giving of advice to debtors or hirers about the liquidation of debts due under consumer credit agreements or consumer hire agreements.

(7) Subject to section 146 (6), debt-collecting is the taking of steps to procure payment of debts due under consumer credit agreements or consumer hire agreements.

(8) A credit reference agency is a person carrying on a business comprising the furnishing of persons with information relevant to the financial standing of individuals, being information collected by the agency for that purpose.

Exceptions from section 145 [31 July1974]

146. (1) A barrister or advocate acting in that capacity is not to be treated as doing so in the course of any ancillary credit business.

(2) A solicitor engaging in contentious business (as defined in section 86 (1) of the Solicitors Act 1957) is not to be treated as doing so in the course of any ancillary credit business.

(3) A solicitor within the meaning of the Solicitors (Scotland) Act 1933 engaging in business done in or for the purposes of proceedings before a court or before an arbiter is not to be treated as doing so in the course of any ancillary credit business.

(4) A solicitor in Northern Ireland engaging in business done, whether as solicitor or advocate, in or for the purposes of proceedings begun before a court (including the Lands Tribunal for Northern Ireland) or before an arbitrator appointed under the Arbitration Act (Northern Ireland) 1937, not being business contained in section 2 of the Probates and Letters of Administration (Ireland) Act 1857, is not to be treated as doing so in the course of any ancillary credit business.

(5) For the purposes of section 145 (2), introductions effected by an individual by canvassing off trade premises either debtor-creditor-supplier agreements falling within section (12) (a) or regulated consumer hire agreements shall be disregarded if—

(a) the introductions are not effected by him in the capacity of an employee, and

(b) he does not by any other method effect introductions falling within section 145 (2).

(6) It is not debt-adjusting, debt-counselling or debt-collecting for a person to do anything in relation to a debt arising under an agreement if—

(a) he is the creditor or owner under the agreement, otherwise than by virtue of an assignment, or

(b) he is the creditor or owner under the agreement by virtue of an assignment made in connection with the transfer to the assignee of any business other than a debt-collecting business, or

(c) he is the supplier in relation to the agreement, or

(d) he is a credit-broker who has acquired the business of the person who was the supplier in relation to the agreement, or

(e) he is a person prevented by subsection (5) from being treated as a credit-broker, and the agreement was made in consequence of an introduction (whether made by him or another person) which, under subsection (5), is to be disregarded.

Licensing

Application of Part III [see Sch 3, para 44, below.]
147. (1) The provisions of Part III (except section 40) apply to an ancillary credit business as they apply to a consumer credit business.

(2) Without prejudice to the generality of section 26, regulations under that section (as applied by subsection (1)) may include provisions regulating the collection and dissemination of information by credit reference agencies.

Agreement for services of unlicensed trader [see Sch 3, para 45, below.]
148. (1) An agreement for the services of a person carrying on an ancillary credit business (the "trader"), if made when the trader was unlicensed, is enforceable against the other pary (the "customer") only where the Director has made an order under subsection (2) which applies to the agreement.

(2) The trader or his successor in title may apply to the Director for an order that agreements within subsection (1) are to be treated as if made when the trader was licensed.

(3) Unless the Director determines to make an order under subsection (2) in accordance with the application, he shall, before determining the application, by notice—

(a) inform the trader, giving his reasons, that, as the case may be, he is minded to refuse the application, or to grant it in terms different from those applied for, describing them, and

(b) invite the trader to submit to the Director representations in support of his application in accordance with section 34.

(4) In determining whether or not to make an order under subsection (2) in respect of any period the Director shall consider, in addition to any other relevant factors,—

    (a) how far, if at all, customers under agreements made by the trader during that period were prejudiced by the trader's conduct,

(b) whether or not the Director would have been likely to grant a licence covering that period on an application by the trader, and

    (c) the degree of culpability for the failure to obtain a licence.

    (5) If the Director thinks fit, he may in an order under subsection (2)—

    (a) limit the order to specified agreements, or agreements of a specified description or made at a specified time;

(b) make the order conditional on the doing of specified acts by the trader.

Regulated agreements made on introduction by unlicensed credit-broker [see Sch 3, para 46, below.]

149. (1) A regulated agreement made by a debtor or hirer who, for the purpose of making that agreement, was introduced to the creditor or owner by an unlicensed credit-broker is enforceable against the debtor or hirer only where—

    (a) on the application of the credit-broker, the Director has made an order under section 148 (2) in respect of a period including the time when the introduction was made, and the order does not (whether in general terms or specifically) exclude the application of this paragraph to the regulated agreement, or

    (b) the Director has made an order under subsection (2) which applies to the agreement.

(2) Where during any period individuals were introduced to a person carrying on a consumer credit business or consumer hire business by an unlicensed credit-broker for the purpose of making regulated agreements with the person carrying on that business, that person or his successor in title may apply to the Director for an order that regulated agreements so made are to be treated as if the credit-broker had been licensed at the time of the introduction.

(3) Unless the Director determines to make an order under subsection (2) in accordance with the application, he shall, before determining the application, by notice—

    (a) inform the applicant, giving his reasons, that, as the case may be, he is minded to refuse the application, or to grant it in terms different from those applied for, describing them, and

    (b) invite the applicant to submit to the Director representations in support of his application in accordance with section 34.

(4) In determining whether or not to make an order under subsection (2) the Director shall consider, in addition to any other relevant factors—

    (a) how far, if at all, debtors or hirers under regulated agreements to which the application relates were prejudiced by the credit-broker's conduct, and

    (b) the degree of culpability of the applicant in facilitating the carrying on by the credit-broker of his business when unlicensed.

(5) If the Director thinks fit, he may in an order under subsection (2)—

(a) limit the order to specified agreements, or agreements of a specified description or made at a specified time;

(b) make the order conditional on the doing of specified acts by the applicant.

.   .   .

No further sanctions for breach of Act [31 July 1974]

170. (1) A breach of any requirement made (otherwise than by any court) by or under this Act shall incur no civil or criminal sanction as being such a breach, except to the extent (if any) expressly provided by or under this Act.

.   .   .

(3) Subsection (1) does not prevent the grant of an injunction, or the making of an order of certiorari, mandamus or prohibition or as respects Scotland the grant of an interdict or of an order under section 91 of the Court of Session Act 1868 (order for specific performance of statutory duty).

Onus of proof in various proceedings [31 July 1974]

171. (1) If an agreement contains a term signifying that in the opinion of the parties section 10 (3) (iii) does not apply to the agreement, it shall be taken not to apply unless the contrary is proved.

(2) It shall be assumed in any proceedings, unless the contrary is proved, that when a person initiated a transaction as mentioned in section 19 (1) (c) he knew the principal agreement had been made, or contemplated that it might be made.

(3) Regulations under section 44 or 52 may make provision as to the onus of proof in any proceedings to enforce the regulations.

(4) In proceedings brought by the creditor under a credit-token agreement—

(a) it is for the creditor to prove that the credit-token was lawfully supplied to the debtor, and was accepted by him, and

(b) if the debtor alleges that any use made of the credit-token was not authorised by him, it is for the creditor to prove either—

(i) that the use was so authorised, or

(ii) that the use occurred before the creditor had been given notice under section 84 (3).

(5) In proceedings under section 50 (1) in respect of a document received by a minor at any school or other educational establishment for minors, it is for the person sending it to him at that establishment to prove that he did not know or suspect it to be such an establishment.

(6) In proceedings under section 119 (1) it is for the pawnee to prove that he had reasonable cause to refuse to allow the pawn to be redeemed.

(7) If, in proceedings referred to in section 139 (1), the debtor or any surety alleges that the credit bargain is extortionate it is for the creditor to prove the contrary.

Statements by creditor or owner to be binding [31 July1974]

172. (1) A statement by a creditor or owner is binding on him if given under—

section 77 (1),
section 78 (1),
section 79 (1),
section 97 (1),
section 107 (1) (c),
section 108 (1) (c), or
section 109 (1) (c).

(2) Where a trader—

(a) gives a customer a notice in compliance with section 103 (1) (b), or
(b) gives a customer a notice under section 103 (1) asserting that the customer is not indebted to him under an agreement,

the notice is binding on the trader.

(3) Where in proceedings before any court—

(a) it is sought to reply on a statement or notice given as mentioned in subsection (1) or (2), and
(b) the statement or notice is shown to be incorrect,

the court may direct such relief (if any) to be given to the creditor or owner from the operation of subsection (1) or (2) as appears to the court to be just.

Contracting-out forbidden [31 July 1974]

173. (1) A term contained in a regulated agreement or linked transaction, or in any other agreement relating to an actual or prospective regulated agreement or linked transaction, is void if, and to the extent that, it is inconsistent with a provision for the protection of the debtor or hirer or his relative or any surety contained in this Act or in any regulation made under this Act.

(2) Where a provision specifies the duty or liability of the debtor or hirer or his relative or any surety in certain circumstances, a term is inconsistent with that provision if it purports to impose, directly or indirectly, an additional duty or liability on him in those circumstances.

(3) Notwithstanding subsection (1), a provision of this Act under which a thing may be done in relation to any person on an order of the court or the Director only shall not be taken to prevent its being done at any time with that person's consent given at that time, but the refusal of such consent shall not give rise to any liability.

PART XII—SUPPLEMENTAL

.   .   .

Interpretation

Associates [31 July 1974]

184. (1) A person is an associate of an individual if that person is the individual's husband or wife, or is a relative, or the husband or wife of a relative, of the individual or of the individual's husband or wife.

(2) A person is an associate of any person with whom he is in partnership, and of the husband or wife or a relative of any individual with whom he is in partnership.

(3) A body corporate is an associate of another body corporate—

(a) if the same person is a controller of both, or a person is a controller of one and persons who are his associates, or he and persons who are his associates, are controllers of the other; or

(b) if a group of two or more persons is a controller of each company, and the groups either consist of the same persons or could be regarded as consisting of the same persons by treating (in one or more cases) a member of either group as replaced by a person of whom he is an associate.

(4) A body corporate is an associate of another person if that person is a controller of it or if that person and persons who are his associates together are controllers of it.

(5) In this section "relative" means brother, sister, uncle, aunt, nephew, niece, lineal ancestor or lineal descendant, and references to a husband or wife include a former husband or wife and a reputed husband or wife; and for the purposes of this subsection a relationship shall be established as if any illegitimate, step-child or adopted child of a person had been a child born to him in wedlock.

Agreement with more than one debtor or hirer [see Sch 3, para 49, below.]

185. (1) Where an actual or prospective regulated agreement has two or more debtors or hirers (not being a partnership or an unincorporated body of persons)—

(a) anything required by or under this Act to be done to or in relation to the debtor or hirer shall be done to or in relation to each of them; and

(b) anything done under this Act by or on behalf of one of them shall have effect as if done by or on behalf of all of them.

(2) Notwithstanding subsection (1) (a), where running-account credit is provided to two or more debtors jointly, any of them may by a notice signed by him (a "dispensing notice") authorise the creditor not to comply in his case with section 78 (4) (giving of periodical statement of account); and the dispensing notice shall have effect accordingly until revoked by a further notice given by the debtor to the creditor:

Provided that:

(a) a dispensing notice shall not take effect if previous dispensing notices are operative in the case of the other debtor, or each of the other debtors, as the case may be;

(b) any dispensing notices operative in relation to an agreement shall cease to have effect if any of the debtors dies;

(c) a dispensing notice which is operative in relation to an agreement shall be operative also in relation to any subsequent agreement which, in relation to the earlier agreement, is a modifying agreement [1979].

(3) Subsection (1) (b) does not apply for the purposes of section 61 (1) (a) or 127 (3).

(4) Where a regulated agreement has two or more debtors or hirers (not being a partnership or an unincorporated body of persons), section 86 applies to the death of any of them.

(5) An agreement for the provision of credit, or the bailment or (in Scotland) the hiring of goods, to two or more persons jointly where —

(a) one or more of those persons is an individual, and

(b) one or more of them is a body corporate,

is a consumer credit agreement or consumer hire agreement if it would have been one had they all been individuals; and the body corporate or bodies corporate shall accordingly be included among the debtors or hirers under the agreement.

(6) Where subsection (5) applies, references in this Act to the signing of any document by the debtor or hirer shall be construed in relation to a body corporate as referring to a signing on behalf of the body corporate.

Agreement with more than one creditor or owner [31 July 1974]

186. Where an actual or prospective regulated agreement has two or more creditors or owners, anything required by or under this Act to be done to, or in relation to, or by, the creditor or owner shall be effective if done to, or in relation to, or by, any one of them.

Arrangements between creditor and supplier [31 July 1974]

187. (1) A consumer credit shall be treated as entered into under pre-existing arrangements between a creditor and a supplier if it is entered into in accordance with, or in furtherance of, arrangements previously made between persons mentioned in subsection (4) (a), (b) or (c).

(2) A consumer credit agreement shall be treated as entered into in contemplation of future arrangements between a creditor and a supplier if it is entered into in the expectation that agreements will subsequently be made between persons mentioned in subsection (4) (a), (b) or (c) for the supply of cash, goods and services (or any of them) to be financed by the consumer credit agreement.

(3) Arrangements shall be disregarded for the purposes of subsection (1) or (2) if—

(a) they are arrangements for the making, in specified circumstances, of payments to the supplier by the creditor, and

(b) the creditor holds himself out as willing to make, in such circumstances, payments of the kind to suppliers generally.

(4) The persons referred to in subsections (1) and (2) are—

(a) the creditor and the supplier;

(b) one of them and an associate of the other's;

(c) an associate of one and an associate of the other's.

(5) Where the creditor is an associate of the supplier's, the consumer credit agreement shall be treated, unless the contrary is proved, as entered into under pre-existing arrangements between the creditor and the supplier.

.   .   .

Definitions [31 July 1974]

189. (1) In this Act, unless the context otherwise requires—

"advertisement" includes every form of advertising, whether in a publication, by

  television or radio, by display of notices; signs, labels, showcards or goods, by distribution of samples, circulars, catalogues, price lists or other material, by exhibition of pictures, models or films, or in any other way, and references to the publishing of advertisements shall be construed accordingly;

"advertiser" in relation to an advertisement, means any person indicated by the advertisement as willing to enter into transactions to which the advertisement relates;

"ancillary credit business" has the meaning given by section 145 (1);

"antecedent negotiations" has the meaning given by section 56;

.   .   .

"associate" shall be construed in accordance with section 184;

"bill of sale" has the meaning given by section 4 of the Bills of Sale Act 1878 or, for Northern Ireland, by section 4 of the Bills of Sale (Ireland) Act 1879;

"building society" has the meaning given by section 1 of the Building Societies Act 1962, and includes a Northern Ireland society as defined by section 134 (4) of that Act;

"business" includes profession or trade, and references to a business apply subject to subsection (2);

"cancellable agreement" means a regulated agreement which, by virtue of section 67, may be cancelled by the debtor or hirer;

"canvass" shall be construed in accordance with sections 48 and 153;

"cash" includes money in any form;

"charity" means as respects England and Wales a charity registered under the Charities Act 1960 or an exempt charity (within the meaning of that Act), and as respects Scotland and Northern Ireland an institution or other organisation established for charitable purposes only ("organisation" including any persons administering a trust and "charitable" being construed in the same way as if it were contained in the Income Tax Acts);

"conditional sale agreement" means an agreement for the sale of goods or land under which the purchase price or part of it is payable by instalments, and the property in the goods or land is to remain in the seller (notwithstanding that the buyer is to be in possession of the goods or land) until such conditions as to the payment of instalments or otherwise as may be specified in the agreement are fulfilled;

"consumer credit agreement" has the meaning given by section 8, and includes a consumer credit agreement which is cancelled under section 69 (1), or becomes subject to section 69 (2), so far as the agreement remains in force;

"consumer credit business" means any business so far as it comprises or relates to the provision of credit under regulated consumer credit agreements;

"consumer hire agreement" has the meaning given by section 15;

"consumer hire business" means any business so far as it comprises or relates to the bailment or (in Scotland) the hiring of goods under regulated consumer hire agreements;

"controller", in relation to a body corporate, means a person—

(a) in accordance with whose directions or instructions the directors of the body corporate or of another body corporate which is its controller (or any of them) are accustomed to act, or

(b) who, either alone or with any associate or associates, is entitled to exercise, or control the exercise of, one third or more of the voting power at any general meeting of the body corporate or of another body corporate which is its controller;

"copy" shall be construed in accordance with section 180;

. . .

"court" means in relation to England and Wales the county court, in relation to Scotland the sheriff court and in relation to Northern Ireland the High Court or the county court;

"credit" shall be construed in accordance with section 9;

"credit-broker" means a person carrying on a business of credit brokerage;

"credit-brokerage" has the meaning given by section 145 (2);

"creditor limit" has the meaning given by section 10 (2);

"creditor" means the person providing credit under a consumer credit agreement or the person to whom his rights and duties under the agreement have passed by assignment or operation of law, and in relation to a prospective consumer credit agreement, includes the prospective creditor;

"credit reference agency" has the meaning given by section 145 (8);

"credit-sale agreement" means an agreement for the sale of goods, under which the purchase price or part of it is payable by instalments, but which is not a conditional sale agreement;

"credit-token" has the meaning given by section 14 (1);

"credit-token agreement" means a regulated agreement for the provision of credit in connection with the use of a credit-token;

"debt-adjusting" has the meaning given by section 145 (5);

"debt-collecting" has the meaning given by section 145 (7);

"debt-counselling" has the meaning given by section 145 (6);

"debtor" means the individual receiving credit under a consumer credit agreement or the person to whom his rights and duties under the agreement have passed by assignment or operation of law, and in relation to a prospective consumer credit agreement includes the prospective debtor;

"debtor-creditor agreement" has the meaning given by section 13;

"debtor-creditor-supplier agreement" has the meaning given by section 12;

"default notice" has the meaning given by section 87 (1);

"deposit" means any sum payable by a debtor or hirer by way of deposit or down payment, or credited or to be credited to him on account of any deposit or down payment, whether the sum is to be or has been paid to the creditor or owner or any other person, or is to be or has been discharged by a payment of money or a transfer or delivery of goods or by any other means;

"Director" means the Director General of Fair Trading;

"electric line" has the meaning given by the Electric Lighting Act 1882 or, for Northern Ireland, the Electricity Supply (Northern Ireland) Order 1972;

"embodies" and related words shall be construed in accordance with subsection (4);

"enforcement authority" has the meaning given by section 161 (1);

"enforcement order" means an order under section 65 (1), 105 (7) (a) or (b), 111 (2) or 124 (1) or (2);

"executed agreement" means a document, signed by or on behalf of the parties embodying the terms of a regulated agreement, or such of them as have been reduced to writing;

"exempt agreement" means an agreement specified in or under section 16;

"finance" means to finance wholly or partly, and "financed" and "refinanced" shall be construed accordingly;

"file" and "copy of the file" have the meanings given by section 158 (5);

"fixed-sum credit" has the meaning given by section 10 (1) (b);

"friendly society" means a society registered under the Friendly Societies Acts 1896 to 1971 or a society within the meaning of the Friendly Societies Act (Northern Ireland) 1970;

"future arrangements" shall be construed in accordance with section 187;

"general notice" means a notice published by the Director at a time and in a manner appearing to him suitable for securing that the notice is seen within a reasonable time by persons likely to be affected by it;

"give" means deliver or send by post to;

"goods" has the meaning given by section 61 (1) of the Sale of Goods Act 1979;

"group licence" has the meaning given by section 22 (1) (b);

"High Court" means Her Majesty's High Court of Justice, of the Court of Session in Scotland or the High Court of Justice in Northern Ireland;

"hire-purchase agreement" means an agreement, other than a conditional sale agreement under which—

(a) goods are bailed or (in Scotland) hired in return for periodical payments by the person to whom they are bailed or hired, and

(b) the property in the goods will pass to that person if the terms of the agreement are complied with and one or more of the following occurs—

    (i) the exercise of an option to purchase by that person,

    (ii) the doing of any other specified act by any party to the agreement,

    (iii) the happening of any other specified event;

"hirer" means the individual to whom goods are bailed or (in Scotland) hired under a consumer hire agreement, or the person to whom his rights and duties under the agreement have passed by assignment or operation of law, and in relation to a prospective consumer hire agreement includes the prospective hirer;

"individual" includes a partnership or other unincorporated body of persons not consisting entirely of bodies corporate;

"installation" means—

(a) the installing of any electric line or any gas or water pipe

(b) the fixing of goods to the premises where they are to be used, and the alteration of premises to enable goods to be used on them,

(c) where it is reasonably necessary that goods should be constructed or erected on the premises where they are to be used, any work carried out for the purpose of constructing or erecting them on those premises;

"insurance company" has the meaning given by section 33 (1) of the Insurance Companies Act 1958, and includes such a company as defined by section 72 (1) of the Insurance Companies Act (Northern Ireland) 1968, but does not include a friendly society or an organisation of workers or organisation of employers;

"judgment" includes an order or decree made by any court;

"land" includes an interest in land, and in relation to Scotland includes heritable subjects of whatever description;

"land improvement company" means an improvement company as defined by section 7 of the Improvement of Land Act 1899;

"land mortgage" includes any security charged on land;

"licence" means a licence under Part III (including that Part as applied to ancillary credit businesses by section 147);

"licensed", in relation to any act, means authorised by a licence to do the act or cause or permit another person to do it;

"licensee", in the case of a group licence, includes any person covered by the licence;

"linked transaction" has the meaning given by section 19 (1);

"local authority", in relation to England and Wales, means the Greater

London Council, a county council, a London borough council, a district council, the Common Council of the City of London, or the Council of the Isles of Scilly, and in relation to Scotland, means a regional, islands or district council, and, in relation to Northern Ireland, means a district council; [see Sch. 3, para 49 below.]

.   .   .

"modifying agreement" has the meaning given by section 82 (2);

.   .   .

"multiple agreement" has the meaning given by section 18 (1);
"negotiator" has the meaning given by section 56 (1);
"non-commercial agreement" means a consumer credit agreement or a consumer hire agreement not made by the creditor or owner in the course of a business carried on by him;
"notice" means notice in writing;
"notice of cancellation" has the meaning given by section 69 (1);
"owner" means a person who bails or (in Scotland) hires out goods under a consumer hire agreement or the person to whom his rights and duties under the agreement have passed by assignment or operation of law, and in relation to a prospective consumer hire agreement, includes the prospective bailor or person from whom the goods are to be hired;

.   .   .

"payment" includes tender;
"personal credit agreement" has the meaning given by section 8 (1);
"pledge" means the pawnee's rights over an article taken in pawn;
"prescribed" means prescribed by regulations made by the Secretary of State;
"pre-existing arrangements" shall be construed in accordance with section 187;
"principal agreement" has the meaning given by section 19 (1);
"protected goods" has the meaning given by section 90 (7);
"quotation" has the meaning given by section 52 (1) (a);
"redemption period" has the meaning given by section 116 (3);
"register" means the register kept by the Director under section 35;
"regulated agreement" means a consumer credit agreement, or consumer hire agreement, other than an exempt agreement, and "regulated" and "unregulated" shall be construed accordingly;
"regulations" means regulations made by the Secretary of State;
"relative", except in section 184, means a person who is an associate by virtue of section 184 (1);
"representation" includes any condition or warranty, and any other statement or undertaking, whether oral or in writing;

203

"restricted-use credit agreement" and "restricted-use credit" have the meanings given by section 11 (1);

.   .   .

"running-account credit" shall be construed in accordance with section 10;

"security", in relation to an actual or prospective consumer credit agreement or consumer hire agreement, or any linked transaction, means a mortgage, charge, pledge, bond, debenture, indemnity, guarantee, bill, note or other right provided by the debtor or hirer, or at his request (express or implied), to secure the carrying out of the obligations of the debtor or hirer under the agreement;

"security instrument" has the meaning given by section 105 (2);

"serve on" means deliver or send by post to;

"signed" shall be construed in accordance with subsection (3);

"small agreement" has the meaning given by section 17 (1), and "small" in relation to an agreement within any category shall be constructed accordingly;

"specified fee" shall be construed in accordance with section 2 (4) and (5);

"standard licence" has the meaning given by section 22 (1) (a);

"supplier" has the meaning given by section 11 (1) (b) or 12 (c) or 13 (c) or, in relation to an agreement falling within section 11 (1) (a), means the creditor, and includes a person to whom the rights and duties of a supplier (as so defined) have passed by assignment or operation of law, or (in relation to a prospective agreement) the prospective supplier;

"surety" means the person by whom any security is provided, or the person to whom his rights and duties in relation to the security have passed by assignment or operation of law;

"technical grounds" shall be construed in accordance with subsection (5);

"time order" has the meaning given by section 129 (1);

"total charge for credit" means a sum calculated in accordance with regulations under section 20 (1);

"total price" means the total sum payable by the debtor under a hire-purchase agreement or a conditional sale agreement, including any sum payable on the exercise of an option to purchase, but excluding any sum payable as a penalty or as compensation or damages for a breach of the agreement;

"unexecuted agreement" means a document embodying the terms of a prospective regulated agreement, or such of them as it is intended to reduce to writing;

"unlicensed" means without a licence, but applies only in relation to acts for which a licence is required;

"unrestricted-use credit agreement" and "unrestricted-use-credit" have the meanings given by section 11 (2);

"working day" means any day other than—

(a) Saturday or Sunday,

(b) Christmas Day or Good Friday,

(c) a bank holiday within the meaning given by section 1 of the Banking and Financial Dealings Act 1971.

(2) A person is not to be treated as carrying on a particular type of business merely because occasionally he enters into transactions belonging to a business of that type.

(3) Any provision of this Act requiring a document to be signed is complied with by a body corporate if the document is sealed by that body.

This subsection does not apply to Scotland.

(4) A document embodies a provision if the provision is set out either in the document itself or in another document referred to in it.

(5) An application dismissed by the court or the Director shall, if the court or the Director (as the case may be) so certifies, be taken to be dismissed on technical grounds only.

(6) Except in so far as the context otherwise requires, any reference in this Act to an enactment, including this Act.

(7) In this Act, except where otherwise indicated—

(a) a reference to a numbered Part, section or Schedule is a reference to the Part or section of, or the Schedule to, this Act so numbered, and

(b) a reference in a section to a numbered subsection is a reference to the subsection of that section so numbered, and

(c) a reference in a section, subsection or Schedule to a numbered paragraph is a reference to the paragraph of that section, subsection or Schedule so numbered.

.   .   .

Miscellaneous

Transitional and commencement provisions amendments and repeals [31 July 1974]

192. (1) The provisions of Schedule 3 shall have effect for the purposes of this Act.

(2) The appointment of a day for the purposes of any provision of Schedule 3 shall be effected by an order of the Secretary of State made by statutory instrument; and any such order shall include a provision amending Schedule 3 so as to insert an express reference to the day appointed.

.   .   .

Short title, and extent [31 July 1974]

193. (1) This Act may be cited as the Consumer Credit Act 1974.

(2) This Act extends to Northern Ireland.

.   .   .

SCHEDULE 3

TRANSITIONAL AND COMMENCEMENT PROVISIONS

Note. Except as otherwise mentioned in this Schedule, the provisions of this Act come into operation on its passing, that is on 31st July 1974.

PART II OF ACT — CREDIT AGREEMENTS, HIRE AGREEMENTS AND LINKED TRANSACTIONS

Regulated agreements

1. (1) An agreement made before 1st April 1977 is not a regulated agreement within the meaning of this Act.

(2) In this Act "prospective regulated agreement" does not include a prospective agreement which, if made as expected, would be made before 1st April 1977.

Linked transactions

2. A transaction may be a linked transaction in relation to a regulated agreement or prospective regulated agreement even though the transaction was entered into before the day appointed for the purposes of paragraph 1.

3. Section 19 (3) applies only to transactions entered into on or after 19th May 1985.

Total charge for credit

4. Section 20 applies to consumer credit agreements whenever made.

PART III OF ACT — LICENSING OF CREDIT AND HIRE BUSINESS

Businesses needing a licence

5. (1) Section 21 does not apply to the carrying on of any description of consumer credit business or consumer hire business—
   (a) before 1st October 1977 in the case of a consumer credit business, not being a consumer credit business which is carried on by an individual and in the course of which only the following regulated consumer credit agreements (excluding agreements made before that date) are made, namely—
      (i) agreements for fixed-sum credit not exceeding £30, and
      (ii) agreements for running-account credit where the credit limit does not exceed that amount,
   (b) before the day appointed for the purposes of this paragraph in the case of any other description of consumer credit business, and
   (c) before 1st October 1977 in the case of any consumer hire business.

(2) Where the person carrying on any description of consumer credit business or consumer hire business applies for a licence before the day specified or referred to in sub-paragraph (1) above in relation to a business

of that description, he shall be deemed to have been granted on that day a licence covering that business and continuing in force until the licence applied for is granted or, if the application is refused, until the end of the appeal period.

.   .   .

Enforcement of agreement made by unlicensed trader

7. Section 40 does not apply to a regulated agreement made in the course of any business before the day specified or referred to in paragraph 5 (1) in relation to the description of business in question.

.   .   .

PART V OF ACT—ENTRY INTO CREDIT OR HIRE AGREEMENTS

Antecedent negotiations

12. (1) Section 56 applies to negotiations in relation to an actual or prospective regulated agreement where the negotiations begin after 16th May 1977.

(2) In section 56 (3), "agreement", where it first occurs, means an agreement whenever made.

General

13. Sections 57 to 59, 61 to 65 and 67 to 73 come into operation on 19th May 1985.

14. Section 66 comes into operation on 19th May 1985.

PART VI OF ACT—MATTERS ARISING DURING CURRENCY OF CREDIT OR HIRE AGREEMENTS

Liability of creditor for breaches by supplier

15. Section 75 comes into operation on 1st July 1977 but only in relation to regulated agreements made on or after that day.

Duty to give notice

16. (1) Section 76 comes into operation on 19th May 1985.

(2) Section 76 applies to an agreement made before 19th May 1985 where the agreement would have been a regulated agreement if made on that day.

Duty to give information

17. (1) Sections 77 to 80 come into operation on 19th May 1985.

(2) Sections 77 to 79 apply to an agreement made before 19th May 1985 where the agreement would have been a regulated agreement if made on that day.

Appendix A

Appropriation of payments

18. Section 81 comes into operation on 19th May 1985.

Variation of agreements

19. Section 82 comes into operation on 1st April 1977.

Misuse of credit facilities

20. (1) Sections 83 and 84 come into operation on 19th May 1985.

(2) Subject to sub-paragraph (4), section 83 applies to an agreement made before 19th May 1985 where the agreement would have been a regulated consumer credit agreement if made on that day.

(3) Subject to sub-paragraph (4), section 84 applies to an agreement made before 19th May 1985 where the agreement would have been a credit-token agreement if made on that day.

(4) Sections 83 and 84 do not apply to losses arising before 19th May 1985.

(5) Section 84 (4) shall be taken to be satisfied in relation to an agreement made before 19th May 1985 if, within 28 days after that day, the creditor gives notice to the debtor of the name, address and telephone number of a person stated in that notice to be the person to whom notice is to be given under section 84 (3).

Duty on issue of new credit-tokens

21. (1) Section 85 comes into operation on 19th May 1985.

(2) Section 85 applies to an agreement made before 19th May 1985 where the agreement would have been a regulated agreement if made on that day.

Death of debtor or hirer

22. (1) Section 86 comes into operation on 19th May 1985.

(2) Section 86 applies to an agreement made before 19th May 1985 where the agreement would have been a regulated agreement if made on that day.

PART VII OF ACT—DEFAULT AND TERMINATION

Default notices

23. Sections 87 to 89 come into operation on 19th May 1985.

Retaking of goods and land

24. Sections 90 and 91 come into operation on 19th May 1985.

25. Section 92 comes into operaton on 19th May 1985.

Interest on default

26. Section 93 comes into operation on 19th May 1985.

208

Early payment by debtor

27. Sections 94 to 97 come into operation on 19th May 1985.

Termination of agreements

28. Section 98 comes into operation on 19th May 1985.

29. Section 99 comes into operation on 19th May 1985.

30. Section 100 comes into operation on 19th May 1985.

31. Section 101 comes into operation on 19th May 1985.

32. Section 102 comes into operation on 19th May 1985.

33. Section 103 comes into operation on 19th May 1985.

. . .

Old agreements

35. Part VII (except sections 90, 91, 93 and 99 to 102 and 104) applies to an agreement made before 19th May 1985 where the agreement would have been a regulated agreement if made on that day.

PART VIII OF ACT—SECURITY

General

36. Section 105 comes into operation on 19th May 1985.

37. (1) Sections 107 to 110 come into operation on 19th May 1985.

(2) Sections 107 to 110 apply to an agreement made before 19th May 1985 where the agreement would have been a regulated agreement if made on that day.

38. (1) Section 111 comes into operation on 19th May1985 where the agreement would have been a regulated agreement if made on that day.

. . .

Negotiable instruments

40. Sections 123 to 125 come into operation on 19th May 1985. [1984]

Land Mortgages

41. Section 126 comes into operation on 19th May 1985.

PART IX OF ACT—JUDICIAL CONTROL

42. Sections 137 to 140 (extortionate credit bargain) come into operation on 16th May 1977 and apply to agreements and transactions whenever made.

43. Subject to paragraph 42, Part IX comes into operation on 19th May 1985.

Licensing

44. (1) Section 21 (1) does not apply (by virtue of section 147 (1)) to the carrying on of any ancillary credit business before 3rd August 1976 in the case of any business so far as it comprises or relates to—

    (a) debt-adjusting,

    (b) debt-counselling,

    (c) debt-collecting, or

    (d) the operation of a credit reference agency,

(1A) Section 21 (1) does not apply (by virtue of section 147 (1)) to the carrying on of any ancillary credit business before 1st July 1978 so far as it comprises or relates to credit brokerage, not being a business which is carried on by an individual and in the course of which introductions are effected only of individuals desiring to obtain credit—

    (a) under debtor-creditor-supplier agreements which fall within section 12 (a) and where, in the case of any such agreement—

      (i) the person carrying on the business would be willing to sell the goods which are the subject of the agreement to the debtor under a transaction not financed by credit, and

      (ii) the amount of credit does not exceed £30; and

    (b) under debtor-creditor-supplier agreements which fall within section 12 (b) or (c) and where, in the case of any such agreement—

      (i) the person carrying on the business is the supplier,

  (ii) the creditor is a person referred to in section 145 (2) (a) (i), and

 (iii) the amount of credit or, in the case of an agreement for running-account credit, the credit limit does not exceed £30.

(1B) Section 21 (1) does not apply (by virtue of section 147 (1)) to the carrying on of any ancillary credit business before the day appointed for the purposes of this paragraph in the case of any description of ancillary credit business in relation to which no day is appointed under the foregoing provisions of this paragraph.

(2) Where the person carrying on an ancillary credit business applies for a licence before—

    (a) 3rd August 1976 in the case of an ancillary credit business of a description to which subparagraph (1) above applies;

    (b) 1st July 1978 in the case of an ancillary credit business of a description to which subparagraph (1A) above applies; or

    (c) the day appointed for the purposes of this paragraph in the case of an ancillary credit business to which subparagraph (1B) above applies,

he shall be deemed to have been granted on 3rd August 1976, 1st July 1978 or the day so appointed, as the case may be, a licence covering the description of ancillary business in question and continuing in force until the licence applied for is granted or, if the application is refused, until the end of the appeal period.

Enforcement of agreements made by unlicensed trader

45. Section 148 (1) does not apply to an agreement made in the course of any business before 3rd August 1976 in the case of any business so far as it comprises or relates to—
(a) debt-adjusting,
(b) debt-counselling,
(c) debt-collecting, or
(d) the operation of a credit reference agency,
or before 1st July 1978 in the case of an ancillary credit business of a description to which subparagraph (1A) of paragraph 44 applies or before the day appointed for the purposes of that paragraph in the case of an ancillary credit business to which subparagraph (1B) of that paragraph applies.

Introductions by unlicensed credit-broker

46. Section 149 does not apply to a regulated agreement made on an introduction effected in the course of any business if the introduction was effected before 1st July 1978 in the case of an ancillary credit business to which subparagraph (1A) of paragraph 44 applies or before the day appointed for the purposes of that paragraph in the case of an ancillary credit business to which subparagraph (1B) of that paragraph applies.

.   .   .

PART XII OF ACT—SUPPLEMENTAL

Interpretation

49. (1) In the case of an agreement—
(a) which was made before 19th May 1985, and
(b) to which (by virtue of paragraph 17 (2)) section 78 (4) applies, section 185 (2) shall have effect as respects a notice given before that day in relation to the agreement (whether given before or after the passing of this Act) as it would have effect if section 78 (4) had been in operation when the notice was given.

(2) Paragraph (1) applies to an agreement made on or after 19th May 1985 to provide credit on a current account opened before that day as it applies to an agreement made before that day.

50. In section 189, the definition of "local authority" shall have effect in relation to matters arising before 16th May 1975 as if for the words "regional islands or district council" there were substituted "a county council or town council".

Supreme Court Act 1981 (c 54)

Power of High Court to award interest on debts and damages

35A. (1) Subject to rules of court, in proceedings (whenever instituted) before the High Court for the recovery of a debt or damages there may be included in any sum for which judgment is given simple interest, at such rate as the court thinks fit or as rules of court may provide, on all or any part of the debt or damages in respect of which judgment is given, or payment is made before judgment, for all or any part of the period between the date when the cause of action arose and—

    (a) in the case of any sum paid before judgment, the date of the payment; and

    (b) in the case of the sum for which judgment is given, the date of the judgment.

(2) In relation to a judgment given for damages for personal injuries or death which exceed £200 subsection (1) shall have effect—

    (a) with the substitution of "shall be included" for "may be included"; and

    (b) with the addition of "unless the court is satisfied that there are special reasons to the contrary" after "given", where first occurring.

(3) Subject to rules of court, where —

    (a) there are proceedings (whenever instituted) before the High Court for the recovery of a debt; and

    (b) the defendant pays the whole debt to the plaintiff (otherwise than in pursuance of a judgment in the proceedings),

the defendant shall be liable to pay the plaintiff simple interest at such rate as the court thinks fit or as rules of court may provide on all or any part of the debt for all or part of the period between the date when the cause of action arose and the date of the payment.

(4) Interest in respect of a debt shall not be awarded under this section for a period during which, for whatever reason, interest on the debt already runs.

(5) Without prejudice to the generality of section 84, rules of court may provide for a rate of interest by reference to the rate specified in section 17 of the Judgments Act 1838 as that section has effect from time to time or by reference to a rate for which any other enactment provides.

(6) Interest under this section may be calculated at different rates in respect of different periods.

(7) In this section "plaintiff" means the person seeking the debt or damages and "defendant" means the person from whom the plaintiff seeks the debt or damages and "personal injuries" includes any disease and any impairment of a person's physical or mental condition.

(8) Nothing in this section affects the damages recoverable for the dishonour of a bill of exchange.

County Courts Act 1984 (c 28)

Interest on debts and damages

Power to award interest on debts and damages

69. (1) Subject to county court rules, in proceedings (whenever instituted) before a county court for the recovery of a debt or damages there may be included in any sum for which judgment is given simple interest, at such rate as the court thinks fit or as may be prescribed, on all or any part of the debt or damages in respect of which judgment is given, or payment is made before judgment, for all or any part of the period between the date when the cause of action arose and—

    (a) in the case of any sum paid before judgment, the date of the payment; and

    (b) in the case of the sum for which judgment is given, the date of the judgment.

(2) In relation to a judgment given for damages for personal injuries or death which exceed £200 subsection (1) shall have effect—

    (a) with the substitution of "shall be included" for "may be included"; and

    (b) with the addition of "unless the court is satisfied that there are special reasons to the contrary" after "given", where first occurring.

(3) Subject to county court rules, where—

    (a) there are proceedings (whenever instituted) before a county court for the recovery of a debt; and

    (b) the defendant pays the whole debt to the plaintiff (otherwise than in pursuance of a judgment in the proceedings),

the defendant shall be liable to pay the plaintiff simple interest, at such rate as the court thinks fit or as may be prescribed, on all or any part of the debt for all or any part of the period between the date when the cause of action arose and the date of the payment.

(4) Interest in respect of a debt shall not be awarded under this section for a period during which, for whatever reason, interest on the debt already runs.

(5) Interest under this section may be calculated at different rates in respect of different periods.

(6) In this section "plaintiff" means the person seeking the debt or damages and "defendant" means the person from whom the plaintiff seeks the debt or damages and "personal injuries" includes any disease and any impairment of a person's physical or mental condition.

(7) Nothing in this section affects the damages recoverable for the dishonour of a bill of exchange.

(8) In determining whether an amount exceeds—

    (a) the county court limit for the purposes of any provision of this Act; or

    (b) an amount specified in any provision of this Act,

no account shall be taken of the provisions of this section or of anything done under it.

       .   .   .

Interest on judgment debts etc

74. (1) The Lord Chancellor may by order made with the concurrence of the Treasury provide that any sums to which this subsection applies shall carry interest at such rate and between such times as may be prescribed by the order.

(2) The sums to which subsection (1) applies are—

(a) sums payable under judgments or orders given or made in a county court, including sums payable by instalments; and

(b) sums which by virtue of any enactment are, if the county court so orders, recoverable as if payable under an order of that court, and in respect of which the county court has so ordered.

(3) The payment of interest due under subsection (1) shall be enforceable as a sum payable under the judgment or order.

(4) The power conferred by subsection (1) includes power—

(a) to specify the descriptions of judgment or order in respect of which interest shall be payable;

(b) to provide that interest shall be payable only on sums exceeding a specified amount;

(c) to make provision for the manner in which and the periods by reference to which the interest is to be calculated and paid;

(d) to provide that any enactment shall or shall not apply in relation to interest payable under subsection (1) or shall apply to it with such modifications as may be specified in the order; and

(e) to make such incidental or supplementary provisions as the Lord Chancellor considers appropriate.

(5) Without prejudice to the generality of subsection (4), an order under subsection (1) may provide that the rate of interest shall be the rate specified in section 17 of the Judgments Act 1838 as that enactment has effect from time to time.

(6) The power to make an order under subsection (1) shall be exercisable by statutory instrument subject to annulment in pursuance of a resolution of either House of Parliament.

.   .   .

Application of practice of High Court

76. In any case not expressly provided for by or in pursuance of this Act, the general principles of practice in the High Court may be adopted and applied to proceedings in a county court.

.   .   .

Execution in county court of judgments and orders of, or enforceable as judgments and orders of, High Court

Execution in county court of judgments and orders of High Court

105. (1) A judgment or order of the High Court for the payment of money to a person, and any judgment, order, decree or award (however called) of any court or arbitrator (including any foreign court or foreign arbitrator) being a judgment, order, decree or award for the payment of money to a person which is or has become enforceable (whether wholly or to a limited extent) as if it were a judgment or order of the High Court shall be enforceable in the county court as it it were a judgment of that court.

(2) Where an application is made to the High Court—

(a) for the attachment of a debt not exceeding the county court limit to answer a judgment or order; or

(b) for leave to issue execution for a debt not exceeding the county court limit against a person as being a member of a firm which a judgment or order has been obtained,

the High Court may make an order either—

(i) transferring the matter to; or

(ii) directing that any issue necessary for determining the matter shall be tried in,

such county court to be named in the order as the court may deem the most convenient to the parties.

(3) Where an order is made under subsection (2) directing an issue to be tried in a county court, the order shall define the issue to be tried, and any party may lodge or cause to be lodged the order, together with the affidavits (if any) filed in the matter, and such other documents (if any) as the High Court may direct, with the registrar of the county court named in the order.

(4) On the documents being lodged the issue shall, subject to county court rules, be tried in the county court so named, and after the issue has been tried the judge shall certify the result of the trial and send the certificate to the High Court together with the documents and any report which he may think fit to make as to costs or otherwise.

Enforcement in High Court of judgments and orders of county courts

Transfer of judgments and orders to High Court

106. (1) If—

(a) a judgment order for the payment of a sum of money has been given or made by a county court; and

(b) an amount in respect of that sum exceeding the amount for the time being specified for the purposes of this section by an order under subsection (3) has become recoverable by execution.

the judgment or order may, subject to rules of court, be transferred to the High Court.

(2) A judgment or order transferred to the High Court under subsection (1) may be enforced in the High Court as if it were a judgment or order of that court and shall be treated as a judgment or order of the High Court for all purposes except—

(a) that powers to set aside, correct, vary or quash a judgment or order of a county court shall continue to be exercisable in relation to it and powers to set aside, correct, vary or quash a judgment or order of the High Court shall not be exercisable; and

(b) that enactments relating to appeals from a judgment or order of a county court shall continue to apply to it and enactments relating to appeals from a judgment or order of the High Court shall not apply.

(3) The Lord Chancellor may by order specify an amount for the purposes of subsection (1); and any such order may specify different amounts for different descriptions of judgment or order.

(4) An order under subsection (3) shall be made by statutory instrument and shall be subject to annulment in pursuance of a resolution of either House of Parliament.

Appendix B

Rules of Court

Contents
Rules of the Supreme Court 1965
County Court Rules 1981

Rules of the Supreme Court 1965

RSC Order 6, rule 2: Indorsement of claim

2. (1) Before a writ is issued it must be indorsed —
  (a) with a statement of claim or, if the statement of claim is not indorsed on the writ, with a concise statement of the nature of the claim made or the relief or remedy required in the action begun thereby;
  (b) where the claim made by the plaintiff is for a debt or liquidated demand only, with a statement of the amount claimed in respect of the debt or demand and for costs and also with a statement that further proceedings will be stayed if, within the time limited for acknowledging service, the defendant pays the amount so claimed to the plaintiff, his solicitor or agent;
  (c) where the claim made by the plaintiff is for possession of land, with a statement showing —
   (i) whether the claim relates to a dwelling-house; and
   (ii) if it does, whether the rateable value of the premises on every day specified by section 4(2) of the Rent Act 1977 in relation to the premises exceeds the sum so specified;
  (d) where the action is brought to enforce a right to recover possession of goods, with a statement showing the value of the goods.

RSC Order 13, rule 1: Claim for liquidated demand

1. (1) Where a writ is indorsed with a claim against a defendant for a liquidated demand only, then, if that defendant fails to give notice of intention to defend, the plaintiff may, after the prescribed time enter final judgment against that defendant for a sum not exceeding that claimed by the writ in respect of the demand and for costs, and proceed with the action against the other defendants, if any.

(2) A claim shall not be prevented from being treated for the purposes of this rule as a claim for a liquidated demand by reason only that part of the claim is for interest under section 35A of the Act at a rate which is not higher than that payable on judgment debts at the date of the writ.

RSC Order 18, rule 8: Matters which must be specifically pleaded

8. (1) A party must in any pleading subsequent to a statement of claim plead specifically any matter, for example, performance, release, any relevant statute of limitation, fraud or any fact showing illegality —
  (a) which he alleges makes any claim or defence of the opposite party not maintainable; or
  (b) which, if not specifically pleaded, might take the opposite party by surprise; or
  (c) which raises issues of fact not arising out of the preceding pleading.

219

(2) Without prejudice to paragraph (1) a defendant to an action for the recovery of land must plead specifically every ground of defence on which he relies, and a plea that he is in possession of the land by himself or his tenant is not sufficient.

(3) A claim for exemplary damages must be specifically pleaded together with the facts on which the party pleading relies.

(4) A party must plead specifically any claim for interest under section 35A of the Act or otherwise.

RSC Order 18, rule 15: Statement of claim

15. (1) A statement of claim must state specifically the relief or remedy which the plaintiff claims; but costs need not be specifically claimed.

(2) A statement of claim must not contain any allegation or claim in respect of a cause of action unless that cause of action is mentioned in the writ or arises from facts which are the same as, or include or form part of facts giving rise to a cause of action so mentioned; but, subject to that, a plaintiff may in his statement of claim alter, modify or extend any claim made by him in the indorsement of the writ without amending the indorsement.

(3) Every statement of claim must bear on its face a statement of the date on which the writ in the action was issued.

RSC Order 22: Payment into and out of court

Payment into court
1. (1) In any action for a debt or damages any defendant may at any time pay into Court a sum of money in satisfaction of the cause of action in respect of which the plaintiff claims or, where two or more causes of action are joined in the action, a sum or sums of money in satisfaction of any or all of those causes of action.

(2) On making any payment into Court under this Rule, and on increasing any such payment already made, the defendant must give notice thereof in Form No. 23 in Appendix A to the plaintiff and every other defendant (if any); and within three days after receiving the notice the plaintiff must send the defendant a written acknowledgment of its receipt.

(3) A defendant may, without leave, give notice of an increase in a payment made under this Rule but subject to that and without prejudice to paragraph (5) a notice of payment may not be withdrawn or amended without the leave of the Court which may be granted on such terms as may be just.

(4) Where two or more causes of action are joined in the action and money is paid into Court under this Rule in respect of all, or some only of, those causes of action, the notice of payment—

   (a) must state that the money is paid in respect of all those causes of action or, as the case may be, must specify the cause or causes of action in respect of which the payment is made, and

(b) where the defendant makes separate payments in respect of each, or any two or more, of those causes of action, must specify the sum paid in respect of that cause or, as the case may be those causes of action.

(5) Where a single sum of money is paid into Court under this Rule in respect of two or more causes of action, then, if it appears to the Court that the plaintiff is embarrassed by the payment, the Court may, subject to paragraph (6) order the defendant to amend the notice of payment so as to specify the sum paid in respect of each cause of action.

Where a cause of action under the Fatal Accidents Act 1976 and a cause of action under the Law Reform (Miscellaneous Provisions) Act, 1934 are joined in an action, with or without any other cause of action the causes of action under the said Acts shall, for the purpose of paragraph (5) be treated as one cause of action.

(7) Where—
(a) an action proceeding in a district registry is being tried at a town within the district of another district registry or at the Royal Courts of Justice, or
(b) an action proceeding in the Royal Courts of Justice is being tried at a town within the district of a district registry,

any payment into court under this rule made after the trial or hearing has begun may, if the defendant so desires, be made at the district registry within the district of which the town is situated or, if the action is being tried at the Royal Courts of Justice, in the same manner as if the action were proceeding there.

(8) For the purposes of this rule, the plaintiff's cause of action in respect of a debt or damages shall be construed as a cause of action in respect, also, of such interest as might be included in the judgment, whether under section 35A of the Act or otherwise, if judgment were given at the date of the payment into Court.

Payment in by defendant who has counterclaimed
2. Where a defendant, who makes by counterclaim a claim against the plaintiff for a debt or damages, pays a sum or sums of money into Court under Rule 1, the notice of payment must state, if it be the case, that in making the payment the defendant has taken into account and intends to satisfy—
(a) the cause of action in respect of which he claims, or
(b) where two or more causes of action are joined in the counter-claim, all those causes of action or, if not all, which of them.

Acceptance of money paid into Court
3. (1) Where money is paid into Court under Rule 1, then subject to paragraph (2) within 21 days after receipt of the notice of payment or, where more than one payment has been made or the notice has been amended, within 21 days after receipt of the notice of the last payment or the amended notice but, in any case, before the trial or hearing of the action begins, the plaintiff may—

(a) where the money was paid in respect of the cause of action or all the causes of action in respect of which he claims, accept the money in satisfaction of that cause of action or those causes of action, as the case may be, or.

(b) where the money was paid in respect of some only of the causes of action in respect of which he claims, accept in satisfaction of any such cause or causes of action the sum specified in respect of that cause or those causes of action in the notice of payment,

by giving notice in Form No. 24 in Appendix A to every defendant to the action.

(2) Where after the trial or hearing of an action has begun—

(a) money is paid into court under rule 1, or

(b) money in court is increased by a further payment into court under that rule,

the plaintiff may accept the money in accordance with paragraph (1) within 2 days after receipt of the notice of payment or notice of the further payment, as the case may be, but, in any case, before the judge begins to deliver judgment or, if the trial is with a jury, before the judge begins his summing up.

(3) Rule 1 (5) shall not apply in relation to money paid into court in an action after the trial or hearing of the action has begun.

(4) On the plaintiff accepting any money paid into court all further proceedings in the action or in respect of the specified cause or causes of action, as the case may be, to which the acceptance relates, both against the defendant making the payment and against any other defendant sued jointly with or in the alternative to him shall be stayed.

(5) Where money is paid into court by a defendant who made a counterclaim and the notice of payment stated, in relation to any sum so paid, that in making the payment the defendant had taken into account and satisfied the cause or causes of action, or the specified cause or causes of action in respect of which he claimed, then, on the plaintiff accepting that sum, all further proceedings on the counterclaim or in respect of the specified cause or causes of action, as the case may be, against the plaintiff shall be stayed.

(6) A plaintiff who has accepted any sum paid into court shall, subject to rules 4 and 10 and Order 80, rule 12, be entitled to receive payment of that sum in satisfaction of the cause or causes of action to which the acceptance relates.

Order for payment out of money accepted required in certain cases
4. (1) Where a plaintiff accepts any sum paid into Court and that sum was paid into Court—

(a) by some but not all of the defendants sued jointly or in the alternative by him, or

(b) with a defence of tender before action, or

(c) in an action to which Order 80, Rule 13, applies, or

(d) in satisfaction either of causes of action arising under the Fatal

Accidents Act 1976 and the Law Reform (Miscellaneous Provisions) Act 1934, or of a cause of action arising under the first mentioned Act where more than one person is entitled to the money,
the money in Court shall not be paid out except under paragraph (2) or in pursuance of an order of the Court, and the order shall deal with the whole costs of the action or of the cause of action to which the payment relates, as the case may be.

(2) Where an order of the Court is required under paragraph (1) by reason only of paragraph (1) (a) then if, either before or after accepting the money paid into Court by some only of the defendants sued jointly or in the alternative by him, the plaintiff discontinues the action against all other defendants and those defendants consent in writing to the payment out of that sum, it may be paid out without an order of the Court.

(3) Where after the trial or hearing of an action has begun a plaintiff accepts any money paid into court and all further proceedings in the action or in respect of the specified cause or causes of action, as the case may be, to which the acceptance relates are stayed by virtue of rule 3(4) then, notwithstanding anything in paragraph (2) the money shall not be paid out except in pursuance of an order of the Court, and the order shall deal with the whole costs of the action.

Money remaining in court
5. If any money paid into court in an action is not accepted in accordance with Rule 3, the money remaining in court shall not be paid out except in pursuance of an order of the Court which may be made at any time before, at or after the trial or hearing of the action; and where such an order is made before the trial or hearing the money shall not be paid out except in satisfaction of the cause or causes of action in respect of which it was paid in.

Counterclaim
6. A plaintiff against whom a counterclaim is made and any other defendant to the counterclaim may pay money into court in accordance with rule 1, and that rules 3 (except paragraph (5)) 4 and 5 shall apply accordingly with the necessary modifications.

Non-disclosure of payment into court
7. Except in an action to which a defence of tender before action is pleaded, and except in an action all further proceedings in which are stayed by virtue of rule 3(4) after the trial or hearing has begun, the fact that money has been paid into court under the foregoing provisions of this Order shall not be pleaded and no communication of that fact shall be made to the Court at the trial or hearing of the action or counterclaim or of any question or issue as to the debt or damages until all questions of liability and of the amount of debt or damages have been decided.

Money paid into court under order

8. Subject to paragraph (2), money paid into court under an order of the Court or a certificate of a master or associate shall not be paid out except in pursuance of an order of the Court.

(2) Unless the Court otherwise orders, a party who has paid money into court in pursuance of an order made under Order 14—

    (a) may by notice to the other party appropriate the whole or any part of the money and any additional payment, if necessary to any particular claim made in the writ or counterclaim, as the case may be, and specified in the notice, or

    (b) if he pleads a tender, may by his pleading appropriate the whole or any part of the money as payment into court of the money alleged to have been tendered;

    and money appropriated in accordance with this rule shall be deemed to be money paid into court in accordance with rule 1 or money paid into court with a plea of tender, as the case may be, and this Order shall apply accordingly.

.   .   .

Investment of money in Court

13. (1) Subject to paragraph (2), cash under the control of or subject to the order of the Court may be invested in any manner specified in Part I and paragraphs 1 to 10 and 12 of Part II of Schedule I to the Trustee Investments Act 1961, as supplemented by the provisions of Part IV of that Schedule.

(2) Nothing in paragraph (1) shall restrict the manner of investment of cash transferred to and held by the Public Trustee under a declaration of trust approved by the Court.

RSC Order 29, Part II: Interim payments

Interpretation of Part II

9. In this Part of this Order—

    "interim payments", in relation to a defendant, means a payment on account of any damages, debt or other sum (excluding costs) which he may be held liable to pay to or for the benefit of the plaintiff; and any reference to the plaintiff or defendant includes a reference to any person who, for the purpose of the proceedings, acts as next friend of the plaintiff or guardian of the defendant.

Application for interim payment

10. (1) The plaintiff may, at any time after the writ has been served on a defendant and the time limited for him to acknowledge service has expired, apply to the Court for an order requiring that defendant to make an interim payment.

(2) An application under this rule shall be made by summons but may be included in a summons for summary judgment under Order 14 or Order 86.

(3) An application under this rule shall be supported by an affidavit which shall—

(a) verify the amount of the damages, debt or other sum to which the application relates and the grounds of the application;

(b) exhibit any documentary evidence relied on by the plaintiff in support of the application; and

(c) if the plaintiff's claim is made under the Fatal Accidents Act 1976, contain the particulars mentioned in section 2 (4) of that Act.

(4) The summons and a copy of the affidavits in support and any document exhibited thereto shall be served on the defendant against whom the order is sought not less than 10 clear days before the return day.

(5) Notwithstanding the making or refusal of an order for an interim payment, a second or subsequent application may be made upon cause shown.

Order for interim payment in respect of damages
11. (1) If, on the hearing of an application under rule 10 in an action for damages, the Court is satisfied—

(a) that the defendant against whom the order is sought (in this paragraph referred to as "the respondent") has admitted liability for the plaintiff's damages, or

(b) that the plaintiff has obtained judgment against the respondent for damages to be assessed; or

(c) that, if the action proceeded to trial, the plaintiff would obtain judgment for substantial damages against the respondent or, where there are two or more defendants against any of them,

the Court may, if it thinks fit and subject to paragraph (2), order the respondent to make an interim payment of such amount as it thinks just, not exceeding a reasonable proportion of the damages which in the opinion of the Court are likely to be recovered by the plaintiff after taking into account any relevant contributory negligence and any set-off, cross-claim or counterclaim on which the respondent may be entitled to rely.

(2) No order shall be made under paragraph (1) in an action for personal injuries if it appears to the Court that the defendant is not a person falling within one of the following categories, namely—

(a) a person who is insured in respect of the plaintiff's claim;

(b) a public authority; or

(c) a person whose means and resources are such as to enable him to make the interim payment.

Order for interim payment in respect of sums other than damages
12. If, on the hearing of an application under rule 10, the Court is satisfied—

(a) that the plaintiff has obtained an order for an account to be taken as between himself and the defendant and for any amount certified due on taking the account to be paid; or

(b) that the plaintiff's action includes a claim for possession of land and, if the action proceeded to trial, the defendant would be held liable to

Appendix B

pay to the plaintiff a sum of money in respect of the defendant's use and occupation of the land during the pendency of the action, even if a final judgment or order were given or made in favour of the defendant; or

(c) that, if the action proceeded to trial the plaintiff would obtain judgment against the defendant for a substantial sum of money apart from any damages or costs,

the Court may, if it thinks fit, and without prejudice to any contentions of the parties as to the nature or character of the sum to be paid by the defendant, order the defendant to make an interim payment of such amount as it thinks just, after taking into account any set-off, cross-claim or counterclaim on which the defendant may be entitled to rely.

Manner of payment
13. (1) Subject to Order 80, rule 12, the amount of any interim payment ordered to be made shall be paid to the plaintiff unless the order provides for it to be paid into court, and where the amount is paid into court, the Court may, on the application of the plaintiff, order the whole or any part of it to be paid out to him at such time or times as the Court thinks fit.

(2) An application under the preceding paragraph for money in court to be paid out may be made *ex parte*, but the Court hearing the application may direct a summons to be issued.

(3) An interim payment may be ordered to be made in one sum or by such instalments as the Court thinks fit.

(4) Where a payment is ordered in respect of the defendant's use and occupation of land the order may provide for periodical payments to be made during the pendency of the action.

Directions on application under rule 10
14. Where an application is made under rule 10, the Court may give directions as to the further conduct of the action, and, so far as may be applicable, Order 25, rules 2 to 7, shall, with the omission of so much of rule 7 (1) as requires the parties to serve a notice specifying the orders and directions which they require and with any other necessary modifications, apply as if the application were a summons for directions, and, in particular, the Court may order an early trial of the action.

Non-disclosure of interim payment
15. The fact that an order has been made under rule 11 or 12 shall not be pleaded and unless the defendant consents or the Court so directs, no communication of that fact or of the fact that an interim payment has been made, whether voluntarily or pursuant to an order, shall be made to the court at the trial, or hearing, of any question or issue as to liability or damages until all questions of liability and amount have been determined.

Payment into court in satisfaction
16. Where, after making an interim payment, whether voluntarily or

226

pursuant to an order, a defendant pays a sum of money into Court under Order 22, rule 1, the notice of payment must state that the defendant has taken into account the interim payment.

Adjustment on final judgment or order or on discontinuance
17. Where a defendant has been ordered to make an interim payment or has in fact made an interim payment, whether voluntarily or pursuant to an order, the Court may, in giving or making a final judgment or order, or granting the plaintiff leave to discontinue his action or to withdraw the claim in respect of which the interim payment has been made, or at any other stage of the proceedings on the application of any party, make such order with respect to the interim payment as may be just, and in particular—
- (a) an order for the repayment by the plaintiff of all or part of the interim payment, or
- (b) an order for the payment to be varied or discharged, or
- (c) an order for the payment by any other defendant of any part of the interim payment which the defendant who made it is entitled to recover from him by way of contribution or indemnity or in respect of any remedy or relief relating to or connected with the plaintiff's claim.

Counterclaims and other proceedings
18. The preceding rules in this Part of this Order shall apply, with the necessary modifications, to any counterclaim or proceeding commenced otherwise than by writ, where one party seeks an order for an interim payment to be made by another.

RSC Order 44, rule 9: Interest on debts
9. (1) Where an account of the debts of a deceased person is directed by any judgment, then, unless the deceased's estate is insolvent or the Court otherwise orders, interest shall be allowed—
- (a) on any such debt as carries interest, at the rate it carries, and
- (b) on any other debt, from the date of the judgment at the rate payable on judgment debts at that date.

(2) A creditor who has established his debt in proceedings under the judgment and whose debt does not carry interest shall be entitled to interest on his debt in accordance with paragraph (1) (*b*) out of any assets which may remain after satisfying the costs of the cause or matter, the debts which have been established and the interest on such of those debts as by law carry interest.

(3) For the purposes of this rule "debt" includes funeral, testamentary or administration expenses and, in relation to expenses incurred after the judgment, for the reference in paragraph (1) (*b*) to the date of the judgment there shall be substituted a reference to the date when the expenses become payable.

Appendix B

RSC Order 44, rule 10: Interest on legacies

10. Where an account of legacies is directed by any judgment, then, subject to any directions contained in the will or codicil in question and to any order made by the Court, interest shall be allowed on each legacy at the rate of £6 per cent. per annum beginning at the expiration of one year after the testator's death.

County Court Rules 1981

CCR Order 6: Particulars of claim

General requirements

1. (1) Subject to the provisions of this rule, a plaintiff shall, at the time of commencing an action, file particulars of his claim specifying his cause of action and the relief or remedy which he seeks and stating briefly the material facts on which he relies.

(2) Where in an action for a debt the particulars of claim can conveniently be incorporated in the form of request for the issue of the summons, they may be incorporated in that form if the proper officer so allows.

(3) Where a plaintiff desires to abandon, under section 17 (1) of the Act, the excess of his claim over the sum mentioned in that section, the abandonment of the excess shall be stated at the end of the particulars.

(4) Except where the particulars are incorporated in the request pursuant to paragraph (2), the plaintiff shall, when filing particulars of his claim, file a copy for each defendant to be served with the summons.

Claim for interest

1A. Where the plaintiff claims interest under section 69 of the Act or otherwise his particulars of claim shall contain a statement to that effect.

.   .   .

Mortgage action

5. (1) Where a plaintiff claims as mortgage payment or moneys secured by a mortgage of real or leasehold property or possession of such property, he shall in his particulars of claim—
  (a) state the date of the mortgage;
  (b) show the state of account between the plaintiff and the defendant with particulars of—
    (i) the amount of the advance,
    (ii) the amount of the periodic payments required to be made,
    (iii) the amount of any interest or instalments in arrear at the commencement of the proceedings, and
    (iv) the amount remaining due under the mortgage;
  (c) state what proceedings, if any, the plaintiff has previously taken against the defendant in respect of the moneys secured by the mortgage or the mortgaged property and, where payment of such

moneys only is claimed, whether the plaintiff has obtained possession of the propery; and

(d) state, where possession of the property is claimed, whether or not the property consists of or includes a dwelling house within the meaning of Part IV of the Administration of Justice Act 1970.

(1A) Where a plaintiff claims as mortgagee possession of land which consists of or includes a dwelling house, he shall state, in his particulars of claim, whether either a land charge of Class F has been registered or a notice or caution pursuant to section 2 (7) of the Matrimonial Homes Act 1967 or a notice pursuant to section 2 (8) of the Matrimonial Homes Act 1983 has been entered and, if so, he shall state the name and address of the person whose interest in the house is so protected and shall file a copy of the particulars of claim for service on that person.

(1B) Where particulars of a charge-holder are given pursuant to paragraph (1A), a copy of the summons and a copy of the particulars of claims together with notice of the action, shall be served on the charge-holder in accordance with Order 7, rule 1.

(2) In this rule "mortgage" includes a legal or equitable mortgage and a legal or equitable charge, and references to the mortgaged property and mortgagee shall be construed accordingly.

Hire-purchase[1]
6. (1) Where a plaintiff claims the delivery of goods let under a hire-purchase agreement to a person other than a body corporate, he shall in his particulars state in the order following—

(i) the date of the agreement and the parties to it with the number of the agreement or sufficient particulars to enable the debtor to identify the agreement;
(ii) where the plaintiff was not one of the original parties to the agreement, the means by which the rights and duties of the creditor under the agreement passed to him;
(iii) whether the agreement is a regulated agreement and, if it is not a regulated agreement, the reason why;
(iv) the place where the agreement was signed by the debtor (if known);
(v) the goods claimed;
(vi) the total price of the goods;
(vii) the paid up sum;
(viii) the unpaid balance of the total price;
(ix) whether a default notice or a notice under section 76(1) or section 98(1) of the Consumer Credit Act 1974 has been served on the debtor, and if it has, the date on which and the maner in which it was so served;
(x) the date when the right to demand delivery of the goods accrued;

---

1 CCR Order 6, r 6, as printed here, replaces the original Order 6, r 6 as from 19 May 1985, except as regards agreements entered into before that date, to which the original Order 6, r 6 still applies: County Court (Amendment) Rules 1985 (SI 1985/566), rr 5 and 10.

    (xi) the amount (if any) claimed as an alternative to the delivery of the goods; and

   (xii) the amount (if any) claimed in addition to the delivery of the goods or any claim under sub-paragraph (xi), stating the cause of action in respect of which each such claim is made.

(2) Where a plaintiff's claim arises out of a hire-purchase agreement but is not for the delivery of goods, he shall in his particulars state in the order following—

    (i) the date of the agreement and the parties to it with the number of the agreement or sufficient particulars to enable the debtor to identify the agreement;

   (ii) where the plaintiff was not one of the original parties to the agreement, the means by which the rights and duties of the creditor under the agreement passed to him;

  (iii) whether the agreement is a regulated agreement and, if it is not a regulated agreement, the reason why;

  (iv) the place where the agreement was signed by the debtor (if known);

   (v) the goods let under the agreement;

  (vi) the amount of the total price;

 (vii) the paid-up sum;

(viii) the amount (if any) claimed as being due and unpaid in respect of any instalment or instalments of the total price; and

  (ix) the nature and amount of any other claim and the circumstances iɪ which it arises.

(3) Expressions used in this rule which are defined in the Consumer Credi Act 1974 have the same meanings in this rule as they have in that Act.

.   .   .

CCR Order 9: Admission, defence, counterclaim and answer

.   .   .

Admission of part or request for time in default action

3. (1) If within the period of 14 days mentioned in rule 2 the defendant in a default action delivers at the court office—

   (a) an admission of part of the plaintiff's claim, or

   (b) an admission of the whole or part of the plaintiff's claim accompanied by a request for payment,

the plaintiff shall, within 14 days of the receipt by him of the proper officer's notice under rule 2 (2), notify the proper officer whether he accepts the amount admitted (if it is not the whole of the plaintiff's claim) and any proposal as to the time of payment.

(2) If the plaintiff notifies the proper officer of his acceptance of the amount admitted (if it is not the whole of the plaintiff's claim) and any proposal as to the time of payment, the registrar shall as soon as practicable enter judgment accordingly.

(3) If the defendant admits the whole of the plaintiff's claim or such part thereof as the plaintiff accepts and the plaintiff notifies the proper officer

that he does not accept the defendant's proposal as to time of payment, the proper officer shall fix a day (in these rules called a day fixed for the disposal of the action) on which the time of payment will be determined and judgment entered by the court, and shall give to the plaintiff and the defendant not less than 8 days' notice of the day so fixed.

(4) If the defendant admits part of the plaintiff's claim and the plaintiff notifies the proper officer that he does not accept the amount admitted, the proper officer shall fix a day for a pre-trial review or if he thinks fit, a day for the hearing of the action and give to the plaintiff and the defendant not less than 8 days' notice of the day so fixed.

(5) The disposal of an action under paragraph (3) may be conducted by the registrar sitting either in court or in chambers.

(6) Where the action is for unliquidated damages and the defendant delivers an admission of liability for the claim but disputes the amount of the plaintiff's damages, then—

(a) if the defendant offers to pay in satisfaction of the claim a specific sum which the plaintiff accepts, the provisions of this rule shall apply as if the defendant had admitted part of the plaintiff's claim; and

(b) in any other case, the plaintiff may apply to the court for such judgment as he may be entitled to upon the admission, and the court may give such judgment, including an interlocutory judgment for damages to be assessed and costs, or make such order on the application as it thinks just.

Admission in fixed date action

4. (1) If within the period of 14 days mentioned in rule 2 the defendant in a fixed date action other than an action for the recovery of land delivers at the court office an admission of the whole or part of the plaintiff's claim, the plaintiff may apply to the court for such judgments as he may be entitled to upon the admission, without waiting for the return day or for the determination of any other question between the parties, and the court may give such judgment or make such order on the application as it thinks just.

(2) An application under paragraph (1) shall, if made before the return day, be made on notice to the defendant.

Defence or counterclaim in default action

5. If within the period of 14 days mentioned in rule 2 the defendant in a default action delivers at the court office either a defence not accompanied by an admission of any part of the plaintiff's claim or a counterclaim, the proper officer shall fix a day for a pre-trial review or, if he thinks fit, a day for the hearing of the action, and shall give to all parties not less than 14 days' notice of the day so fixed.

Judgment in default or on admission in default action

6. (1) Subject to paragraphs 2 (2) and (3) and rule 7, if the defendant in a default action—

(a) does not within 14 days after service of the summons on him, pay into court the total amount of the claim and costs on the summons or deliver at the court office an admission, defence or counterclaim, or

(b) delivers at the court office an admission of the whole of the plaintiff's claim unaccompanied by a counterclaim or a request for time for payment,

the plaintiff may, upon filing a request in that behalf and, unless otherwise directed, producing the plaint note, have judgment entered against the defendant for the amount of the claim and costs, and the order shall be for payment forthwith or at such time or times as the plaintiff may specify.

(2) If the plaintiff's claim is for unliquidated damages, any judgment entered under paragraph (1) (a) shall be an interlocutory judgment for damages to be assessed and costs.

(3) Where the defendant is a State as defined in section 14 of the State Immunity Act 1978—

(a) the plaintiff may not enter judgment under paragraph (1) (a) without the leave of the judge and RSC Order 13, rule 7A, shall apply to an application for such leave as it applies to an application for leave to enter judgment against a State in the High Court;

(b) the plaintiff may not enforce a judgment entered pursuant to such leave until two months after a copy of it has been served on the State.

Default judgment for mortgage money

7. (1) No judgment shall be entered under rule 6 (1) (a) for money secured by a mortgage except with the leave of the court.

(2) An application for the grant of leave under this rule shall be made on notice to the defendant.

(3) The application may be heard and determined by the registrar.

(4) In this rule "mortgage" includes a legal and an equitable mortgage and a legal and an equitable charge.

Recovery of interest

8. (1) The sum for which judgment is entered under rule 3 (2) or 6 (1) may include interest down to the date of issue of the summons or, where it is claimed at the same rate in respect of the period down to judgment, to the date of the request for entry of judgment, provided that—

(a) particulars of the amount claimed down to issue, rate and period are set out in the particulars of claim; and

(b) in the case of interest claimed under section 69 of the Act the rate is not higher than that payable on judgment debts in the High Court at the date of issue of the summons.

(2) Where, in accordance with paragraph (1), the plaintiff requests the entry of judgment for interest in respect of a period subsequent to issue, he shall enter such interest on the appropriate form of request as an additional item, with particulars of the amount, rate and period.

(3) Save as provided by paragraph (1), where a judgment is sought under rule 3 (2) or 6 (1) in respect of a claim which includes a claim for interest,

and the plaintiff so requests, the judgment shall, as regards the interest, be an interlocutory judgment for interest to be assessed.

.　　.　　.

CCR Order 11: Payment into and out of court

Payment into court before judgment
1. (1) In any action for a debt or damages any defendant may at any time before judgment pay money into court—
  (a) in satisfaction of the plaintiff's cause of action or, where two or more causes of action are joined in the action, in satisfaction of any or all of those causes of action; or
  (b) on account of a sum admitted by him to be due to the plaintiff in respect of the plaintiff's cause or causes of action.

(2) Where the amount paid into court under paragraph (1) is less than the amount claimed, the payment shall be treated as being made under sub-paragraph (b) unless it is accompanied by notice stating that it is made in satisfaction of the plaintiff's cause or causes of action.

(3) Where a payment under paragraph (1) is made by one or more but not all of several defendants, it shall be accompanied by a notice stating the name and address of each defendant making the payment.

(4) A defendant may, without leave, give notice of an increase in a payment made under paragraph (1) (a) but, subject to that and without prejudice to paragraph (6), a notice of payment may not be withdrawn or amended without the leave of the court, which may be granted on such terms as may be just.

(5) Where two or more causes of action are joined in the action, any notice given under paragraph (2) shall—
  (a) state that the payment is made in respect of all those causes of action or specify the cause or causes of action in respect of which the payment is made, and
  (b) where the defendant desires to make separate payments in respect of any two or more of the causes of action, specify the sum paid in respect of each.

For the purposes of this paragraph stated to be made in satisfaction of the plaintiff's claim shall be treated as being made in satisfaction of all the causes of action.

(6) Where a single sum of money is paid into court under this rule in respect of two or more causes of action, then, if it appears to the court that the plaintiff is embarrassed by the payment, the court may, subject to paragraph (7), order the defendant to amend the notice of payment so as to specify the sum paid in respect of each cause of action.

(7) Where a cause of action under the Fatal Accidents Act 1976 and a cause of action under the Law Reform (Miscellaneous Provisions) Act 1934 are joined in an action, with or without any other cause of action, the causes of action under the said Acts shall, for the purpose of paragraph (6), be treated as one cause of action.

(8) For the purposes of this rule a plaintiff's cause of action in respect of a debt or damages shall be construed as a cause of action in respect of such interest as might be included in the judgment, whether under section 69 of the Act or otherwise, if judgment were given at the date of the payment into court.

(9) Where a payment under paragraph (1) is made by a defendant who makes a counterclaim against the plaintiff for a debt or damages, the notice given under paragraph (2) must state, if it be the case, that in making the payment the defendant has taken into account and intends to satisfy the cause of action in respect of which he counterclaims or, if two more causes of action are joined in the counterclaim, all those causes of action or such of them as may be specified in the notice.

(10) On receipt of a payment by a defendant under paragraph (1) the proper officer shall, if time permits, send notice thereof to every other party to the action.

Payment of whole sum

2. (1) Where the only relief claimed in an action is the payment of money and the whole amount is paid into court under rule 1, the action shall be stayed except for the purposes of paragraphs (2) and (3) of this rule and rules 4 and 6.

(2) Where the action is for a debt or liquidated demand and the money was paid by the defendant within 14 days after the service of the summons on him, together with the costs stated on the summons, the defendant shall not be liable for any further costs unless the court otherwise orders.

(3) In any case to which paragraph (2) does not apply, the defendant shall not be liable for any costs incurred after receipt by the plaintiff of the notice of payment into court, but—
  (a) except as provided in sub-paragraph (b), the plaintiff may lodge for taxation a bill of costs incurred by him before receipt of the notice and, if the costs allowed on taxation are not paid within 14 days after taxation, may have judgment entered for them and the costs of entering judgment;
  (b) if an order is required under rule 4 (2) for payment of the money out of court, the plaintiff may apply for an order for such costs.

(4) Paragraphs (2) and (3) are without prejudice to the provisions of Order 10, rules 10 and 11, Order 19, rule 6, and Order 38, rule 3 (4).

Acceptance of lesser sum

3. (1) Where the amount paid into court by the defendant under rule 1 (1) (a) in satisfaction of the plaintiff's cause or causes of action is less than the amount claimed or there is also a claim for some relief other than the payment of money, then subject to paragraph (2); the plaintiff may—
  (a) where the money was paid in respect of the cause of action or all of the causes of action in respect of which he claims, accept the money in satisfaction of such cause or causes or action, or
  (b) where the money was paid in respect of some only of the causes of

action in respect of which he claims, accept in satisfaction of any such cause or causes of action the sum specified in the notice of payment into court,

by giving notice of acceptance to the proper office and to every other party to the action within 14 days after the receipt by the plaintiff of notice of payment into court but in any case not less than 3 days before the hearing of the action begins.

(2) Where after the hearing of an action has begun—

(a) money is paid into court under rule 1 (1) (a), or

(b) money in court is increased by a further payment into court under that rule,

the plaintiff may accept the money in accordance with paragraph (1) within 14 days after receipt of notice of the payment but in any case before the court begins to deliver judgment.

(3) On receipt by the proper officer of the plaintiff's notice of acceptance, proceedings in respect of the cause or causes of action to which the notice relates shall be stayed except for the purposes of this rule.

(4) Where notice of acceptance is given in a case to which paragraph (1) (a) applies and—

(a) the action is for a debt or liquidated demand and

(b) the money was paid by the defendant within 14 days after the service of the summons on him, together with the costs which would be stated on a summons for that amount,

the defendant shall not be liable for any further costs unless the court otherwise orders.

(5) Where notice of acceptance is given in any case to which paragraph (4) does not apply and the notice relates to the whole claim or, if it relates to one or more of several causes of action, the plaintiff at the same time gives notice that he abandons the other cause or causes of action, then—

(a) except as provided in sub-paragraph (b) the plaintiff may lodge for taxation a bill of costs incurred by him before receipt of the notice of payment into court and, if the costs allowed on taxation are not paid within 14 days after taxation, may have judgment entered for them and the costs of entering judgement;

(b) if an order is required under rule 4 (2) for payment of the money out of court, the plaintiff may apply for an order for such costs.

(6) Where money is paid into court by a defendant who made a counterclaim and the notice of payment stated, in relation to any sum so paid, that in making the payment the defendant had taken into account and satisfied the cause or causes of action, or the specified cause or causes of action in respect of which he claimed, then, on the plaintiff accepting that sum, all further proceedings on the counterclaim or in respect of the specified cause or causes of action, as the case may be, against the plaintiff shall be stayed.

(7) The foregoing paragraphs are without prejudice to the provisions of Order 10, rules 10 and 11, Order 19, rule 6, and Order 38, rule 3 (4).

Payment out of court

4. (1) Where proceedings are stayed under rule 2 (1) or 3 (3), the plaintiff shall, subject to the following paragraphs of this rule, be entitled to have paid out to him the sum paid into court in satisfaction of his claim or, if the stay is in respect of some only of the plaintiff's causes of action, in satisfaction of that cause or those causes of action.

(2) Subject to the provisions of this rule, money paid into court—

(a) by one or more but not all of defendants sued jointly or in the alternative;

(b) with a defence of tender before action;

(c) in an Admiralty action;

(d) in proceedings to which Order 10, rule 11, relates, or

(e) in satisfaction either of causes of action arising under the Fatal Accidents Act 1976 and the Law Reform (Miscellaneous Provisions) Act where more than one person is entitled to the money,

shall not be paid out of court except in pursuance of an order of the court.

(3) Where in a case to which paragraph (2) (a) relates the plaintiff discontinues the action against the other defendants and those defendants consent in writing to the payment out of the money, it may be paid out without an order of the court.

(4) Where a party entitled to money in court is a person in respect of whom a certificate is or has been in force entitling him to legal aid under Part I of the Legal Aid 1974, payment shall be made only to that party's solicitor or, if he is no longer represented by a solicitor, to the Law Society.

Late acceptance

5. (1) If in a case to which rule 3 (1) relates the plaintiff fails to give notice of acceptance within the time limited by that rule, he may give notice at any subsequent time before the hearing of the action begins and thereupon, subject to the provisions of this rule, rule 3 shall apply as if the notice had been given within the time so limited.

(2) Paragraph (5) (a) of rule 3 shall not apply but in the circumstances to which that paragraph relates the plaintiff may apply for an order for the costs incurred by him before the receipt of the notice of payment into court.

(3) Notwithstanding the provisions of rule (4) (1) the money in court shall not be paid out without an order of the court.

(4) An application for an order under paragraph (2) or (3) shall be made on notice to the defendant, and on the application the court may order the plaintiff to pay any costs reasonably incurred by the defendant since the date of payment into court.

.   .   .

Money paid into court under order

9. (1) Subject to paragraph (2), money paid into court under an order shall not be paid out except in pursuance of an order of the court.

(2) Unless the court otherwise orders, a party who has paid money into

court in pursuance of an order made under Order 9, rule 14, or Order 13, rule 1 (8) (c), or Order 37, rule 8 (1)—

(a) may by notice to the proper officer and to every other party appropriate the whole or any part of the money and any additional payment, if necessary, to any particular claim made by the other party and specified in the notice, or

(b) if he pleads a tender, may by his defence appropriate the whole or part of the money as payment into court of the money alleged to be tendered;

and money appropriated in accordance with this rule shall be deemed to be money paid into court in accordance with rule 1 or money paid into court with a plea of tender, as the case may be, and this Order shall apply accordingly.

CCR Order 49, rule 4: Consumer Credit Act 1974[1]

4. (1) In this rule 'the Act' means the Consumer Credit Act 1974, a section referred to by number means the section so numbered in the Act and expressions which are defined in the Act have the same meaning in this rule as they have in the Act.

(2) an action to recover possession of goods to which a regulated hire-purchase agreement relates shall be commenced in the court for the district in which the debtor resides or carries on business or resided or carried on business at the date when he last made a payment under the agreement.

(3) Where in any action or matter relating to a regulated agreement the debtor or any surety has not been served with the originating process, the court may, on the ex parte application of the plaintiff made at or before the hearing of the action or matter, dispense with the requirement in section 141(5) that the debtor or surety, as the case may be, shall be made a party to the proceedings.

(4) Where an action or matter relating to a regulated agreement is brought by a person to whom a former creditor's rights and duties under the agreement have passed by assignment or by operation of law, the requirement in section 141(5) that all the parties to the agreement shall be made parties to the action shall not apply to the former creditor unless the court so directs.

(5) An application under section 129(1) (b) may be made by originating application and the application—

(a) shall be filed in the court for the district in which the applicant resides or carries on business; and

(b) shall state—

(i) the date of the agreement and the parties to it with the number of the agreement or sufficient particulars to enable the respondent to identify the agreement and details of any sureties;

---

1 The provisions of this rule apply to agreements entered into after 19 May 1985, but not to agreements entered into before, except in relation to provisions of the Consumer Credit Act 1974 which so apply: County Court (Amendment) Rules 1985 (SI 1985/566), rr 7 and 10.

(ii) if the respondent was not one of the original parties to the agreement, the name of the original party to the agreement;

(iii) the names and addresses of the persons intended to be served with the application;

(iv) the place where the agreement was signed by the applicant;

(v) details of the notice served by the respondent giving rise to the application;

(vi) the total unpaid balance admitted to be due under the agreement and the amount of any arrears (if known) together with the amount and frequency of the payments specified by the agreement;

(vii) the applicant's proposals as to payment of any arrears and of future instalments together with details of his means;

(viii) where the application relates to a breach of the agreement other than the non-payment of money, the applicant's proposals for remedying it.

(6) Any application under section 131 may be heard and determined by the judge or by the registrar.

(7) In an action brought by the creditor to recover possession of goods comprised in an agreement to which section 90(1) applies, Order 9 shall have effect with the following modifications:—

(a) subject to sub-paragraph (b), rules 2 and 3(1) and 3(2) of the said Order shall apply, with the necessary modifications, in relation to a debtor who makes an offer as to conditions for the suspension of a return order under section 135(1) (b) as they apply in relation to a defendant in a default action who admits the whole or part of the plaintiff's claim and desires time for payment;

(b) where the plaintiff elects to accept such an offer as is mentioned in sub-paragraph (a) and a surety is a party to the action, judgment shall not be entered before the return day save with the consent of the surety;

(c) rule 4 of the said Order shall not apply where judgment is entered under rule 3(2) thereof;

(d) where such an offer as is mentioned in sub-paragraph (a) is made on the form appended to the summons but the plaintiff elects not to accept it, the court may, if the debtor does not attend on the return day, treat the form as evidence of the facts stated therein for the purposes of sections 129(2)(a) and 135(2).

(8) Where in relation to a regulated hire-purchase agreement the registrar has made a time order or an order for the return to the creditor of the goods suspended under section 135(1)(b), any application under section 130(6), 133(6) or 135(4) may be heard and determined by the registrar.

(9) An application for an enforcement order may be made—

(a) by originating application asking for leave to enforce the agreement in respect of which the order is sought, or

(b) if, apart from the need to obtain an enforcement order, the creditor is entitled to payment of the money or possession of the goods or land to which the agreement relates, by fixed date action to recover the money, goods or land.

(10) An originating application under paragraph (9) (a) and the particulars of claim in an action brought pursuant to paragraph (9) (b) shall state the circumstances rendering an enforcement order necessary.

(11) Paragraph (9) shall apply to an order under section 86(2), 92(2) or 126 as it applies to an enforcement order, so however that in the case of an order under section 86(2) the personal representatives of the deceased debtor or hirer shall be made parties to the proceedings in which the order is sought, or, if no grant of representation has been made to his estate, the applicant shall, forthwith after commencing the proceedings, apply to the court for directions as to what persons, if any, shall be made parties to the proceedings as being affected or likely to be affected by the enforcement of the agreement.

(12) Where by virtue of section 90(1) the creditor is not entitled to recover possession of the goods comprised in an agreement except on an order of the court, an application for such an order may be made only by action claiming possession of the goods.

(13) An application for an order under section 92(1) entitling a creditor or owner to enter any premises to take possession of goods shall be made by originating application.

(14) An application to a county court under section 139(1)(a) for a credit agreement to be reopened shall be made by originating application.

(15) Where in any such proceedings in a county court as are mentioned in section 139(1)(b) or (c), the debtor or a surety desires to have a credit agreement reopened, he shall, within 14 days after the service of the originating process on him, give notice to that effect to the proper officer and to every other party to the proceedings and thereafter the debtor or surety, as the case may be, shall be treated as having delivered a defence or answer and accordingly, if the proceedings are a default action, no judgment shall be entered under Order 9, rule 6(1).

Appendix C

Practice directions

Contents

Practice Direction 1—Claims in foreign currency

[1976] 1 All ER 669, [1976] 1 WLR 83

1. Subject to any order or directions which the court may make or give in any particular case, the following practice shall be followed in relation to the making of claims and the enforcement of judgments expressed in a foreign currency.

Claims for debts or liquidated demands in foreign currency
2. For the purpose of ascertaining the proper amount of the costs to be indorsed on the writ pursuant to RSC Ord 6, r 2(1)(*b*), before a writ of summons is issued in which the plaintiff makes a claim for a debt or liquidated demand expressed in a foreign currency, the writ must be indorsed with the following certificate, which must be signed by or on behalf of the solicitor of the plaintiff or by the plaintiff if he is acting in person:

'*Sterling equivalent of amount claimed*
'I/We certify that the rate current in London for the purchase of [*state the unit of the foreign currency claimed*] at the close of business on the
day of   19
[*being the date next or most nearly preceding the date of the issue of the writ*] was   to the £ sterling and at this rate the debt or liquidated demand claimed herein, namely [*state the sum of the foreign currency claimed*] amounts to £   or exceeds £650 [*as the case may be*].'

'Dated the   day of   19
Signed
(Solicitor for the plaintiff).'

Pleading claims in foreign currency
3. Where the plaintiff seeks to obtain a judgment expressed in a foreign currency, he should expressly state in his writ of summons, whether indorsed into a statement of claim or not, that he makes his claim for payment in a specified foreign currency and unless the facts themselves clearly show this, he should plead the facts relied on to support such a claim in his statement of claim. [*Substituted by Direction of 21 December 1976* [1977] 1 All ER 544, [1971] 1 WLR 197.]

Default judgment for debts or liquidated demands in foreign currency
4. A judgment in default of appearance or in default of defence may be entered in foreign currency by adapting RSC Appendix A, Form 39, as follows:

'It is this day adjudged that the Defendant do pay the Plaintiff [*state the*

---

1 The relevant current figure, to secure High Court costs, under County Courts Act 1984, s 20(2) and (9), is now £3,000.

sum in which foreign currency is claimed] or the Sterling equivalent at the time of payment.'

Judgment under RSC Ord 14

5. Wherever appropriate, a judgment under RSC Ord 14, r 3, may be entered for a debt or liquidated demand in foreign currency by adapting RSC Appendix A, Form 44, as follows:

'It is this day adjudged that the Defendant do pay the Plaintiff [*state the sum in foreign currency for which the court has ordered judgment to be entered*] or the Sterling equivalent at the time of payment and £   cost) [*or* cost to be taxed]'.

The amount of the fixed costs will be calculated on the sterling equivalent of the amount of the foreign currency claimed as indorsed and certified on the writ, unless the court otherwise orders.

Transfer to the county court

6. On the hearing of an application for an order under the County Courts Act 1959, s 45, for the transfer to a county court of an action for a debt or liquidated demand expressed in foreign currency, on the ground that the amount claimed or remaining in dispute does not exceed £1,000, the court will have regard to the sterling equivalent of the foreign currency claimed as indorsed and certified on the writ, unless at the time of the application it is shown to the court that the said sterling equivalent does exceed the sum of £1,000.[1]

Payment of foreign currency into court in satisfaction

7. In an action for the recovery of a debt or liquidated demand, whether in sterling or in foreign currency, the defendant may, subject to the requirements of the Exchange Control Act 1947, pay into court in satisfaction of the claim, under RSC Ord 22, r 1, a sum of money in foreign currency by adapting Form 2 of the Supreme Court Funds Rules 1975 [SI 1975/1803]. If it is desired that the money should be placed on deposit after the expiry of 21 days, the necessary directions must be given on a Part II order.

Orders for conditional payment of foreign currency into court

8. Where the court makes a conditional order for payment of money into court, e g when granting conditional leave to defend an application for summary judgment under RSC Ord 14, or when setting aside a default judgment or granting an adjournment of the hearing of a summons or the trial hearing of an action or making any other order conditional on payment of money into court may order that such money be paid into court in a foreign currency, and the court may further order that such money should be placed in a foreign currency account and if practicable should be placed in such an account which is an interest-bearing account.

---

1 The relevant provision is now County Courts 1984, s 40 and the limit is £5,000.

Entry of judgment in foreign currency
9. A judgment may be entered in foreign currency by adapting the relevant forms in RSC Appendix A as follows:
'It is this day adjudged that the Defendant do pay the Plaintiff [*state the sum in foreign currency in which judgment has been ordered to be entered*] or the sterling equivalent at the time of payment.'

Interest on judgment debt in foreign currency
10. A judgment entered in foreign currency will carry the statutory rate of interest on the amount of the judgment in foreign currency and such interest will be added to the amount of the judgment itself for the purposes of enforcement of the judgment.

Enforcement of judgment debt in foreign currency writ of fi fa
11. (a) Where the plaintiff desires to proceed to enforce a judgment expressed in foreign currency by the issue of a writ of fieri facias, the praecipe for the issue of the writ must first be indorsed and signed by or on behalf of the solicitor of the plaintiff or by the plaintiff if he is acting in person with the following certificate:

'*Sterling equivalent of judgment*
'I/We certify that the rate current in London for the purpose of [*state the unit of the foreign currency in which the judgment is expressed*] at the close of business on the   day of   19   [*being the date nearest or most nearly preceding the date of the issue of the writ of fi fa*] was   to the £ sterling and at this rate the sum of [*state the amount of the judgment debt in foreign currency*] amounts to £
'Dated the   day of   19   Signed
(Solicitor for the Plaintiff)'.

(b) The amount so certified will then be entered in the writ of fi fa by adapting RSC Appendix A, Form 53, to meet the circumstances of the case, but substituting the following recital:

'Whereas in the above named action it was on the   day of 19   adjudged [*or* ordered] that the Defendant C D do pay the Plaintiff A B [*state the sum of the foreign currency for which judgment was entered*] or the sterling equivalent at the time of payment, and whereas the sterling equivalent at the date of issue of this writ is £   as appears by the certificate indorsed and signed by or on behalf of the Plaintiff on the praecipe for the issue of this writ.'

Enforcement of judgment debt in foreign currency by garnishee proceedings
12. (a) Where the plaintiff desires to proceed to enforce a judgment expressed in foreign currency by garnishee proceedings, the affidavit made in support of an application for an order under RSC Ord 49, r 1, must contain words to the following effect:

Appendix C

'The rate current in London for the purchase of [*state the amount of the judgment in foreign currency*] at the close of business on the   day of   19   was   to the £ sterling, and at this rate the said sum of   amounts to £   sterling. I have ascertained the above information [*state the source of the information*] and verily believe the same to be true.'

The master will then make an order nisi for the sterling equivalent of the judgment debt so verified.

(b) Where the plaintiff desires to attach a debt or accruing due to the defendant within the jurisdiction in the same unit of foreign currency as the judgment debt is itself expressed, the affidavit made in support of an application for an order under RSC Ord 49, r 1, must state all the relevant facts relied on and in such event the master may make the order to attach such debt due or accruing due in *that* foreign currency.

Enforcement of judgment debt in foreign currency by other modes of enforcement
13. Where the plaintiff desires to proceed to enforce a judgment expressed in a foreign currency by other means of enforcement, e g by obtaining an order imposing a charge on land or interest under RSC Ord 50, r 1, or by obtaining an order imposing a charge on securities under RSC Ord 50, r 2, or some other similar order, or by obtaining an order for the appointment of a receiver by way of equitable execution, under RSC Ord 51, r 1, the affidavit made in respect of any such application shall contain words similar to those set out in para 1(a) above. The master will then make an order for the sterling equivalent of the judgment expressed in foreign currency as so verified by such affidavit.

14. These directions are issued with the concurrence of the Chief Chancery Master acting on the authority of the Vice-Chancellor so far as they apply to the practice in the Chancery Division, and of the Senior Registrar of the Family Division so far as they apply to the practice in that division.

I H Jacob
18th December 1975   Senior Master of the Supreme Court.

Practice Direction 2—Transfer of funds
[1983] 1 All ER 800, [1983] 1 WLR 278

QUEEN'S BENCH DIVISION

Pursuant to s 174A of the County Courts Act 1959 many county courts are now transferring the funds held by them to the High Court.

By r 22(4) of the Supreme Court Funds Rules 1975 (as substituted by the Supreme Court Funds (Amendment) Rules 1981, SI 1981/1589, r 10),

'Where money is lodged at a District Registry it shall be forwarded forthwith to the Court Funds Office . . .'

Hitherto in cases in which it was desirable that there should be local control over investment or disposal of the funds of minors it was the practice to order payment into the appropriate county court, unless those funds were substantial.

For the future in the London county courts areas the appropriate local control will be exercised by the master making the order. Outside the London county courts areas it will normally be the appropriate district registrar.

Accordingly, the following order should be applied for in appropriate cases where the next friend resides outside the London county courts areas (unless the next friend wishes that the minor's money should remain under the control of the master):

'The defendant within   days do pay the sum of £   into the Court Funds Office to be invested and accumulated in Short Term Investment Account for the benefit of the minor   pending further order, and that all further proceedings relating to the investment and application of the said fund be transferred to the District Registry.'

Masters' Practice Forms 165 to 172 will be amended accordingly in due course.

J B Elton
7 February   Senior Master, Queen's Bench Division

Practice Direction 3—Investment of funds

[1983] 1 All ER 928

The Lord Chancellor's Department has issued the following notice:

On 1 April 1983 the Supreme Court Funds (Amendment) Rules 1983 and the County Court Funds (Amendment) Rules 1983, SI 1983/290 and 291 respectively, come into force. The main purpose of these two instruments is to alter the way in which satisfaction payments and payments into court under order to abide the event will be treated with regard to earning interest.

At present such payments may be placed, at the appropriate time, to a short-term investment account on the application of one of the parties to the proceedings. The new rules will change the present system in the following respects:(a) such payments will in future be placed to a deposit account and not to a short-term investment account; (b) the deposit rate is to be raised from its present level (5%) to $9\frac{1}{2}$% per annum; (c) deposit interest will be paid on a day-to-day basis instead of in respect of whole months only; (d)

Appendix C

money eligible for interest will be placed automatically to deposit after the appropriate interval so that there will be no need for an application for this purpose by any party.

In future the short-term investment will be available only to 'funds' in the narrower sense, ie money held in court for the benefit of successful plaintiffs under disability.

The new rules apply generally to all payments into court made after 1 April 1983, with the following exceptions: (a) money which the court had ordered to be placed to a short-term investment account before 1 April 1983 will be so placed even if it is not lodged in court until after 1 April 1983; (b) money which has started to earn short-term investment interest before 1 April 1983 will continue to do so in accordance with the previous rules.

Money lodged in court before 1 April 1983 but which does not fall within categories (a) or (b) above will not be eligible for short-term investment interest and may be placed to a deposit account only on an application by a party.

11 March 1983

Practice Direction 4—Pleading claim for interest

[1983] 1 All ER 934, [1983] 1 WLR 377

QUEEN'S BENCH DIVISION

1. *Interest under s 35A of the Supreme Court Act 1981*

(A) *Indorsements complying with RSC Ord 13, r 1(2)*
The procedure, including procedure under RSC Ord 6, r 2(1)(*b*), will be as for claims for contractual interest. See para 2 below.

(a) The statement of claim must plead (i) the cause of action, with particulars, the sum claimed and the date when payment was due, (ii) the claim for interest under 35A of the Supreme Court Act 1981, the rate of interest claimed and the amount of interest claimed from the date when payment was due to the date of issue of the writ (the rate of interest claimed must not exceed the rate of interest on judgment debts current at the date of issue of the writ; the current rate is 12% (see the Judgment Debts (Rate of Interest) (No 2) Order 1982/1427).[1]

(b) The statement of claim should also include a claim for further interest at the aforesaid rate under the 1981 Act from the date of issue of writ to judgment or sooner payment. This should be shown as a daily rate to assist calculation when judgment is entered.

(c) See para 2(b) below for the 14-day costs indorsement.

(B) *Indorsements for interest to be assessed*
If the plaintiff seeks interest at a higher rate than current judgment debts interest, or for any other reason requires interest on a debt to be assessed, he

---

1 Now 15%: see Appendix E.

must plead a claim for interest under s 35A of the Supreme Court Act 1981 and enter judgment for interest to be assessed.

Contractual interest

2. (a) The statement of claim must give sufficient particulars of the contract relied on and, in particular, must show (i) the date from which interest is payable, (ii) the rate of interest fixed by the contract, (iii) the amount of interest due at the issue of the writ.

(b) The interest up to the issue of the writ should be claimed in the prayer and included in the sum entered in the indorsement for 14-day costs. This indorsement must be made; if the defendant pays the principal sum, the interest to the date of the writ and the 14-day costs within the 14 days, the action is stayed and no further interest is payable.

(c) The statement of claim should also contain a prayer for further interest at the contract rate from the issue of the writ to judgment or sooner payment. It is often helpful to work out and show this interest also as a daily rate.

(d) If the defendant makes default in giving notice of intention to defend or in serving a defence, the plaintiff may sign judgment for the principal sum, interest to the date of the writ, further interest calculated to the date of judgment and scale costs. This last calculation is checked by the court when judgment is entered, and it is for this reason that the statement of claim must give sufficient information to enable this to be done quickly.

3. *Interest under the Bills of Exchange Act 1882*

(a) By s 57 of the Bills of Exchange Act 1882 the holder of a cheque (or other bill of exchange) which is dishonoured when duly presented is entitled to recover, in addition to the amount of the cheque, interest as liquidated damages from the date of dishonour until the date of judgment or sooner payment.

(b) There is no prescribed rate of interest; the plaintiff may properly ask for a reasonable rate around or somewhat above base rate. If a high rate is asked, there may be difficulty in entering a default judgment while the matter is referred to the Practice Master (see s 57(3) of the 1882 Act). Short-term investment account rate is a safe guide.

(c) The statement of claim should set out the date of dishonour, the rate of interest claimed, a calculation of the interest due at the date of the issue of the writ, and prayers for this interest and further interest until judgment or sooner payment. The procedure is as explained for contractual interest in para 2(b) to(d) above.

Note: The expression 'judgment or sooner payment' is used in this direction because the right to interest after judgment is almost always under the Judgments Act 1838 *only*.

John Elton
24 February 1983   Senior Master, Queen's Bench Division.

Appendix C

Practice Directions 5 and 6—Enforcement in the High Court of county court judgments

[1984] 3 All ER 155, [1984] 1 WLR 1126

QUEEN'S BENCH DIVISION

The practice for the enforcement in the High Court of county court judgments shall be as follows:

1 Attendance shall first be made in the alphabetical section of the judgment room appropriate to the plaintiff's surname. The applicant shall present to the judgment clerk a certificate of judgment of the county court, sealed with the seal of that court, setting out details of the judgment or order to be enforced, together with a copy of the same.

2 The judgment clerk will: (a) allot to the matter a reference number and endorse that number on the certificate and copy; (b) seal the certificate and the copy, return the certificate to the applicant and retain the copy for the court records; (c) enter the matter in a special register. The certificate so sealed shall be treated, for the procedure of enforcement, as a High Court judgment, with the modifications set out in paras 4 and 5.

3 All subsequent documents shall be intituled as follows:

'In the High Court of Justice . . . High Court no . . . Queen's Bench Division . . . county court plaint no . . . (on transfer from the . . . county court) between . . . AB . . . plaintiff and . . . CD . . . defendant'.

4 *Fieri facias* (a) The praecipe shall refer to the county court judgment and Queen's Bench Master's practice form no PF 87 shall be amended as in para 3 above and by adding immediately after the words '[or order]' the words 'of the . . . county court'. (b) When the writ of execution is issued, the certificate of judgment retained by the applicant shall be again sealed by the High Court on the bottom left corner and endorsed with the designation of the sheriff to whom the process is directed.

5 *Other forms of execution* The affidavit to lead to a garnishee order, charging order or other execution shall be intituled as in para 3 and shall, in its body, refer to the county court judgment and depose to it having been duly transferred for execution to the High Court.

6 *Stay of execution* Any application for stay of execution shall be by summons in the High Court, intituled as in para 3.

7 *District registries* The above practice shall be followed in the district registries with such variations as the circumstances may require.

J R Bickford Smith,
1 August 1984   Senior Master, Queen's Bench Division

[1984] 3 All ER 1002

QUEEN'S BENCH DIVISION

1. Before the High Court can issue execution on a county court judgment transferred to the High Court under the County Courts Act1984, s 106 and CCR Ord 25, r 13, there must be presented to the High Court in accordance with the Practice Direction of 1 August 1984 ([1984] 3 All ER 155, [1984]1 WLR 1126) a certificate of the judgment regularly granted under CCR Ord 22, r 8(1), together with a copy.

2. To comply with Ord 22, r 8(1), as amended by the County Court (Amendment No 2) Rules 1984, SI 1984/878, the certificate must on its face state that it is granted 'for the purpose of enforcing the judgment [*or* order] in the High Court'. It is undesirable to add any other words. If the words '(for evidence only)' appear on the printed form of certificate they should be deleted.

3. The certificate must be signed by the registrar (see County Courts Act 1984, s 12(2) and the revised Form N293). A rubber stamp is insufficient. The copy certificate may be a facsimile.

J R Bickford Smith
Senior Master.

15 November 1984

Appendix D

Forms and precedents

Contents

D1   **Action for debt (goods sold and delivered) and statutory
                                interest**

(a)   *General Indorsement*

The Plaintiff claims

(1)	the price of goods sold and delivered	£4,000
(2)	interest thereon pursuant to section 35A of the Supreme Court Act 1981 at the rate of 12 per cent. per annum[1] (i) from . . . . when the price was due, until the issue of the writ on	£. . . . . .
	(ii) thereafter until judgment or sooner payment	£1.315 for every day of default

---

1 As regards the choice of rate, see paras 4.10, 4.15 and 4.28, above, and Appendix E, below.

Appendix D

(b) *Statement (*or, *in the County Court, Particulars) of Claim:*

STATEMENT [*OR* PARTICULARS] OF CLAIM

1. On   the Plaintiff sold and delivered the following goods to the Defendant for a total price of £4,000, which was payable forthwith:

PARTICULARS OF GOODS SOLD AND DELIVERED

. . . .

2. Further, the price of £4,000 is a debt to which section 35A of the Supreme Court Act 1981 [*or* section 69 of the County Courts Act 1984] applies and pursuant thereto the Plaintiff claims interest on the said price at the rate of 12 per cent. per annum[1] from   when the debt was due to be paid until judgment, or sooner payment; the interest so claimed for the period down to the issue of the writ (*or* summons) amounts to £

AND THE PLAINTIFF CLAIMS

(1)	the price	£4,000
(2)	interest thereon at the rate of 12 per cent. per annum	
	(i) from . . . . . to the issue of the writ (*or* summons)	£ . . . . . .
	(ii) thereafter until judgment or sooner payment	£1.315 for every day of default

---

1 As regards the choice of rate, see paras 4.10, 4.15 and 4.28, above, and Appendix E, below.

D2   **Action for liquidated damages, including interest,
upon the dishonour of a cheque**

(a)   General Indorsement:

The Plaintiff claims liquidated damages for the dishonour of a bill of
exchange:–

(1) the amount of the principal sum	£4,000
(2) interest thereon pursuant to section 57 of the Bills of Exchange Act 1882 at the rate of 12 per cent. per annum[1] (i) from when the bill was presented until the issue of the writ on	£
(ii) thereafter until judgment or sooner payment	£1.315 for every day of default

---

1 As regards the choice of rate, see para 3.05, above, and Appendix E, below.

Appendix D

*(b)   Statement (*or, in the County Court, Particulars*) of Claim:*

STATEMENT [*OR* PARTICULARS] OF CLAIM

1.   On   the Defendant delivered to the Plaintiff a bill of exchange, namely a cheque dated   drawn on the XY Bank, whereby the Defendant directed the said bank to pay the sum of £4,000 to the Plaintiff.

2.   On   the Plaintiff presented the said cheque to the said bank for payment but it was dishonoured and the Plaintiff gave the Defendant notice thereof by a letter dated

3.   By the dishonour of the cheque as aforesaid the Defendant caused the Plaintiff to suffer damages which are deemed, by section 57 of the Bills of Exchange Act 1882, to be liquidated, as follows:–

PARTICULARS OF DAMAGES

(1)	The amount of the principal sum	£4,000
(2)	interest thereon at the rate of 12 per cent. per annum[1]	
	(i) from presentation of the cheque until issue of the writ (*or* summons)	£ .
	(ii) thereafter until judgment or sooner payment	£1.315 for every day of default

AND THE PLAINTIFF CLAIMS, AS LIQUIDATED DAMAGES

(1)	the principal sum	£4,000
(2)	interest thereon at the rate of 12 per cent. per annum[1]	
	(i) from . . . . . . to the issue of the writ (*or* summons)	£ .
	(ii) thereafter until judgment or sooner payment	£1.315 for every day of default

---

1 As regards the choice of rate, see para 3.05, above, and Appendix E, below.

258

D3   **Action for damages (personal injury)**
and statutory interest

General Indorsement
The Plaintiff claims

(1) damages for personal injury and loss arising out of the negligent driving of the Defendant; and
(2) interest thereon, pursuant to section 35A of the Supreme Court Act 1981, at such rate and for such period as the Court thinks fit.

D4   **Default judgment in the High Court for principal debt and**
interest to be assessed

[*Heading as in action*]

The day of   19   .
No notice of intention to defend having been given [*or* no defence having been served] by the Defendant herein, it is this day adjudged that the Defendant do pay the Plaintiff £   and £   costs and interest to be assessed.

Appendix D

D5 Final judgment in the High Court after assessment of interest

The day of   19   .

The Plaintiff having on   day of   19
obtained interlocutory judgment herein against the Defendant for interest
to be assessed, and the amount found due to the Plaintiff having been
certified at £   as appears by the   's certificate, filed the
day of   19   .
It is this day adjudged that the Defendant to pay the Plaintiff £   and
costs to be taxed.

D6   Notice to reopen credit agreement

(RSC Ord 83, r2(1): CCR Ord 49, r4(15)

[Title as in action]

Take Notice that the Defendant desires to have the agreement made
between himself and the plaintiffs on   19   reopened under
section 139(1) of the Consumer Credit Act 1974 on the ground that the
credit bargain is extortionate.

Dated
To the Plaintiff. [and every other Party]
                and to the Court

                                        (Signed)
                            [Solicitors for the] Defendant.

D7   **Request for entry of judgment in the county court,**
including interest for the period after issue[1]

To the Court

I request you to enter judgment by default against . . . . . . Defendant(s)
[2](Payable forthwith)
[2](Payable on the . . . . . .)
[2](Payable by instalments of £. . . . per . . . . commencing on . . . .)

Amount of claim as stated in Summons[3]	£. . . . . .
Court fees on Summons	£. . . . . .
Solicitor's Charge (if any) entered on Summons. . .	£. . . . . .
Solicitor's Charge (if any) on entering Judgment	£. . . . . .

Interest on the principal debt of £. . . . . .[4]
at the rate of . . . .[5]
from the date of issue to
[. . . . . when £. . . was paid
off the principal (. . . . . . days) . . . .   £. . . . . .]
[and on the balance of £
at the same rate thereafter to][6]

the date of this request (. . . . . . days)	£. . . . . .
	Sub total £. . . . . .
Deduct amount (if any) paid into court by Defendant	
Deduct amount (if any) paid Plaintiff direct	
since issue	£. . . . . .
Balance payable by Defendant and for	
which judgment is to be entered	£. . . . . .

Dated   (Signed)
Plaintiff (or Plaintiff's Solicitor)

---

1 This precedent is an adaptation of Prescribed Form N14, with additional material required by
   CCR Ord 9, r 8(2).
2 Delete as appropriate.
3 This means the debt and interest claimed down to issue.
4 Exclude from this figure any interest claimed down to issue, as well as court fees and Solicitors'
   charges.
5 The rate must be specified and must be the same as the rate at which interest is claimed down
   to issue.
6 The passages in square brackets are applicable where, after issue, the Defendant pays money
   off the principal, so that interest runs thereafter on a lesser sum. The Plaintiff may not
   appropriate the payment to statutory interest under s 69 of the County Courts Act 1984, but
   may appropriate it to contractual interest if any is outstanding (see paras 2.06 and 4.22,
   above).

Appendix E

Rates of interest payable on judgments and on the Short Term Investment Account

1. Interest payable on judgments and orders under Judgments Act 1938, s 17

Rate	Date of Change	Statutory Instrument No
$7\frac{1}{2}\%$	20 April 1971	1971/491
10%	1 March 1977	1977/141
$12\frac{1}{2}\%$	3 December 1979	1979/1382
15%	9 June 1980	1980/672
14%	8 June 1982	1982/696
12%	10 November 1982	1982/1427
15%	16 April 1985	1985/437

2. Interest payable on the Short Term Investment Account

Rate	Date of Change	Statutory Instrument No
$7\frac{1}{2}\%$	1 April 1971	1971/259
8%	1 March 1973	1973/231
9%	1 March 1974	1974/207
10%	1 February 1977	1976/2235
$12\frac{1}{2}\%$	1 March 1979	1979/106
15%	1 January 1980	1979/1620
$12\frac{1}{2}\%$	1 January 1981	1980/1858
15%	1 December 1981	1981/1589
14%	1 March 1982	1982/123
13%	1 July 1982	1982/787
$12\frac{1}{2}\%$	1 April 1983	1983/290
12%	1 April 1984	1984/285

Interest on county court judgments and orders: consultation paper

Introduction

1. In October 1981, the Lord Chancellor's Department published a consultation paper seeking views about a proposed scheme for the payment of interest on judgment debts in the county courts, under section 101A of the County Courts Act 1959. Since it was clear that the simple system applicable in the High Court by virtue of section 17 of the Judgments Act 1838 was not suitable for the county court, the consultation paper proposed a more elaborate scheme. It was made clear in that paper that an essential condition of any scheme was that it should be a limited one so as to comply with Government policy limiting the size of the public service and restricting the burden placed upon it.

2. The main features of the original proposals were as follows:–
   (1) A judgment or order must produce an indebtedness of £2,000 or more at the date of judgment to qualify for interest.
   (2) There should be a separate lower limit of £100, below which an eligible judgment would cease to attract interest.
   (3) Interest would be compounded monthly on the outstanding balance and payments made under the order were to be applied first to interest.
   (4) The rate of interest would be the same as that on High Court judgments.
It was suggested that the scheme should apply to all judgments or orders to which the above criteria applied, including those made in matrimonial proceedings.

Response to Consultation

3. A wide and helpful response was provoked by the consultation document and much constructive comment was offered. The following were the main points which were made:–
   (1) The proposed £2,000 ceiling was arbitrary and unrealistically high. Less than 2 per cent. of county court judgment debts would be eligible for interest.
   (2) Even this limited scheme as proposed was complex and would require a disproportionate amount of staff time in the courts.
   (3) A scheme whereby a debtor was required to pay off interest before principal would be unduly harsh; a debtor could very quickly find that even while he was making payments, the amount of his total indebtedness was still growing.
   (4) The High Court system, under which the burden of seeking and calculating interest is in effect thrown upon the creditor, should be considered for adoption in the county courts.

New Proposals

4. In order to meet the criticisms described above as far as possible new,

269

and considerably different, proposals are now put forward. It must be emphasised, however, that the necessity to limit the impact of changes on the county court system remains a paramount one. The new proposals are set out in the Annex to this paper.

5. The main features of the scheme as now put forward are as follows:–
   (1) The judgment creditor would be responsible for initiating a claim for interest and for calculating it.
   (2) Many more cases would be brought within the scheme by reducing the qualifying limit.
   (3) Interest would be simple rather than compound.

Comments

6. The Department would be pleased to receive comments on the proposals in this paper.

7. Replies should be sent by 30th November 1983 to—
   M. Kron, Esq.,
   Lord Chancellor's Department,
   Neville House,
   Page Street,
   LONDON, SW1

   Telephone 211 8430

   Lord Chancellor's Department.
   24 August 1983

ANNEX—THE SCHEME

Rate of Interest

1. It is proposed that the rate of interest payable on judgment debts under the scheme will be that which is in force for the time being under section 17 of the Judgments Act 1838. The advantages of applying the same interest rate in both the High Court and the county courts are self-evident.

Entitlement to Interest

2. Interest will accrue on all county court judgment debts of more than £500, but excluding any order for interim maintenance or maintenance pending suit under sections 22 and 23 of the Matrimonial Causes Act 1973. It is for consideration whether interest should run on lump sum awards payable by instalments under section 27 of the Matrimonial Causes Act, and if so, whether interest should run automatically from the date of the order or only from the date of any default in the payment of an instalment. Interest will not run on any costs incurred after the final order or judgment (e.g.

execution costs), nor will it run on a High Court judgment or order which is enforceable in the county court under section 139 of the County Courts Act 1959. Interest would of course continue to run on such a judgment or order by virtue of the Judgments Act itself. However, tribunal awards which are enforceable through the county courts, under Order 25, rule 12 of the County Court Rules 1981, will qualify for interest.

Qualifying Limit

3.   The reduction in this limit from £2,000 to £500 is accompanied by the abandonment of the suggested lower qualifying limit of £100. £500 is the upper limit of the "small claims" procedure, defended claims beneath this amount automatically being referred to arbitration; claims below this amount should be kept free of the additional complication of interest. Under this proposal some 20 per cent. of money judgments will be within the scope of the scheme, which amounts to about 200,000 cases per year.

Calculation of Interest

4.   Interest will be simple and calculated on a day-to-day basis by the judgment creditor and will start to run from the date of judgment or the order, if it is for a liquidated sum; from the date of assessment, if judgment is for a sum to be assessed and, where the judgment or order includes an order for costs to be taxed then in relation to the costs only, from the date of taxation.

5.   Interest will run on the outstanding part of the judgment debt until it is finally satisfied; a judgment debt, or part of it, will be considered to be outstanding even if it is payable by instalments and the unsatisfied part is not yet due. If judgment or enforcement has been stayed, interest will continue to accrue.

Application for Interest

6.   As indicated previously, it will be the judgment creditor's responsibility to calculate the interest to be credited to the judgment debt. It is proposed, however, that he should be permitted to apply only when he is seeking enforcement of the whole outstanding balance or when the principal sum has been paid off, and in any case on not more than two occasions in any twelve months. When the judgment debt has been paid in full, a final application in respect of any interest due must be made within one month of receipt of the final payment.

7.   The application for interest will be made to the proper officer (the chief clerk) of the county court by a written request in a form which will be appended to the statutory instrument containing the scheme. The creditor would be required to serve a duplicate notice on the debtor. Adding the interest to the judgment debt would normally be an administrative rather than a judicial function, unless the judgment debtor applied, within 14 days

of service of the application, for the court to set aside the award on the grounds that the judgment creditor was not entitled to it or that the amount claimed was incorrect. A date would then be fixed for hearing and the parties notified by the court. At the hearing the registrar would decide the amount of interest due, if any, and it would be added to the judgment debt.

8. Court staff would not be expected to check the calculation made by the judgment creditor unless it was plainly quite inaccurate.

9. It is emphasised that under these proposals it would be entirely for the creditor to choose whether or not to seek interest; he would be under no obligation to do so and, without an application, it will not be automatically added to the judgment debt.

Payment

10. The judgment debt would cease to be outstanding and the judgment or order become satisfied when payment was received by the judgment creditor, whether by cash or payable order or other negotiable instrument.

11. No payment by the judgment debtor would be attributed to interest until the whole of the principal judgment debt had first been satisfied.

Enforcement

2. Interest added to a judgment debt would be enforceable to the same extent, and in the same manner, as the principal money due under the judgment or order, but no interest would be payable on it.

Certificate of Satisfaction

13. It is proposed that the debtor could apply for a certificate of satisfaction either when the total judgment and interest had been paid or when the judgment creditor was out of time to claim interest, i.e. when one month had expired from the date of payment of the judgment debt. The Register of the County Court Judgments Regulations 1936 will need to be amended accordingly.

Appendix G

Deduction of tax

Contents

G1   Inland Revenue statements

(published in the Law Society's Gazette, 2 September 1981)

The Solicitors' Account (Deposit Interest) Rules 1975[1]

A solicitor who is required by the rules to pay interest to a client may do so by either of two methods. He may —

(a) under r 2(1) (a) deposit the money in a separate designated account and account to the client for the interest earned thereon ('method (a)'); or

(b) under r 2(1) (b) pay to the client an equivalent sum out of his own money ('method (b)').

Where solicitor pays interest by either method to a client who is resident in the UK he should do so without deducting tax. Although s 114(1) of the Income and Corporation Taxes Act 1970 can be used to assess a person in receipt of income on behalf of another the Inland Revenue have stated that they will not in practice use that section to assess a solicitor who receives interest on a designated deposit account held for a client resident in the UK. However, whether method (a) or (b) is used, a solicitor may be required under s 18 of the Taxes Management Act 1970 to furnish information about the client and the payments made.

The Inland Revenue accept that interest paid by either method will normally be 'short' rather than annual interest, and will accordingly not expect solicitors to deduct and account for tax under s 54 of the Income and Corporation Taxes Act 1970 even where the client's usual place of abode is outside the UK.

Where the client is resident outside the UK the Revenue will assess a solicitor receiving interest on a designated deposit account to income tax at the basic rate under either s 114 of the Income and Corporation Taxes Act 1970 or s 78 of the Taxes Management Act 1970 (agents of non-residents), both sections being regarded as applicable. To cover this liability the solicitor should therefore retain tax at the basic rate for the year in which the interest is paid or credited by the bank when transmitting or accounting for the interest to the client. He should also, for each year of assessment in which he receives designated deposit account interest for one or more non-resident clients, notify the inspector of taxes of the fact, and after the end of the year the inspector will issue the appropriate return form requiring details. Where method (b) is used the interest should be paid to the non-resident client without deduction of tax.

---

1 The statement regarding the deduction of tax in respect of client account interest was made before the introduction of the Composite Rate Tax scheme for banks (CRT). It must therefore be reviewed, in the light of that scheme, for present day purposes. A Law Society statement on the implications of CRT for client account interest follows, as G2.

If a solicitor pays interest by method (b) the payments are regarded as the client's income and not as the solicitor's. The solicitor himself will accordingly be assessed to income tax only on the net interest retained on undesignated clients' accounts in the year and, correspondingly, the interest paid to clients in respect of money held in undesignated accounts will not be admitted as a deduction in computing the profits of the practice. This relieves solicitors of investment income surcharge in respect of interest on undesignated accounts which has, in effect, been accounted for to clients and profits will not be reduced for pension premium purposes. The Inland Revenue will continue to charge to income tax and investment income surcharge interest on undesignated clients' accounts retained by the solicitor and will not treat such interest as earned income.

INTEREST ON THE BALANCE OF PURCHASE MONEYS

1. *Should interest payable on the balance of purchase money be paid net or gross?*

(a)   Where interest becomes payable for the period between the date fixed for completion and the date of actual completion it should be paid gross (subject to what is said in subpara (c) below).

(b)   If part of the purchase money is left outstanding after completion so that interest is payable thereon the interest should be paid gross (subject to what is said in subpara (c) below).

(c)   If the vendor's usual place of abode is outside the UK or if the payment of interest is made other than in a fiduciary or representative capacity by a company or local authority or if the payment of interest is made by a partnership of which a company is a member the interest should in all cases be paid under deduction of tax.

2. *Is it possible to make an arrangement with the Revenue whereby it is not necessary for a purchaser's solicitor to enquire if the vendor's usual place of abode is outside the UK?*

This is not thought to be possible. The Income and Corporation Taxes Act 1970 by s 54(1) clearly throws on the person by or through whom payment is made a duty to deduct tax at the basic rate in force at the time of the payment from any yearly interest paid to a person whose usual place of abode is outside the UK.

However, if a paying solicitor mistakenly pays interest gross on the faith of an assurance by the recipient's solicitor that to the best of his knowledge the recipient's usual place of abode is in the UK the Revenue will not seek to make the paying solicitor accountable for the tax that ought to have been deducted.

3. *Can a solicitor be personally liable for the tax on the interest paid by his client through him?*

If a client pays through a solicitor interest from which tax ought to be deducted the solicitor may be liable to be assessed to that tax. For example, if a solicitor, having funds to pay the full amount of the interest on behalf of his client fails to deduct tax which ought to be deducted when making the payment to a person whose usual place of abode is outside the UK the solicitor may be liable under s 54 Income and Corporation Taxes Act 1970 to be assessed in respect of the sum which ought to have been deducted.

4. Can a solicitor be personally liable for tax on any gross interest received by him and paid gross to his client?

Under s 114 of the Income and Corporation Taxes Act 1970 the tax on such interest can be assessed either on the solicitor or on his client. If the client is resident in the UK the practice of the Revenue will be to assess the client; in that case the solicitor will not be assessed and should account to his client gross. If the client is not resident in the UK the solicitor will be assessed; he will have to pay the tax and should account to his client net.

5. If there is a possible personal tax liability to a solicitor under questions 3 or 4 above, can this be avoided if the paying client gives his solicitor a cheque to be handed over without using the solicitor's clients' account?

If the paying client hands to his solicitor a cheque made out in favour of his creditor and the solicitors concerned have nothing more to do than see that the cheque is transmitted to the creditor, it is not considered that the payment could be regarded as made through the paying client's solicitor for the purposes of s 54 of the Income and Corporation Taxes Act 1970, nor is it thought that the solicitor for the creditor could be regarded as receiving the income. In these circumstances therefore neither solicitor would be liable to be assessed.

G2   Law Society statement on Composite Rate Tax and interest payable to clients

[This is an extract from a Law Society statement, published in the Law Society's Gazette, 13 March 1985, pp 738–740, on the application of the Composite Rate Tax scheme (CRT) to interest on solicitors' client account balances. References in it to interest payable by method A are to bank interest on a separate designated account for which the solicitor must account to the client under r 2(1)(a) of the Solicitors' Accounts (Deposit Interest) Rules 1975. References in the statement, as published, to interest payable under r 2(1)(b) (ie by method B) have been deleted from the following extract, in anticipation of an amendment of Schedule 8 to the Finance Act 1984 which will disapply CRT in relation to any general client account deposit, as from 5 April 1985 when CRT came into operation.]

Introduction

The statement which follows is a summary of the way in which the CRT scheme will apply to interest earned on money held on behalf of clients and reference should always be made to the statutory provisions when in doubt.

The tax implications of using method A

Where method A is used, the bank will either deduct CRT or continue to pay interest gross according to the status of the client to whom the interest belongs. Banks are required to deduct CRT except where they are satisfied that the deposit in question is outside the scheme and they will seek information from solicitors to enable them to establish whether any particular deposit is within the scheme or not. Where interest is paid net of CRT the solicitor will pay over that net sum to the client who will be treated for tax purposes as though he had received it from the bank in respect of a deposit in his sole name. (Although s 114 of the Taxes Act 1970 can be used to assess a person in receipt of income on behalf of another, the Inland Revenue have stated that they will not in practice assess tax under s 114 on a solicitor who pays interest from a designated account to a client resident in the UK—see below in relation to non-resident clients.)

Thus, if for example the client is an individual ordinarily resident in the UK or a trust with a UK resident life tenant, CRT will apply, but if the client is a company, a charity or a discretionary or accumulation trust, CRT will not apply. Examples of those to whom it does apply and those to whom it does not apply are appended.

Even assuming that the declaration and undertaking have been given in relation to a non-resident client, and that the CRT scheme therefore does not apply and interest is received from the bank gross, s 78 of the Taxes Managment Act 1970 and s 114 of the Taxes Act 1970 will still apply, and require the solicitor to deduct basic rate tax from the gross interest before remitting it to the overseas client in order to protect himself against the possibility of an assessment on behalf of that client. If the client is entitled under a double taxation treaty to recover the basic rate tax so deducted, it will be necessary for him to make the appropriate claim to the Inland Revenue for its repayment.

Deposits held outside the UK

It may be noted that under r 9(2)(a) of the Solicitors' Accounts Rules 1975 a solicitor is not obliged to pay clients' money into client account (and therefore to a bank in England or Wales which has to operate the CRT scheme) if the client, for his own convenience, requests the solicitor to withhold the money from client account and the client's request is made in writing, or acknowledged in writing by the solicitor. A client may therefore request that his money be held in a solicitor's account with a bank outside the UK and thereby avoid the operation of the CRT scheme, but solicitors should be careful to note that if the account is in their name, or if any interest passes through their hands, they may still be liable to assessment on behalf of the client under ss 78 and 114 mentioned above, and they would therefore want to deduct basic rate tax as before in order to protect themselves against the possibility of such an assessment.

Deposits held in the client's own name

Under r 9(2)(a) of the Solicitors' Accounts Rules 1975 (see above) it is possible for a client's money to be held in an account solely in the client's name and for the solicitor to have no involvement in its opening or operation at all. Where this is done, the Solicitors' Accounts Rules will not normally apply and the implications of the CRT scheme will be a matter entirely for the client. In view of the necessity, if this method is to be followed, of the solicitor avoiding any contact with the account or the remittance of the interest due on it there will evidently be few occasions on which the use of a deposit held in the client's own name is practicable, even if the client otherwise desires it.

Interest paid over to a client under deduction of CRT will be treated for tax purposes in the same way as building society interest and the client will have no further liability to income tax at the basic rate. For the purpose of computing the client's total income, and hence any liability to tax at the higher rates, the interest received will be treated as a net amount from which income tax at the basic rate has been deducted at source. Thus, if a client receives interest of £210 net of CRT and the basic rate is 30%, any higher rate liability will be calculated as if he had received a gross amount of £300 from which £90 basic rate tax had been deducted at source. A client who is not subject to income tax and who receives interest net of CRT will not be able to claim repayment, either of the CRT deducted or of any notional basic rate income tax.

Non-resident clients—method A

A non-resident client who is an individual, whether resident in a treaty country or not, will be outside the scheme provided that the 'appropriate person' lodges with the bank a written declaration that the person beneficially entitled to the interest (or where there is more than one, all the persons beneficially entitled to the interest) is not ordinarily resident in the UK and at the same time undertakes to notify the bank should this ever cease to be the case. These arrangements also apply to a deposit by a trust, provided that all the beneficiaries entitled to interest on a deposit are not ordinarily resident in the UK. The same procedure is available where the client is the personal representative of a deceased person who, immediately before his death, was not ordinarily resident in the UK. The 'appropriate person' means any person beneficially entitled to the interest, or entitled to it as a personal representative, or to whom the interest is payable: the solicitor is therefore one of the 'appropriate persons' for this purpose, but it will seldom be advisable for him to give the undertaking which forms part of the declaration and he may often have difficulty in establishing the tax residence of the deceased, or the person entitled to the interest. He may therefore think it better for the personal representatives, or the person beneficially entitled to the interest, to make the declaration and give the undertaking.

Trusts

Where the clients are trustees the solicitor must first decide whether the CRT scheme applies to the trust or not: if all the persons beneficially entitled to the interest on any deposit of the trust's money are individuals the CRT scheme usually will apply, but if the trust is a discretionary or accumulation trust, or a charitable trust, the scheme will not apply and it will not apply to any trust where any of those beneficially entitled to the interest from a depost are not individuals. Once this classification has been made the solicitor will either proceed under method A or method B above.

Where one of the trustees of a trust is a solicitor (whether or not he is a 'solicitor-trustee' as defined by the Solicitors' Accounts Rules 1975), it will of course be imperative that the trust money is either deposited in a non-interest bearing account or in a designated account. If the former is done, there is clearly no question of the CRT scheme applying because no interest will be involved, and if the latter is the case, the position will be as for method A above: there will normally be no occasion in such cases for the use of method B.

Attention is drawn to the position in relation to personal representatives whose deposits will always be within the CRT scheme irrespective of the nature of the the underlying beneficial interests (unless a declaration is made that the deceased was immediately before his death not ordinarily resident in the UK). The Revenue have confirmed that Statement of Practice 7/80 will however apply in relation to bank interest subject to CRT in the same way as it does to building society interest.

280

APPENDIX

Below, for ease of reference, is a summary of the effect of the CRT scheme on solicitors' client accounts and a list of examples of those either within or without the scheme.

Effect of CRT Scheme on Solicitors' Client Accounts

Status of Client	*Solicitor's Designated Deposit Account (Method A)*
Individual ordinarily resident or personal representative	CRT scheme applies and payment made to client net but with tax credit
Non ordinarily resident individual	Interest paid gross (if declaration given) but solicitor assessable under s 114 TA or s 78 TMA; client receives net of basic rate tax but possibility of reclaim under treaty
UK resident company	Interest paid gross by the bank (in practice no assessment on solicitor under s 114 TA)
Non-resident company	Interest paid gross by bank (no declaration required) but solicitor assessable under s 114 TA or s 78 TMA; client receives net of basic rate tax but possibility of reclaim under treaty.

Examples of Persons within the Composite Rate Tax Scheme	*Examples of Persons outside the Composite Rate Tax Scheme*
Personal accounts of individuals (sole and joint)	Companies (Ltd, plc, unlimited)
Accounts of unincorporated businesses—sole traders and partnerships of individuals (including Scottish partnerships)	Liquidators' accounts for companies
	Corporations sole
	Nationalised industries
	Local authorities
Receivers' accounts for bankruptcies (but not trustees for bankruptcies)	Public bodies—health authorities, education authorities, *etc*
Accounts of receivers (including Court of Protection) appointed under s 105, Mental Health Act 1959	Pension funds
	Trade unions
	Building societies
Accounts of personal representatives of deceased persons during administration of the estate—executors, administrators, *etc*	Friendly societies
	Industrial and provident societies
	Credit unions
	Charities
Thrift funds and annual savings clubs such as holiday clubs and Christmas clubs	Accumulation and discretionary trusts
	Unit trusts (authorised and

Trusts (*other than* discretionary, accumulation and charitable trusts, unit trusts, and investment trusts)

The examples given are subject to the rules for non-residents.

unauthorised)

Investment trusts

Trustees accounts for bankruptcies

Societies (*eg*, the ... local history society)

Associations (*eg*, the ... ratepayers association)

Members' clubs (*eg*, the ... tennis club)

Churches

Sequestrators

Regimental accounts

Masonic lodges

Deposits from other deposit-takers

Stock Exchange money brokers

Index